ON THE POSSIBILITY OF JEWISH MYSTICISM IN OUR TIME

& Other Essays

ON THE POSSIBILITY OF JEWISH MYSTICISM IN OUR TIME

& Other Essays

GERSHOM SCHOLEM

EDITED AND SELECTED WITH AN
INTRODUCTION BY AVRAHAM SHAPIRA
TRANSLATED BY JONATHAN CHIPMAN

THE JEWISH PUBLICATION SOCIETY
PHILADELPHIA   JERUSALEM
5758   1997

**The publication of this book was assisted
by a generous grant from
THE LUCIUS N. LITTAUER FOUNDATION**

Copyright © 1997 by Gershom Scholem

First Edition All rights reserved.

No part of this publication may be reproduced or transmitted in any form or by
any means, electronic or mechanical, including photocopy, recording, or any
information storage or retrieval system, except for brief passages in connection
with a critical review, without permission in writing from the publisher:
The Jewish Publication Society, 1930 Chestnut Street, Philadelphia, PA 19103-4599.

Manufactured in the United States of America

Library of Congress Cataloging-in-Publication Data

Scholem, Gershom Gerhard, 1897–1982
    [Essays. English. Selections]
    On the possibility of Jewish mysticism in our time and other
essays / by Gershom Scholem; edited and selected with an
introduction by Avraham Shapira; translated by Jonathan Chipman.
        p.   cm.
    Includes bibliographical references.
    ISBN 0-8276-0579-X
    1. Judaism. 2. Mysticism—Judaism. 3. Zionism. 4. Judaism—20th
century.   I. Shapira, Avraham, 1935–   . II. Title.
BM45.S44132   1997
296—dc21   97-48613
                                                                CIP

Designed and typeset by Book Design Studio II

02 01 00 99 98 97

Contents

Acknowledgments

Grateful acknowledgment is made to the following:

"On Education and Judaism" from *Dispersion and Unity*, 1971. Reprinted by permission of the World Zionist Organization.

"Judaism" by Gershom Scholem. Reprinted with permission of Charles Scribner's Sons, an imprint of Simon & Schuster Macmillan, from *Contemporary Jewish Religious Thought,* edited by Arthur A. Cohen and Paul Mendes-Flohr. Copyright ©1987 Charles Scribner's Sons.

"Three Types of Jewish Piety" published in © *Ariel: The Israel Review of Arts and Letters*. First published in *Ariel* no. 32, 1973.

The Philosophy of Franz Rosenzweig edited by Paul Mendes-Flohr, "Franz Rosenzweig and His Book: The Star of Redemption" by Gershom Scholem, © 1988 by Trustees of Brandeis University, by permission of University Press of New England.

"Our Historical Debt to Russian Society" published in *The Jerusalem Post*, February 1971.

"Messianism: A Never-ending Quest" published in Hebrew in *Ha-Ra'ayon ha-Meshiḥi be-Yisrael*, pp. 254–62.

Editor's Acknowledgments

I would like to thank all those who assisted me in bringing this book into existence, as a fitting tribute to the memory of the late teacher and scholar, Prof. Gershom Scholem. First and foremost, Dr. Ellen Frankel, editor-in-chief of the Jewish Publication Society, who played an active role both in the conception of the book and in the fashioning of its contents, a task to which she brought both extensive professional knowledge and cultural breadth. Dr. Asi Farber-Ginat of Haifa University and Dr. Amira Eran of the School of Overseas Studies of the Hebrew University assisted both in the choice of the selections to be included in the book, and as consultants regarding various academic issues. The following assisted the translator by reading and commenting on the drafts of the various chapters: Prof. Rachel Elior of the Hebrew University, Mr. Shlomo Zucker of the Institute of Hebrew manuscripts at the National and University Library in Jerusalem, Dr. Haviva Pedaya and Prof. Bracha Sack of Ben-Gurion University, Dr. Amira Eran, and Dr. Daniel Abrams of the College of Judaea and Samaria in Ariel. Finally, my heartfelt thanks to the translator, Rabbi Jonathan Chipman, for his rendering of Scholem's words into English, with sensitivity both to the contents and stylistic nuances of the essays. During the course of his work, he troubled to elucidate various ambiguous points, as well as adding notes which help to clarify various matters for the reader.

Avraham Shapira
Tel Aviv University

Translator's Introduction

Readers of Gershom Scholem's scholarly studies in Kabbalah, with their punctilious attention to philological and bibliographical detail, are no doubt familiar with the strict spiritual and intellectual austerity with which he approached the scholarly calling. The essays chosen for the present volume include a number which shed light upon several aspects of Scholem's personal experience and own spiritual world, together with some major historiosophical and historiographical essays hitherto unknown in English. One encounters here a Scholem passionately concerned with the renaissance of the Jewish people in its own land, specifically in its cultural and spiritual dimensions; one whose concerns encompassed issues of cultural life, language, the nature of scholarship, and the religious quest. Albeit not a practitioner of religion in the conventional sense, he was a religious believer and seeker, one who was troubled by the difficulty presented to the possibility of religious experience by the modern consciousness, which made himself and those of his ilk into "religious anarchists."

As Ehud Ben-Ezer notes in the introduction to his own collection of "conversations" on Zionism and Jewish identity, *Unease in Zion,* Scholem's ability to deal with the quintessential problematics of burning contemporary issues "in all their sharpness and severity," was second to none. In the essays "Reflections on the Possibility of Jewish Mysticism in Our Time," "Reflections on Modern Jewish Studies," and "Exile Today Is Devoid of the Seeds of Redemption" presented here, Scholem addresses himself with penetrating insight to the problematics of three central issues with which he was engaged throughout his life: Jewish mysticism, Jewish scholarship, and Zionism.

All of the essays in this volume are taken from the volumes *Devarim be-go*, 2 vols. (Tel Aviv: Am Oved, 1976), and *'Od Davar* (Tel Aviv: Am Oved, 1992) [collectively subtitled *Pirkei Morashah u-Teḥiyah*; in English: *Explications and Implications: Writings on Jewish Heritage and Renaissance*], compiled and edited by Avraham Shapira, who was likewise the guiding spirit behind the present volume.

In some places footnotes have been added to the essays, so as to provide certain background material for the edification of the reader. Except where otherwise noted (i.e., esp. Chs. 20 and 23), all notes in this volume were added by the translator.

Several chapters already existed in English, both those which were originally composed by Scholem in English and those which were translated during his lifetime and reviewed by him. Many of these were originally delivered as public speeches and reconstructed from recordings and, as such, were not always in form appropriate to the present volume. In such cases, I have taken the liberty of editing them very slightly, taking care not to alter or detract in any way from the sense or intent of Scholem.

In conclusion, it seems to me peculiarly appropriate that this book should appear at the present historical moment. With the apparent dawning of a peace between Israel and its Arab neighbors, both without and within (a development which Scholem much wished)—problematic as it may be—the "cultural question," the issues of Jewishness and Jewish identity which have long been muted or postponed in face of more immediate existential threats, will doubtless present themselves upon the public life of the State with greater force and urgency. Scholem's discussion of these difficult problems may provide, if not "answers"—Scholem was not a man for facile solutions to vexing problems—at least some guidance and understanding of the issues confronting Israeli society and world Jewry in these difficult times.

Finally, I wish to express my gratitude to Avraham Shapira, editor of this volume, for his invaluable guidance and advice throughout the preparation of this translation. Conveying Scholem's grace of language and subtlety of thought was a formidable challenge. It is my hope that the present volume will prove a fitting representation of the manifold and profound thought of one of the geniuses of modern Judaism.

Jonathan Chipman
Jerusalem
Tishrei 5756, October 1995

Introduction

The Dialectics of Continuity and Revolt*

by Avraham Shapira

Gershom Scholem (Berlin 1897–Jerusalem 1982) was one of those creative giants whose lifework breaks down the commonly accepted borders between disciplines. One cannot understand his approach to Jewish studies, for example, without taking into account both his conception of Judaism and his personal sense of religiosity. Furthermore, these two factors were inextricably linked to his spiritual identity and to his profound identification with Zionism as the embodiment of Jewish life.

In understanding the traditionalist aspect of Scholem's identity, we come to appreciate the universal dimensions of his work, including its significance for contemporary Western culture in general. Unfortunately, Gershom Scholem's identification in the public mind with the rediscovery of the history of Jewish mysticism overshadows these other aspects of his work. Thus, many readers of his biographical work, *Walter Benjamin: The Story of a Friendship* (Philadelphia, 1981), were surprised to discover how deeply rooted Scholem was in European cultures and how often his spiri-

*Introduction translated by Jeffrey M. Green.

xi

tual biography intersected the worlds of the great creators in the fields of twentieth century literature, poetry, visual arts, philosophy, and the history of religion, among others.

Perhaps only those not directly involved in similar scholarly fields can appreciate Scholem's creative genius from such a broad perspective. Such, for instance, is the vantage point of Cynthia Ozick:

> Gershom Scholem is a historian who has remade the world. He has remade it the way Freud is said to have remade it—by breaking open the shell of the rational to uncover the spiraling demons inside. But if Freud is regarded as one of the century's originals, there are nevertheless those who, without necessarily reducing Freud's stature, think the oceanic work of Gershom Scholem envelops Freud's discoveries as the sea includes even its most heroic whitecaps. Or, to alter the image: Freud is a peephole into a dark chamber—a camera obscura; but Scholem is a radio telescope monitoring the universe, with its myriads of dark chambers. . . .
>
> . . . Freud struck loose also from the sustenance of Jewish ideas, turning instead to classical mythology and claiming Hannibal as his hero. Scholem delved beyond the Greek and Roman roots of the conventional European education common to them both. Scholem went in pursuit of the cosmos—and that took him straight to the perplexities of Genesis and the Hebrew language.[1]

Every contemporary culture experiences tensions between the patterns and paradigms of its traditions and the rapid changes characteristic of our post-modern era. These crises have spared neither the great historical religions of the West, nor those of the Far East.[2] Analyzing the history of Judaism and its break from tradition in the early eighteenth century, Scholem defined two movements—Ḥasidism in Eastern Europe and the Haskalah in Western Europe—as together heralding a decisive turning point, a revolution in traditional Jewish culture.[3] Although most Jewish historians note the crisis entailed by the emergence of these two movements, Scholem took the analysis further. He excavated the paradoxes and contradictory tendencies underlying their emergence, refusing to oversimplify or falsify their complexity, paying particular attention to the subterranean trends, invisible to the eye, that occasionally burst into the active historical arena. He noted the tension between tradition and renewal. His gaze was fastened on the dialectical processes that promised to heal the crisis of fissure. We shall return to this matter later.

The title of Scholem's autobiographical work, *From Berlin to Jerusalem,*[4] points to the single direction that defined his intellectual life: Zionism. He was born with the Zionist movement, the same year that the first Zionist Congress convened in Basel, dominated by the figure of Theodor

Herzl. While still only thirteen or fourteen, Scholem began to seek his own path and to discover himself. From that time on, from within himself, and in brilliant isolation, he began to turn away from the path of assimilation and accommodation that characterized his parents' home and their circle, and began moving toward a rooted Jewish identity. Thus, even before he emigrated to the Land of Israel in the early 1920s, he had begun his journey from "Berlin" to "Jerusalem." Yet, he remained rooted in the language and culture of his native Germany. For him, Zionism embodied the tension between his Germanness and his Judaism. He experienced this tension most intimately as he shuttled intellectually between his mother-tongue and Hebrew, which he mastered as a second language.[5]

Scholem's one-way journey from Berlin to Jerusalem was not a smooth one. Enroute, he encountered moments of exaltation and of faltering. But all along his spiritual path, a journey lasting nearly seventy continuous years, he was guided by a utopian vision: Zionist self-realization. He persisted in believing in a Jewish renaissance in the Land of Israel even as he despaired over the vagaries of Jewish history and the dominant strain of political, messianic Zionism. He also struggled against those he called the modern "prophets of falsehood"—people who themselves were in error and who misled others—and against those with closed eyes and little faith.[6] Yet he kept these feelings of despair to himself, neither speaking nor writing about them. To him, these were disappointments solely with people and with doctrines, not with the utopian path with which he identified his life: "Paradox is a characteristic of truth. What *communis opinio* has of truth is surely no more than an elementary deposit of generalizing partial understanding, related to truth even as sulfurous fumes are to lightning." Scholem recognized the "deep truth of the dialectic in history. . . . In the realization of one trait its opposite is revealed."[7]

The dialectical oscillation that animated his research and thought was not, for him, an abstract structure. Of himself, he declared: "I did not learn dialectics from Hegel or the Marxists, but from my own experiences and from pondering the labyrinths of Zionism as I was trying to implement it."[8] He observed that "in my youthful jottings you will not find a single clue to a dialectical understanding of processes. I came to see the force of dialectics only gradually, in the course of careful study, especially after I came to Eretz Yisra'el and saw the contradictions in the constructive processes here: the inner contradictions in reviving a secular language and the silence overpowering the language."[9]

It is somewhat reductionist to define Scholem as an "historian." His old friend and colleague, the great historian Yitzhak Baer, described him as "by propensity a metaphysician and against his will a great historian who has enriched the study of Jewish history more than anyone else in our generation. . . . A realistic historian by force of his transcendentalist tendencies."[10]

We are thus dealing here with a great intellectual who, through his insights and deep intuitions, broke through the conventions of scholarship yet remained faithful to his commitments. He defined himself once in a lecture as an archaeologist of the spiritual past of the Jewish people.

But he did far more than break open and lay bare the blocked wells of the past, revealing its subterranean veins. Rather, his historical vision extended beyond the past, beyond collective memory, toward the horizons of future development. "We are interested in history," he declared, "because therein lie the experiences of mankind, just as therein lies the dynamic light of the future." In a profound and brilliant essay, published posthumously, he discussed the reciprocal links between past and future: "Not only are the symbols of the past buried in our consciousness, . . . but also the utopian hopes for the future give shape to those symbols (of the past)."[11] Scholem thus understood Jewish history as an ongoing development present within Jewish culture and embodied in Jewish hermeneutics, i.e., in Midrash. Jewish culture is based on an ongoing creative interpretation of its classics. In the words of Ismar Schorsch, its canon is not "closed."[12]

Scholem's conception of Judaism assumed the existence of utopian elements that have not yet been actualized, fruit yet to ripen on the boughs of the past. Some of his writings about this idea were collected for the first time in *'Od Davar*, and appear here for the first time in translation.

The creative dynamic of Jewish history—what Scholem called "a new spiritual perspective on the exegesis of primary sources" (see his article with that title in Chapter Ten)—is what makes historical tradition possible in Judaism. According to him, the modern period in Jewish history is not one of "tradition and crisis," but rather a period of "heritage and renaissance." But, not only does this renaissance grow out of the heritage of the past; it also gains strength from a utopian vision of the future.

Gershom Scholem was one of the youngest of that unorganized group of Jewish spiritual giants who arose during the transitional period beginning in the late nineteenth century: Ḥayyim Naḥman Bialik, Berl Katznelson, Aharon David Gordon, Rabbi Abraham Isaac Kook, Yosef Ḥayim Brenner, Shlomo Zemach, and others who emerged from Eastern Europe. From central Europe came others of equal spiritual stature: Martin Buber, Franz Kafka, Franz Rosenzweig, Sigmund Freud, Albert Einstein, and Gustav Landauer, as well as those who contributed mainly to cultures beyond that of their own people. All of these men were marked by the crisis in European culture known as *fin de siècle*, which gave rise to a volcanic eruption of Jewish genius, the last to date in Jewish history. Such a concentration of creative cultural power has never before coalesced within such a short period of Jewish history.

We can discern the outlines of Scholem's own sources and beliefs in the portraits he drew of his contemporaries. Prominent among these is Scholem's profile of Agnon,[13] as well as his ambivalent portrayal of Buber. We can also find him partially revealed in his evocations of Kafka's work, particularly in the many references to *The Trial* throughout Scholem's writings.[14] In these expressions of his affinity with Kafka, we can glimpse the intellectual friction which kindled Scholem's own creative genius: on the one hand, the absurdity and incomprehensibility that characterized Kafka's universe; on the other, the world of faith. Between the two worlds prevails constant tension. To Scholem, Kafka exemplified the "infinite drive" to seek the key unlocking the meaning of revelation, even when the key itself has been lost. This striving, according to Gershom Scholem, typifies the Jewish mystical tradition.

Generally, Scholem's essays devoted to specific personalities offered only the outlines of a portrait. To flesh out the picture requires further research into other places. For example, when he asked of Ernst Bloch—"Does God Dwell in the Heart of an Atheist?" (see Chapter Twenty-four) his answer unfolded in two other works, "Towards an Understanding of the Messianic Idea in Judaism," and in *Walter Benjamin: The Story of a Friendship.*

A certain aura enveloped Gershom Scholem, one that inspired distance and awe (though he himself seemed unaware of this). Partially, this impression was created by the mysticism he devoted himself to as a scholar. It was reinforced by his habits as the veteran professor and by his German manners. Yet this man who inspired dread without intending to do so, transcended all the formalities of status. When in his company, one realized that he was not a "distant" man after all, but rather someone who listened and responded.

Although he often seemed a sphinx-like individual, Scholem was also a social person who made friends. He had a number of very close friends as well as numerous associates (some of them his colleagues), but these were not full spiritual partners. Despite all of his involvement and conviviality, he was a man enclosed within his own secret world. Even those closest to him realized this only after his passing: Scholem was a solitary man. "Scholem is a genius," Akiva Ernst Simon once told me, "and every genius is solitary." But it should be emphasized that with respect to Scholem, solitary does not mean isolated. From childhood he became accustomed to live estranged in spiritual detachment from his family. Later in life he found it difficult to locate someone after his own heart, and so he maintained the secret patterns of solitude he had cultivated as a child. His essay,

"If We Could Only Tell How We Became Zionists" (1919),[15] poignantly testifies to the roots of that solitude and to his being accustomed to it. There
he writes to himself about "the friendship which has been taken away."
His descriptions of how his bond with Walter Benjamin was formed (see
below) also demonstrate his longing for companionship. On rare occa-
sions this solitude cries out in personal letters. Typically, such letters have
not been included in his published correspondence.

Among his many relationships, one of the most complex was with
Martin Buber, twenty years his senior. Scholem published critiques of
Buber only toward the end of his own life.[16] But while Buber was still alive,
Scholem refrained from criticizing him in writing, aware of Buber's great
sensitivity to criticism, especially from someone like himself. As the years
passed, the connection between these two men, based on deep and mutual personal respect, deepened. When Buber became ill near the end of
his life, Scholem showed great concern for Buber, even going from pharmacy to pharmacy in search of medicine for him.

Yet despite their deep feeling toward each other, these two spiritual giants were both extremely solitary and did not stretch their cordiality into
true friendship. It is even possible to view their mutual respect as a barrier
to such friendship. In contrast, Buber had a much more relaxed relationship with Scholem's wife Fanya, who became his friend and confidante.
He preferred to visit the Scholem home while the master of the house was
absent, attending meetings of the faculty senate of the Hebrew University.

And, despite their many differences of opinion regarding their conceptions of Judaism and their methods of investigating Ḥasidism, Scholem
acknowledged Buber as an exalted spiritual personality. He once told his
wife Fanya, "While Buber did not hear the [Divine] voice, he did hear a
Bat-kol." Only about Buber could he have said such a thing.

Another of Scholem's special friendships was with Walter Benjamin, a
relationship that inspired him to break out of the walls of his solitude. In
a letter from Benjamin that reached Scholem on his twentieth birthday
(December 5, 1917), one catches a glimpse of the secret of that friendship.
Responding to an earlier letter from Scholem, Benjamin speaks of a "revelation," defining "revelation" as that particular personal bond that united
the two men and nurtured their friendship, the special connection that
"has reached you and has entered our life again for a moment. I have entered a new phase of my life." Gershom Scholem chose to include this letter in *From Berlin to Jerusalem,*[17] saying that it was one, "the likes of which
I never received from him again." But according to Fanya Scholem,
Scholem's unshakable bond with Benjamin revealed within this letter prevented her husband from seeing Benjamin in appropriate perspective,
from objectively noting the less positive sides of his personality. In his

book, *The Story of a Friendship,* which Scholem devoted to Benjamin, we find that Scholem repeatedly blinded himself to Benjamin's flaws and to evidence of his friend's immoral behavior. Those close to Scholem found it difficult to understand and accept this uncritical attitude toward Benjamin. And yet, Scholem's friendship with Benjamin, like that with Buber, remained incomplete. Though Scholem could enter their worlds, they could not encompass his. According to Fanya, they fell short because only Scholem "was gifted with the intuitive power of a genius."

Though endowed with extraordinary intellectual talents and a phenomenal memory, Scholem acknowledged the equal power of inner penetration which transcends rational analysis. More than once he granted a higher authority to an intuitive feeling than to a stronger logical proof. About the philological-historical method, he once admitted that he did not "tend to exaggerate" the value of "historical criticism" or view it as "the be all and the end all." It is "not the key that opens all of the locked chambers. There are proofs that see further; there are intuitions and reflections that penetrate (or claim to penetrate) to the depths. In contrast to them, historical criticism is like a daughter of the 'petite bourgeoisie.' Yet nevertheless—how great is its power, as it protects us from the illusions and self-deceits that we all love so much."[18] In an article in honor of Gershom Scholem's eightieth birthday, David Flusser described the role of intuitive thinking in Scholem's approach to historical research:

> Perhaps in order to clarify the essence of the intuition which the scholar needs, one should recall the words of Cincius, a sage who lived in about the fourth century C.E. He said that one can understand the book one is dealing with only when one can guess correctly what is written on the page which is missing in one's copy of it—and who could doubt that ability in Gershom Scholem?[19]

In Scholem we find at work a unique alchemy of creative forces that transformed a talented scholar into a creative genius. On the one hand, Scholem considered himself a scholar subject to the rules of the philological and historical method who, to the end of his days, devoted long stretches of time to the scrupulous philological decipherment of texts. Yet, at the same time, his work blurs the accepted boundaries among the separate disciplines comprising Jewish studies. His research was not merely a scientific, intellectual activity; rather it drew upon, to use the words of Erich Neumann, "the fervor of the entire person."[20] Indeed, Gershom Scholem's works are an expression of his entire personality. He did not follow a set path of pre-established patterns, but instead rediscovered them for himself each time afresh. Though a marvelous consistency binds together his work from his youth until the end of his days, his work also crackles with original and unexpected ideas. His truths broke out from within.

In all creative genius, something essential to that genius springs into being fully formed. According to the Midrash:

> It is characteristic of flesh and blood that when it wishes to create a form it begins with the head or with one of the limbs and then finishes it. However, the Holy One, blessed be He, creates an entire form all at once, as it is said, "for He creates all" (Jeremiah 10:16), and it says: "and there is no Form [a play on the Hebrew *tzur,* meaning "rock," but which also means "form"] but our Lord" (1 Samuel 2:2), there is no Maker of Forms but our Lord.[21]

In Scholem, this essence can be found in early compositions and entirely personal writings such as "If We Could Only Tell How We Became Zionists" (mentioned above), and also in his longest and most comprehensive work, *Sabbatai Ṣevi—The Mystical Messiah.*[22] That book was written in its entirety almost all at once, in one draft, first and final, without early studies or partial preparations. Such a creative birth, of which perhaps only geniuses are capable, testifies to an extensive process of gestation.

Several souls struggled within Gershom Scholem, and his spirit frequented several circles. Vying with each other, various intellectual tendencies joined together within his works, especially the general ones published from 1949 on, when he began taking part in the Eranos Conferences in Ascona.[23] Hidden dimensions burst forth from his creative core, and then it was possible to be burned in the intense heat.

Scholem had a complex and intense relationship with Judaism. He wrestled with the question that "thrust itself" upon him: "Was Judaism still alive as a heritage or an experience, even as something constantly evolving, or did it exist only as an object of cognition?"[24] This was a question to which he continued to compose answers throughout his life. Here, especially, he placed his faith in the utopian element of Judaism. Dov Sadan, one of the greatest Hebrew scholars of our time (neither a mystic nor a visionary), relates a conversation he once held with Berl Katznelson, concerning the place of Gershom Scholem's books in the future life of Judaism: "We started from the shared assumption that the study of Judaism would ultimately become Jewish doctrine. However, there was a difference between us in the way we put it. He [Berl] said: 'perhaps even in Jewish faith'; and I said: 'especially in Jewish faith, for that is what is determining.' He said: 'in any event, if I knew where his books will stand in coming generations, I would be able to tell you what Jewish faith will be like.' I answered: 'they will stand where the books of the Jews have stood and stand forever [meaning in synagogues and houses of study], especially those which strip away their own time and extend over all time.'"[25]

Gershom Scholem's path to Judaism overlapped with his path to Zionism. He viewed the Jewish national rebirth not as a separate and independent stage in Jewish history, but rather as an expression and realization of Judaism. His Zionism was not ideology, nor personal world view. "That which we call Zionism," he wrote in an unpublished note to himself in June 1913, "belonged to the essence of our life." That essence suffused his entire being, and was congruent with his entire spiritual biography. It shaped his way of life, provided an impulse for his creativity, formed the basis of his thinking, and directed the course of his work.

His Judaism was rooted in a faith in God. Perhaps because this faith served as the foundation of his life, he spoke little about it, but referred instead to possible paths of faith and attitudes to Judaism. Not surprisingly, he only expressed his own faith in God within a limited, inner circle.[26]

The Zionist conviction expressed in his immigration to the Land of Israel in the early 1920s and his submission to the obligations entailed by his identity did not emerge out of a naive utopianism. From his first steps in the Land of Israel, Gershom Scholem showed an acute awareness of the contrasts roiling within the new historical reality being created there and of the paradoxes within it. He gave expression to it mostly in private, in unpublished personal notebooks that have come to light only since his death.

Within Gershom Scholem we witness a confrontation between the wide vistas of Jewish history and "the day of small beginnings" (Zech. 4:10). This dual focus is what gave him a unique perspective for understanding the "living experiment" of Zionist renewal:

> The Jews built their historical experience into their cosmogony. Kabbalistic myth had "meaning," because it sprang from a fully conscious relation to a reality which, experienced symbolically even in its horror, was able to project mighty symbols of Jewish life as an extreme case of human life, pure and simple. We can no longer fully perceive, I might say, "live," the symbols of the Kabbalah without a considerable effort, if at all. We confront the old questions in a new way. But if symbols spring from a reality that is pregnant with feeling and illumined by the colorless light of intuition, . . . then surely we may say this: what greater opportunity has the Jewish people ever had than in the horror of defeat, in the struggle and victory of these last years, in its utopian withdrawal into its own history, to fulfill its encounter with its own genius, its true and "perfect nature?"[27]

From his youth onward, "The troubles of his people touched his heart," as Bialik wrote. He was always tormented by the tension between *heritage,* which had perished, unaware of itself, within deracinated German Jewry, and *renaissance,* which expresses "living continuity" over the generations. His work resolved this tension by weaving together the yearnings of the individual and the "higher aspirations" of the nation.

Part One

Scholem's Personal
Relationship to the
Study of Mysticism

Chapter One

A Candid Letter About My True Intentions in Studying Kabbalah (1937)*

Remembering the many hours of friendly conversation between us filled with unpretentious exchange of ideas and opinions, I should like to share with you a candid word as to my true intentions in studying the Kabbalah.

I have not, under any circumstance, become a Kabbalist. I knew what I was doing—except that the task that I took upon myself seemed to me far easier than it is in fact. It is true that, when I first began preparing myself to assume the mantle of the philologist, abandoning the disciplines of mathematics and epistemology for a far more ambiguous field, I did not have any real knowledge of the subject, but was filled with numerous insights.

Behind me were three years, 1916–1918, which were to be decisive for the course my entire life was to take. Years of highly stimulating thought had brought me to a rationalistic skepticism concerning the object of my study, coupled with an intuitive affirmation of those mystical theses that lie on the narrow boundary between religion and nihilism.

I found the fullest and unsurpassed expression of this boundary in the writings of Kafka, which are themselves a secularized description for a con-

---

* A letter sent to Salman Z. Schocken, founder of Schocken Verlag in Berlin, on the occasion of his sixtieth birthday. Dated October 29, 1937. Published in Hebrew translation in *Ha-Aretz*, Erev Pesaḥ 5741 (1981); reprinted in *'Od Davar*, 29–31.

temporary person of the feeling of a Kabbalistic world. Indeed, at a later stage this led me to look on them as possessing an almost canonical halo.

But in those days I was subject to the magical influence of that curious book by Molitor, *The Philosophy of History*, or, *Concerning Tradition*,[1] which I came across at Poppelauer's. Notwithstanding the fact that everything he said about history was utterly groundless, he nevertheless did note a place in which the hidden life of Judaism had once dwelled, to which I attached myself in my meditations.

I did not enter this field with the intention of writing the history of Kabbalah, but rather its metaphysics. I was struck by the impoverishment of what people were fond of designating as the philosophy of Judaism. The only three authors I knew—Saadiah Ga'on, Maimonides, and Hermann Cohen—annoyed me, in that they saw their primary function as setting up antitheses to myth and pantheism and disproving them. It would have been more beneficial had they attempted to raise them to a higher level within which they would be negated.

It is not difficult to prove that myth and pantheism are mistaken. The comment, which I first heard from a pious Jew, that they nevertheless do possess some substance, seems to me far more significant. I felt that same higher level to be found in Kabbalah, even if it is perhaps expressed there in a distorted way. It seemed to me that here, beyond the distinctions drawn by our contemporaries, there was a realm of associations that should touch upon our most human experiences.

It is true that, judging from the obtuse Enlightenment standard that Jewish scholars have offered on the subject, the key to their understanding seems to have been lost. Nevertheless, in those first Kabbalistic works that I read with the enthusiasm of ignorance, there seemed to flash forth a way of thinking that—to use simple language—had not yet found a home.

Molitor's profound insight, even if derived from the distorted perspective of Franz von Baader, is unlikely to be misleading. Perhaps it was not so much the key that was missing as the courage: the courage to risk the descent into the abyss that might one day swallow us up. That, and the daring to penetrate beyond the symbolic plane and to break through the wall of history.

The mountain itself—the things themselves—does not need a key at all; it is only the misty wall of history that surrounds it that must be penetrated. To penetrate it—that is the task I have set for myself. Would I remain stuck in the mist, suffering a professorial death, so to speak? Yet even if it demands sacrifices, the compelling need for a critique of history and for historical criticism cannot be provided in any other way.

It may, of course, be that fundamentally history is no more than an illusion. However, without this illusion it is impossible to penetrate through temporal reality to the essence of the things themselves. Through the unique perspective of philological criticism, there has been reflected to contemporary man for the first time, in the neatest possible way, that mystical totality of Truth *(des Systems)* whose existence disappears specifically because of its being thrust upon historical time.

My work is sustained today, as it was at the very beginning of my path, by virtue of this paradox, and in anticipation of being answered from the mountain, through that slight, almost invisible motion of history, allowing the truth to break through from what is called development.

Chapter Two

Reflections on the Possibility of Jewish Mysticism in Our Time (1963)*

I am afraid that, more than a well-ordered doctrine, what you will hear from me are certain doubts, as is perhaps appropriate to this place.

If we are to conduct an inquiry concerning mysticism in our day, or the specific question being asked here about Jewish mysticism in our day, it must be set against a certain framework and within a more general background. In the final analysis, one may say that there is no authentic original mysticism in our generation, either in the Jewish people or among the nations of the world. Those expressions of feeling or consciousness on the part of people possessing mystical knowledge, involving the giving of form and its transmission to future generations, have long since ceased. It is clear that in recent generations there have been no awakenings of individuals leading to new forms of mystical teachings or to significant movements in public life. This applies equally well to Judaism, Christianity, and Islam.

Two centuries have passed since the two most recent major awakenings in the history of Jewish mysticism, which represented a new and, for the present, last stage of those wishes or yearnings of the soul known as mysticism.

* Based upon a public lecture given at Har-El Synagogue in Jerusalem, 1963. Published in Hebrew in *Amot* 8 (Tishrei–Ḥeshvan 5724 [Fall 1963]); reprinted in *Devarim be-go*, 71–83.

Two hundred years ago there was founded in Jerusalem Yeshivat Beth-El, the center of those Kabbalists who came from the Sephardic communities and of the Jews from Arab lands (as well as of the Yemenites). This center existed for many generations, almost until the present, providing a certain expression for the feeling of an entire public, and not only of those isolated individuals involved—one that was considered the height of inner awareness of the meaning of Jewish experience. The Ḥasidic movement in Poland and Russia, which provided an anchor for Jewish mysticism as a broad and multi-faceted public phenomenon in our history, was likewise created two centuries ago.

It is true that since then there have been, here and there, continuations of such impulses. Nevertheless, our period has generally speaking been impoverished in original awakenings of public significance. Here and there one can find certain wild growths of mysticism which grew out of the intuitions of individuals, and which found a sectarian echo in narrower or wider circles. Less than ten years ago, the most recent flourishing of unbridled mysticism of this type appeared in certain manifestations of the movement known as *Subud* that emerged in Indonesia.[1] These phenomena, which spread throughout the world, originated in a man of mystical consciousness from Java. However, it is doubtful whether these will remain of lasting significance as a mystical phenomenon of general value, rather than as a wild growth of the human spirit. It is, nevertheless, interesting to note the speed with which such an impulse, originating in an individual of intense personal charisma, spreads today to all corners of the globe by means of contact or a type of quasi-contact.

People may rightly ask to what I refer when I speak of mysticism. I am in fact hesitant to trouble you with definitions, as no one apart from the mystics themselves really knows what mysticism is—and even they have different opinions, each one according to his own attainments or the attainments of his spirit. Every author writing about this subject proposes a different definition. Nevertheless, as it is impossible to avoid the subject completely, allow me to begin by saying that Jewish mysticism as such does not exist at all, in the sense of direct, unmediated union with the Godhead. There is no such thing within the framework of the Jewish tradition, as such a union requires a level of daring which seems impossible within the context of the concepts traditionally accepted by one who calls himself a Jew. If mysticism is defined, however, as a consciousness or experience of divine matters, there certainly is Jewish mysticism, of many and varied forms and shades. It has existed over the course of two thousand years, from the time of the Merkabah mystics and of that extraordinary mystic known as Paul of Tarsus down to our own day. The question confronting us may of course only arise in the context of the second definition, which is both more cautious and more all-encompassing. In this case, we may inquire concerning the existence of people blessed with spiritual sensitivity who have any sort of experience of divine matters.

Of course, mysticism in the sense of experience belongs to the individual rather than the public realm. Indeed, on the face of it, the center of gravity of all those phenomena known as mysticism pertains first and foremost to the realm of the individual. Nevertheless, when we speak of such questions in general, certainly in the context of such reflections as these, we are not concerned with the private domain of mysticism. Isolated individuals, undergoing experiences known or comprehended only to themselves, which suddenly shed new light and understanding upon their inner world, drawing upon inner sources of inspiration, vision, and comprehension—such persons have existed in every generation, and were not unknown even after the Ḥasidic movement; that is, even after the degeneration of Ḥasidism. Such people may and do exist in every circle. But these phenomena are confined to the experience of the individual, are not translated into public language, and do not have any public significance. Many have drunk from these wells and many will drink; they have not and will not find it possible to translate their experience, which is beyond the framework of human language. They sufficed with their own apprehension of what was given to them, or did not talk of it at all. If they did reveal it, they remained on the level of translators, without any echo or response.

Let me mention a well-known example, which many people certainly knew about at the time without realizing that it had any connection to mysticism. I refer to the emergence of Nathan Birnbaum as a religious teacher. One day this Birnbaum, who had undergone many transformations, and not for naught called himself a latter-day Mattathias, became an extremely Orthodox Jew. I doubt whether he ever publicly revealed or recorded in writing the basis on which he became what he did—namely, a spokesman for the strictest, most extreme version of Orthodox Judaism. This happened on the basis of mystical experiences, which he underwent while engaged in entirely different matters. These experiences led to a profound change of orientation in this man—who, notwithstanding his many weaknesses, was in certain respects a great man.

Birnbaum's experiences on his way into Judaism did not leave any discernible result. He lived these experiences and made use of them, but did not continue with them. Whatever may have happened between himself and his Creator was not translated into the language of literature, save for the slightest hints. Whoever does not know how to read the writings of Nathan Birnbaum—and today he is not read at all—and does not know this secret tradition, will not know from whence he derived the feeling of mission that is so prominent in several of his later writings.

As for that mysticism that is in some way concerned with public eluci-dation (I deliberately express myself with extreme caution): it has in it an element of the public domain. It seeks to influence the generation as a whole, to show a path, not only to that individual whose eyes have been opened and who sees and comprehends something of the root of our being, but to transmit this knowledge to others. Here there begins the paradox of the mystics in each generation, and hence the great interest that mystics have for us. One who does not wish to influence, but keeps his prophecy to himself, does not enter into the historical chain of the history of mysticism. The very concept is paradoxical from beginning to end. How can one speak of a history of the private realm or of those things that are between man and his Creator?! Yet nevertheless, there certainly is! The entire history of religions is built upon the development of these im-pulses and their translation into the language of each generation accord-ing to its own concepts—all in accordance with the accepted language. Those who felt such impulses attempted to energize human beings toward new forms of organization and society, toward a unique type of society, as the spirit moved them.

In this sense, we are speaking of Jewish mysticism as an historical phe-nomenon within the people, one that took shape beyond all those wild flourishings of private mysticism of which we know nothing and which existed without leaving a trace in the living literature and tradition. The public as such does not undergo those revolutionary events and enthusi-asms which frequently mark mysticism. Nevertheless, an echo of these primal impulses does reverberate within the public. Thus, even if we are concerned here with a particular individual and a personal matter, it nev-ertheless imbues a particular spirit upon entire phenomena, upon entire communities, upon certain circles within society, or upon the public as a whole. Only from this point of view may we ask: What is the position of our generation with respect to this matter? Where do we stand? All that I can offer in this respect are certain reflections, as I have no answer; a few reflections that have bearing on this basic problem, about which many people ask.

The question is, of course, based upon the assumption that our history has a certain continuity: an assumption with which not everyone in our generation would agree, and without which there is no basis for my fol-lowing remarks. The question is: Are there yet, and will there continue to

be, Jews who have undergone a living and authentic religious experience,
one drawing upon the realm which is beyond routine performances, or
even beyond living faith, because they have come to the sources of that
faith itself, upon which they drew and to which they returned. Beyond
that, we inquire as to the possible form such a living experience may assume for the public.

Our generation, being a generation of crisis, is seemingly ready for such
a manifestation. There are no greater hours of inspiration in the history of
religion, no times of greater creativity in the public realm of mysticism,
than times of historical crisis. All of the great outbreaks of mysticism in
the monotheistic religions (of which we know a considerable amount,
after four generations of research) are associated with crises. I will not elaborate this point here. The same holds true for the history of Jewish mysticism, in all of its various forms. Indeed, we are now at such a propitious
moment: the Jewish people has undergone a crisis and catastrophe that
are beyond the power of human words and language to express. We must
nevertheless ask: What will become of this? What can emerge from it?

There is of course an element of rashness in anticipating immediate results from crises. The Kabbalah of Safed, one of the best-formulated and
best-understood mystical manifestations in terms of its historical significance in the history of Judaism, was a response of the Jewish people to
the expulsion from Spain, which constituted a tremendous crisis in the
life of the nation. Yet two or three generations passed until this legitimate
response was articulated in the language of its contemporaries in a form
that carried historical meaning for the public, beyond the two or three
Safed Kabbalists whose names are associated with this phenomenon as
original visionaries. The same holds true for the phenomenon of Ḥasidism
(without undertaking here a discussion of the issue of Sabbatianism). It
too emerged after the crisis had passed, and not immediately after the
shock. Only after some time does an historical shock penetrate to those
productive depths from which such impulses emerge. Sometimes a great
deal of time must pass until the reaction becomes visible. True, there are
some people who will say that concepts of time have changed since the
idea of relativity was introduced into the world, and that which in our ancestors' time took generations now requires only a short time, due to the
change in circumstances and conditions. But there are limits to this insight concerning relativity, and it remains to be proven that human reac-
tions and the pace of their depth have indeed changed.

It is therefore understandable why the response to the Holocaust, which
was such a profound shock—whether that reaction be destructive or productive—is not yet in sight. We hope that this shock will be productive,

and it is for that reason that we live here, in this country. Therefore, in my opinion, it is not at all surprising that we have yet to see mystical manifestations as a reaction to those events. This should serve as a warning to those who ask: Where is the religious and universal-human reaction of our generation to what happened, to what so shook the very roots of the existence of our people?

The immediate function of a creative mystical religious awakening is based, as we said, upon a profound and living personal religious experience. The time needed to react and respond to such an event is in direct proportion to the depth of the shock. There may be other questions involved, and other reflections evoked, to which I shall need to return so as to provide something of an additional response to this point concerning the stance of this generation and its relation to a fundamental human experience, which may perhaps cause man to confront his Creator.

One can find in this generation a continuation of earlier forms, in the sense of a precious living heritage, or one which has degenerated but nevertheless continues to exist in its external forms, even though it has lost its soul. There are phenomena of authentic awakening among circles in whom we would expect such a mystical renewal, such as those of Hasidism. In this respect, there is something to tell and to explain. Here and there one finds striking examples of phenomena occurring deep within the Judaism of the last generation, bearing a certain echo pertaining to our subject: phenomena which draw upon the sources of our people's mystical tradition as embodied in many forms of Kabbalah and Hasidism.

There are at least three phenomena, which may provoke thought regarding our problem, which I would like to mention here, even though I am not among their devotees. I refer, first of all, to the figure of Rav Kook, whom I see as an example *par excellence* of a great Jewish mystic, as expressed in the three volumes of his book *Orot ha-Kodesh*. This book is an esoteric and strange one in several respects: a remarkable combination of thought, with its own inner logic, and of reflections, which contain rather less systematic thought and more an outpouring of the heart, which is renewed and awakened from time to time, and behind which there lies a profound mystical upheaval.

I would also like to refer to a living innovation which has emerged in Hasidism in only one place. Hasidism still exists in all kinds of forms—a point that I will not discuss here. While much is said in the larger world about parlor Hasidism, here in Jerusalem in our own day, some thirty years ago, we witnessed the growth of a new, living Hasidic community as an authentic historical phenomenon. This is not merely a continuation of the dynasty of such-and-such a rebbe who was the son of a *tzaddik,* one of those numerous "grandchildren" *(eineklakh)* who today fill the world of pious Jewry, but rather a person who became a Ḥasidic leader in his own right, without any pedigree. This is a unique phenomenon in the history of Ḥasidism during the generation preceding the Holocaust. I refer to Rabbi Arele Roth and his circle. Rabbi Arele came to Jerusalem in 1928, returned to Europe during the 1930s, came back again in 1940, and died in 1946. In this case, we can see that there still exists the possibility of spiritual ascent by means of pious attachment to the tradition, which originally doubtless drew upon an individual of mystical inspiration. Just as the world-view of a Jew with unique contemplative powers emerges in the volumes of Rabbi Kook's *Orot ha-Kodesh,* so do the volumes of the book *Shomer Emunim* by Rabbi Arele Roth present one of the most remarkable documents to the contemporary Jew, even if he himself is far removed from the traditional framework within which such a phenomenon was possible.

These two outstanding, inspired figures were still able to develop their own thoughts while identifying with the world of Kabbalah which preceded them. They are no longer Kabbalists in the strict sense, like the Kabbalists of Beth-El or those who preceded them. Anyone reading Rav Kook's *Orot ha-Kodesh* can immediately see that he is not a Kabbalist; rather, we see here a great man, who translated his own religious experience into human language, drawing upon the heritage of the generations. It is clear that he altered various linguistic usages, both in its details and in general, and that he is still capable of freshly adapting the words and tradition of his predecessors. These two figures still have the great quality of faith, for which there is no substitute. I will explain immediately what I mean by this. In what did they have faith? What was the basis upon which people like Rav Kook and Rabbi Arele Roth were able to build?

A third example of Ḥasidic renewal, better known than either of the other two, is that of contemporary Ḥabad Ḥasidism, which has been widely discussed among people generally and in the press, and whose nature is well-known.

All three of these manifestations share something in common that is peculiar to our present concern: namely, that they minimize insofar as possible the mystical component of their inspiration, to the point of barely acknowledging it at all. It is clear, however, that they derive their inspiration from something like a genuine shock. In the famous declaration issued some twenty years ago by the former Lubavitcher Rebbe, "Redemption Immediately!" *(le-'altar le-ge'ulah),* one detects a clear reliance upon the private realm of mysticism, albeit things have assumed a guise that has hardly anything of the mystical about it; they accompany accepted, institutionalized Orthodoxy in a striking and extreme way. The mystical side remains as a kind of hint to the individual whose soul may be touched by God, but not to the public whom they wish to organize or to build up. The public success of Ḥabad Ḥasidim stems, to a large extent, from their deliberate ignoring of the mystical realm.

At the beginning of my remarks, I mentioned the resemblance between these phenomena and that of Nathan Birnbaum. However, the latter failed because there was no response or sequel to his activity, even though from a personal standpoint, as a spiritual phenomenon in our generation, he was far more significant than the Rebbe of Lubavitch.

All of these manifestations could only have developed within the framework of the ancestral tradition, not in the breaking out from it nor in the renewal of life that seeks free or new expression. When Rav Kook— who is closest to an explicitly mystical viewpoint in terms of the conclusions which he derived from his inspiration as well as in his understanding of it—sought to maintain and to derive conclusions from his definitions, he encountered an opposition which is well-known to many of us, who remember the bitter controversy here in Jerusalem, because Rav Kook sought to understand the phenomenon of secularization of his generation. I shall return to this point later on. Rav Kook attempted to understand the secular phenomena of his generation as a positive manifestation of the great mystical experience expressed in the creation of the nation and in the manifestations of the national spirit. It was that selfsame new and original impulse which led Rav Kook on his part to attempt to understand the acts of the pioneers, who violated or were prepared to violate the prohibitions of the Torah, who did not observe any of the practical precepts of the Torah, and yet whom he nevertheless wished to defend to the public or to the leaders of the public. His approach to the people was that of an advocate, whose language regarding this matter was filled with concepts from the world of Jewish mystical tradition. This attempt immediately aroused a hostile reaction on the part of those same circles, who saw no possibility of leaving their own framework by so much as a hair's breadth.

Hence, in reality there exist certain phenomena of struggle surrounding the public expression of mystical impulses (i.e., whether limited or extensive), even though generally speaking this struggle did not elicit a broad echo. I imagine that in reality there existed more than that known to me.

The principal question to which we must now return is the following: What is the difference between this world, in which mysticism is a living phenomenon, and ourselves, who do not pretend to, are not able to, and do not wish to wear the mantle of pious, Orthodox Jews following the tradition of our forefathers? What is the difference between a contemporary

Jew, who has experienced whatever he has experienced, and the creative, productive individual? Is there anything by way of a public crystallization which might bridge between them? And a second question: Is there any possibility of renewal within the world of Kabbalah, such as that manifested in so striking a way in the writings of Rav Kook? And is there any room for such continuity even for one who is outside the realm of those who observe the halakhic tradition?

Is a new Kabbalah possible? (I have been asked this question an endless number of times.) This question elicits numerous thoughts, and particularly doubtful ones. The basis of these doubts lies in the central problem to which these inquirers shut their eyes, even when they reflect upon the manifestations of religious Jewry in these areas.

What is the basic assumption upon which all traditional Jewish mysticism in Kabbalah and Ḥasidism is based? The acceptance of the Torah, in the strictest and most precise understanding of the concept of the word of God. In other words: one must clearly emphasize the significance of the concept of Torah from heaven and the belief in it as a factor in the existence of Jewish mysticism as an historical phenomenon.

One cannot overemphasize the significance and necessity of this element in the productive lives of Kabbalists or Ḥasidic masters. Each and every word and letter, and not merely something general and amorphous lacking in specific meaning, is an aspect of the revelation of the Divine Presence; and it is this specific revelation of holiness that is meant by Torah from heaven. It is only for this reason that they were able to find infinite illuminating lights in every word and letter, in the sense of seventy faces to the Torah—of the infinite interpretation and endless understandings of each sentence.

How did all of those streams, which were to become self-contained units within the history of Jewish mysticism, develop the form in which their ideas were expressed? They uncovered new layers within the divine word, which is in principle infinite. Thus, once a person has accepted the strictures of this faith and this quality of faith, as did Rav Kook or Rabbi Arele Roth and others, together with this strict, exact concept of Torah from heaven, without any whitewashing—from then on, he enjoys an extraordinary measure of freedom, to which the history of the Kabbalah gives abundant testimony. He becomes so to speak a member of the family, and is able to uncover level upon level, layer upon layer, in the understanding that the gates of exegesis are never closed—and not necessarily because the talents of the person himself are unlimited.

All of the teachings agree with regard to this great principle. The infinite wealth of the word of God present in the Torah, which is the divine reality, is not withheld from them. From the viewpoint of Jewish mysticism, it is absurd to inquire as to the true significance of the Torah, as its meaning is infinite and every layer reveals some new aspect of its subject matter. There is no more general expression of this sense of the supreme and infinite significance of the Torah, together with its individual significance for each person according to the root of his soul, than the formula given to this view in the school of R. Isaac Luria of Safed. That is: not only does the Torah have seventy faces, each one of which is revealed in accordance with the generation and its consciousness, but it also has sixty myriad meanings. These Kabbalists explicitly stated that each Jewish soul has its own unique mystical path by which to read the Torah, in the sense of it being a living body and a true manifestation of the divine word; a path connected with the root of each person's soul in the upper worlds, which he, and he alone, is able to reveal.

The awesome faith in the power hidden within the divine word, a faith than which there is none higher, served in the past as the basis for the mystical decision based upon the exegesis of this word. This decision allows wide latitude for religious individualism, without leaving the fixed framework of the Torah, which reserves to itself the possibility of unique inspiration, which is only granted to a particular individual whose soul is hewn from the same source or from its sparks.

This view was the culmination of the position of the Kabbalists in the earlier generations, and it was that which opened the gates to mysticism. There was an absolute belief here in something, but for many of us that very thing was a tremendous obstacle, if not an absolute obstacle. We do not believe in Torah from heaven in the specific sense of a fixed body of revelation having infinite significance. And without this basic assumption one cannot move.

The moment this assumption falls, the entire structure upon which mysticism was built, and by means of which it was to be accepted among the people as legitimate, likewise falls. And once this sense of faith in Torah from heaven ceased, it fell—and I dare say that for most of our people this sense of faith no longer exists. This being the case, one must ask the question: Where can one find a firm basis for that same continuity, for that same feeling that the gates of exegesis have not been shut to the infinite wealth of the divine word known in its expansion?

It is this stumbling block which stands in the way of the formulation today of a Jewish mysticism bearing public significance. Anyone attempting today to bring matters of inspiration and mystical cognition within the range of public understanding, without seeing himself, with a clear conscience, as being connected in an unqualified way with the great prin-

ciple of Torah from heaven, of that selfsame Torah with those selfsame
letters as it is, is a religious anarchist. I cannot emphasize too strongly the
extent to which this issue is the foundation of the entire tradition of Jewish mysticism, without which it is impossible to formulate patterns bearing general significance.

One who is unwilling or unable to accept this upon himself; one who
does not share the firm faith of our forebears, whether he is engaged in
other paths toward faith, or whether his path has become clouded by history and historical criticism (for there are many sources for doubt regarding this matter of Torah from heaven), may be objectively considered a
religious anarchist. All of us today may to a great extent be considered anarchists regarding religious matters, and it should be stated openly. There
are some who know it and admit it openly, while others beat around the
bush in order to evade the fundamental fact that a religious understanding
of Jewish continuity today goes beyond the principle of Torah from
heaven. This conclusion leads us necessarily to anarchistic forms of religion. This is why the difficulty entailed in these reflections is so great. Can
one find a clear, objective basis for a new Jewish translation of our generation, which is a translation of experiences of no less significance than
those of other generations? For this is a generation which has lost the basis
upon which the earlier ones stood firm.

It follows from all this that, if we inquire about manifestations of mystical impulses in Judaism today, we find ourselves confronting a reality of
Jewish religious anarchy. It is this problem which confronts the present
generation, which asks whether there is any hope of creating public forms
of fundamentally mystic inspiration even in the absence of any positive
dogmatic basis. We have no answer to this question. Such a thing may be
possible. There may be upheavals of varying intensity until they acquire
the proper tools by which to give expression to the feelings of the heart or
to a recognition of general significance drawing upon an experiential-mys-
tical religious basis, an experience which achieves self-consciousness. In
any event, it is only possible to think a fundamentally melancholy
thought regarding the divine basis of such a thing. But this is the truth of
our generation.

If there is to be a mysticism that reflects the experience of an individual
or individuals, it will not easily, if at all, assume the simultaneously free
and obligatory expression that derives from its being bound to an historical revelation, to the living word of God; a feeling, if not a conviction of
certain knowledge, that whatever one wishes to express is already hinted
at in the Torah; the sense that "There is nothing that is not hinted at in

the Torah,"[2] as the early ones understood the significance of this talmudic saying.

It is not surprising that, within this path to anarchy, and within anarchy itself—a way that is no way, yet one nevertheless walked by thousands and tens of thousands of people, every day, every hour—we have no clear knowledge as to whether mystical experience can in our generation assume a crystallized form obligating any sort of community. In my humble opinion, for the present we need to leave this question unresolved.

I would like to raise one final point, which I cannot refrain from touching upon in brief: namely, the matter of secularization, or the sanctity of the secular, in our lives. That is, the problem of secularization and its possible connection to the issue of mysticism in our generation.

During this generation, most of the creative energies of our people have been invested in other and different forms of building than those established in the earlier tradition. This is a fundamental fact, whether or not it is pleasant for us to hear.

It is a basic fact that the creative element, drawing upon the authentic consciousness of this generation, has been invested in secular forms of building. This building or reconstruction of the life of the nation was and still is difficult, demanding energies of both will and execution leaving little room for productive expression of traditional forms. This power includes much that would under different circumstances have been invested in the world of religious mysticism. This power has now been invested in things which are seemingly bereft of religious sanctity, but are entirely secular, the most secular thing imaginable—and therein lies the greatest problem.

Who knows where the boundaries of holiness lie? It was to this problem that Rav Kook addressed himself in the most controversial parts of his teaching. He was unprepared to accept—from the traditional viewpoint—the opinion that this building was purely secular. We find it difficult today to judge the possibility of secularization as a camouflage for holiness that has not yet been recognized as such. This is our secular reality here in Eretz Yisra'el, into which most of the paradoxical power present in the Jewish people during this generation has entered. Having entered into this productive life, is there any energy left for the creation of forms through which the connection of these forms to the realm of holiness may be recognized, yet will nevertheless have eternal significance for us beyond that? One may express some doubt as to whether there is a positive answer to this question. Or perhaps there is the possibility of a double path of holiness and secularity, toward which we are moving? Perhaps mysticism will be revealed, not in the traditional garb of holiness, but as Rav Kook saw it, in his daring words, as somehow seeking to restore things to their traditional perception. Perhaps holiness will be revealed within the innermost sanctums of this secularity, and the traditional concepts fail to recognize mysticism in its new forms? Perhaps this type of mysticism will not fit into the conservative traditional conceptions of the mystics, but will have a secular significance. One should note that the idea to which I am now alluding is not pulled out of thin air: there are those who see in the secularity of our lives and the rebuilding of the nation a reflection of the mystical significance of the secret of the world.[3]

We do not have any outstanding examples of this type of our own (unless one would wish to consider here the teaching of A. D. Gordon). But those of us who labor here as Jews in the Land of Israel may find great interest in the book of poems by Walt Whitman,[4] who a hundred years ago sang the song of America with a feeling of the absolute sanctity of the absolutely secular. Whitman is a striking example of this phenomenon, which has had many advocates and representatives over the past three generations among those who saw that mystical experiences may continue to flourish among human beings so long as the human race exists because mysticism is a basic human experience, connected to the very nature of man. However, in the coming generations this mystical experience was to be embodied in naturalistic and secular forms of consciousness which do not, to all appearances, involve the recognition of traditional religious concepts, even though the substance of the mystical experience still exists, and is preserved and echoing.

The new consciousness of man is a category which has been accepted for about one hundred years, since the appearance of the book by Richard Bucke (the classical text of secular mysticism, as an extreme expression of what I have said here).[5] Such a phenomenon has existed over the course of the last three or four generations, although it has not reached down to the public at large. It acquired a certain sectarian form, and was known to people concerned with the human spirit, or human consciousness, or what has been called human mind—that is, consciousness in the broadest sense of the word. The latter believed that in the future human consciousness will change and be expanded, undergoing new forms and transformations, in which there will appear the mystical attempt of the mystics. They may have erred regarding this: it is not my task here to discuss the truth or error of these categories. Indeed, I doubt whether any *ab initio* non-dogmatic approach can measure these things by dogmatic criteria of truth and falsehood. These are things which may perhaps allude to the possibility of a mystical embodiment in nontraditional forms.

I have spoken here at some length. If I have been aware that I am unable to bring any concrete tidings, I have at least sought to explain what was in my heart.

Chapter Three

My Way to Kabbalah (1974)*

In expressing my gratitude upon being awarded the distinguished honor of the Literary Prize of the Bavarian Academy of Arts, I ought by rights to say a few words about the circumstances which brought me to this happy—and not unparadoxical—state of having been found deserving of such a prize. A German literary prize is about the least expected honor for a person such as myself who, over the past fifty years, has had only the most tenuous connection with the German language, and who is presently toiling over the gathering of his scattered writings written over that same half century in the Hebrew language.

During the past ten years, I have set myself the goal of gathering the fruit of my scientific work, a task to which I shall also devote the coming days. This work has been dedicated to the discovery of a hidden chapter in the history of the spirit of Judaism, one that has been virtually unknown among extensive circles within the Jewish people, and even more so in the world outside of Judaism. I began this task fifty-five years ago here in Munich as a young man who, as a result of his origin and upbringing, was completely alienated from the living springs of the Jewish tradition. I found my way toward them with much struggle and great effort. This demanded much spiritual daring, bordering upon madness. An even more important role was played by a kind of inner compass which guided my

---

* A lecture given upon the occasion of being awarded the Literary Prize of the Bavarian Academy of Arts in 1974. Printed in *'Od Davar,* 301–05.

life decisions, including those which determined my path and my choice of work.

When I began to study the Hebrew language in my youth, against my parents' wishes and in clear rebellion against their authority, an intense attraction toward the tradition awakened within me. Although its archaic character was clear to me, I nevertheless sensed something in its heartbeat that indicated its ability to undergo a vital transformation—something toward which I wished to call attention by my work. What gave a unique character to the vision underlying my work was the dialectical, and possibly paradoxical mix into a significant complex of conservative persistence, restoration, and utopia, which I believed was to be found within Judaism. I believed to have distinguished its historical breadth in a progressively growing manner in mysticism. To provide a basis for this outlook, which differed substantially from the traditional image of Jewish spirituality— an outlook which at the beginning of my path I only vaguely perceived, and which over the course of time came into sharper and sharper focus— required that same inner compass and daring of which I spoke earlier. But it also demanded a certain enthusiasm and ability for clear thought, to which my university training in mathematics contributed.

In the fall of 1919 I arrived in Munich in order to study the Kabbalistic manuscripts found in the Royal Library. My original intention was to write a dissertation on the linguistic doctrine of Kabbalah, and thereby attain the degree of doctor of philosophy from Clemens Baumker, to whom I owe a great debt of gratitude to this very day. Once it became clear to me that my knowledge was totally inadequate to realize this grandiose goal, I abandoned this plan. There began a long march through ancient books and manuscripts, which ultimately brought me, in this distinguished hour, to the present gathering. The work which I was unable to perform in my youth was ultimately written in Jerusalem, with a somewhat quieter conscience, fifty years later.

I would like to relate a brief incident which took place at the start of this path. When I arrived in Berlin during the summer of 1922 with a fresh doctorate in the study of Kabbalah, I discovered that the only Jewish scholar who had engaged in the study of Kabbalah during the previous generation, an individual who had written several books on the subject and had also been a student of the distinguished Jewish historian Heinrich Graetz, had come to live in Berlin[1]—and so, I went to visit him. He was an unusually alert elderly gentleman of eighty-two years, who had received the title of professor from Kaiser Wilhelm, and had formerly been rabbi of the city of Poznan. He received me in a warm manner and said: "You and I, we are the only two crazy people dealing with these matters."

He then showed me his library. At the time, he was the only person in Germany owning a reasonably large collection of Kabbalistic works, including an imposing-looking manuscript from the school of R. Isaac Luria. In youthful enthusiasm upon seeing these treasures spread before me, I said: "How wonderful it is, Herr Professor, that you have read and learned all this." To which the elderly gentleman replied: "What! I also have to read all this nonsense?"

Allow me to say a few words about the problem I had with regard to the German language and to the Hebrew language, which has accompanied me throughout my entire life. When I immigrated to the Land of Israel in 1923—Palestine of those days—I thoroughly prepared myself for the transition to the Hebrew language. Over the course of twelve years "I studied it diligently, with warm effort" (Goethe, *Faust,* Pt. I), thanks to which I was able to enter into a conservative world of language, whose traditional forms of expression deeply impressed me. However, the standard Hebrew in which the majority of my writings were composed underwent far-reaching changes and transformations in Israel. Having migrated from the ancient books to the mouths of babes and sucklings, it has given way to an extremely vital language, characterized by an anarchistic lack of rules. Only by the confrontation between these two linguistic worlds will the Hebrew of the future develop, deriving its image from the fruitful experience of the meeting between them—a fertile, but also dangerous process. I found much of interest in these transformations. On the other hand, the German which I brought with me was the language of the first twenty-five years of my life—and remained such. I brought with me the collected writings of only two German authors, or at least what I was able to obtain of their writings. These were Jean Paul and Paul Scheerbart, whose writings spoke to me in a unique manner. Among the figures of the German heritage, these two figures were closest to me. I was then—and have perhaps remained today—evidently the only person to have collected all the writings of Scheerbart, an author who has been completely forgotten and whom I liked so much. I knew nothing at all of his life, except for the fact that he died of starvation during the First World War.

I did not take any part in the transformations undergone by the German language thereafter, first and foremost during the period of Nazi rule. I can still see in my mind's eye the giant red posters of the new National-Socialist Workers Party, posted on the notice boards in Munich, heralding the future horrors of the murder of the Jews, together with the barbaric degeneration of language which accompanied it. Even earlier, I had made my decision to bind my lot with the new life developing in the ancient land, for which reason I absorbed very little of all these events. During

those days, I spent most of my time in the peaceful manuscript department of the Royal Library in Bavaria and in the study of the old rabbi who
led a small Orthodox group, with whom I daily "learned" a page of Talmud together with a handful of people of similar outlook to my own. During the period when my path began to turn in the direction of Hebrew,
German remained a living language for me, albeit to a certain degree a static one. For this reason, it is not particularly surprising that during the following years, in Israel, there were only three books which I read and reread
with true attentiveness, with an open heart, and with spiritual tension—
strange as this combination of words may seem in relation to the great
texts of which we are speaking, suggesting as they do an inner contradiction. These texts were: the Hebrew Bible; *Sefer ha-Zohar,* the sacred text of
the Kabbalists, written in Aramaic; and the collected works of Franz Kafka,
written in German by a Jew from Prague, who was conscious of being a
German author, even though he himself was not German. Three collections, on which over the course of three thousand years were impressed
that spirit customarily referred to as the spirit of Judaism. One might say—
that is not much. In my life, this was a great deal indeed.

Kafka's writings, with their distinctive characteristics, connect in a peculiar way to the other two works mentioned. In extensive portions of his
work there is also a kind of canonicity: that is to say, they are subject to infinite interpretation; and many of them, specifically the more impressive
among them, in themselves constitute works of interpretation. Indeed, as
one may read in one or another fine place, regarding such writings it is
forbidden to engage in interpretation that departs from the work itself.
How then is the independent-minded reader to react to critical literature
which does not hesitate at any means so as to avoid the Jewish significance of Kafka's last story, "Josephine the Singer, or the Mouse People,"[2]
with the ludicrous argument that the word "Jew" does not appear at all
in that work? I will not even consider the peculiar arrogance which seeks
to refute the interpretation of an author whose writing has touched the
center of existence of so many among us and shaken them up—interpretations propounded by people who testified to that selfsame shock, with
the convoluted argument that the forms of poetic statement, which are
the precondition for all science and for all poetry—were not sufficiently
taken into account, or were ignored completely, by the interpreter. A person such as myself, who throughout those years of his life devoted to
scholarship was a philologist, at times serious and at times ironic, and who
is left with very few illusions as to the limits of what is called the science of
literature, may perhaps be allowed to relate with a certain measure of displeasure toward such claims.

The three collections mentioned above are certainly also literature, and from this point of view the criteria of literary study are valid regarding them—assuming that in our day valid criteria of this type still indeed exist. But who will doubt that they are also far more than literature alone? Is it improper for us to turn our gaze upon this "more" and to seek frameworks which describe it and which are capable of attaining it? The forms of biblical speech or of Kabbalistic reflection certainly have bearing upon this matter. But do they truly wish to convince us—even if only by the fact that they hide behind the author within Kafka, who sought, out of a feeling of shame (the least literary of all feelings), to destroy his manuscripts—do they truly wish to convince us that the cry uttered by him, or which is still uttered by him, can be comprehended or rejected by studies of the type to which I alluded, whatever their value?

In 1946, I was sent to Germany with the special mission of examining the destiny of the Jewish libraries, to report on those remnants which survived, and to present overall proposals pertaining to their care. It is difficult for me to describe the shock that I experienced in my encounter with the German language of those days. There was in it something Medusa-like, something paralyzing, something that had absorbed the events of those years in a manner which cannot be explained. And if, in 1949, I began to write more extensively in the German language, this too had a certain bearing upon that selfsame shock. My lectures at the Eranos Conferences in Ascona were an additional factor. There I was given the opportunity to arrive at a synthesis of things upon which I had worked for thirty years, without sacrificing historical criticism or philosophical thought. In the atmosphere of those conferences, I felt that I could once again express myself properly in the German language without submitting to the provocation originating in that same shock. I was assisted in this, not only by my extended abstention from this language, but also by the obligation, so rare and so much sought by a lecturer, to speak of what I wished for two solid hours. As is well-known, the speaker is generally subjected to the instruction: say whatever you wish, but for not more than fifty minutes. There I was given that same breathing space required for explanations, such as those I have given here. I must therefore note that the prose which has enjoyed your recognition, ladies and gentlemen, was composed thanks to the double impulse of severity and pleasure. It is my hope that the reader will discover in it both of these qualities.

Part Two

Zionism as Spiritual and Cultural Identity

Chapter Four

Thoughts About Our Language (1926)*

The land is a volcano, and it hosts the language. People talk a great deal here about many things which may make us fail—particularly these days about the Arabs. But another, more serious danger than that of the Arab people threatens us, a danger which follows of necessity from the Zionist enterprise. What will be the result of updating the Hebrew language? Is not the holy language, which we have planted among our children, an abyss that must open up? People here do not know the meaning of what they have done. They think that they have turned Hebrew into a secular language and that they have removed its apocalyptic sting, but it is not so. The secularization of the language is merely empty words, a rhetorical turn of phrase. In reality, it is impossible to empty the words which are filled to bursting with meaning, save at the expense of the language itself. And indeed, this *Volapük*,[1] this ghostly language spoken in our streets, precisely represents that expressionless linguistic universe which alone may be secularized. But if we pass on to our children the language that we have received, if we, the generation of the transition, revive the language of the old books that it may be revealed to them anew—will not the religious power latent therein one day break out against its speakers? And what will be the image of the generation toward whom its expressions are directed?

* A letter to Franz Rosenzweig, dated December 26, 1926. Published in *'Od Davar,* 59–60.

We live with this language as on the edge of an abyss, yet nearly all of us walk there with confidence, like blind men. Does no one fear that, once our eyes are opened, we or those who follow us will roll down into it? Nor can we know whether the sacrifice of those lost in the abyss will suffice to cover it up again.

The creators of the Hebrew renaissance believed in the magical powers of language with a blind, almost fanatical faith. Had their eyes been open, they would have been unable to find in their souls the demonic courage to revive a language within an environment in which it could only become a kind of Esperanto. And yet they walked—and continue to walk—on the edge of an abyss, as if in a trance—and the abyss is silent. They pass on the old names and signs to others, to the youth. At times, when, in the course of a totally unimportant speech by an anonymous speaker, we hear a religious term, we shudder—even if it might have been meant to comfort us. This Hebrew language is pregnant with catastrophe; it cannot remain in its present state—nor will it remain there. Our children will no longer have any other language; truth be told, they, and they alone, will pay the price for this encounter which we have imposed upon them unasked, or without even asking ourselves. One day the language will turn against its own speakers—and there are moments when it does so even now; moments which it is difficult to forget, leaving wounds in which all the presumptuousness of our goal is revealed. Will we then have a youth who will be able to hold fast against the rebellion of a holy tongue?

A language is composed of names. The power of the language is hidden within the name; its abyss is sealed therein. After invoking the ancient names day after day, we shall no longer be able to hold off their power. We have awakened them, and they shall appear, for we have summoned them up with awesome power. True, we speak inarticulately, in a ghost language. Names walk about in our sentences like ghosts. Journalists play with them, pretending to themselves or to God that it is really meaningless. But at times the holiness of our language leaps out and speaks to us from within its spectral degradation. Names have a life of their own. Were it not so—woe to our children, who have been abandoned to emptiness.

All those words which were not created arbitrarily and out of nothing, but were taken from the good old lexicon, are filled to the brim with explosive meaning. A generation which has inherited the most fruitful of all of the holy traditions, our language, cannot live without tradition—even should it wish to do so a thousandfold. When the power inherent in the language, when the spoken word—that is, the content of the language—will again assume form, our nation will once more be confronted by the holy tradition as a decisive example. And the people will then need to choose between the two: either to submit to it, or to perish in oblivion. God cannot remain silent in a language in which He has been evoked thousands of times to return to our life. The inevitable revolution of a language in which His voice is again heard—that is the only subject not discussed here in the land, because those who renewed the Hebrew language did not believe in the Day of Judgment which they set up for us through their deeds. Would that the lightness of mind which guided us on this apocalyptic path not lead us to destruction.

Chapter Five

Exile Today Is Devoid of the Seeds of Redemption (1963)*

The question being asked here is similar to (and in a sense also somewhat related to) another question for which there is no clear or unequivocal answer: namely, are the Jews a nation? The answer depends upon a mixture of objective and subjective considerations, the answer depending upon the degree of emphasis placed upon one or another aspect.

There was a time when there was no contradiction between the objective and subjective factor: we considered ourselves to be in exile, both in terms of our consciousness and in terms of the everyday and historical experience of our contact with the nations of the world; others likewise considered us to be in exile and accepted our self-evaluation. Indeed, they added to it and imposed it upon us. This exile was the fundamental reality of our being, as individuals and as a nation, and there were no disagreements concerning its understanding, as well as its concrete and historical significance. All sides involved, each one for his own reasons, agreed to those. If disagreements did arise, these pertained to the religious and metaphysical interpretation of this reality.

* From a round-table discussion on the issue of the sense and meaning of exile today, moderated by Geulah Cohen, with the participation, in addition to Scholem, of Rabbi Tzvi Yehudah Kook, Nathan Rotenstreich, Ḥayyim Hazzaz, Abraham Joshua Heschel. Published in Ma'ariv, April 8, 1963; reprinted in Devarim be-go, 217–220.

The non-Jews had one view concerning this matter, while we, the Jews, held a different view or views. This reality was interpreted in a variety of ways among us, depending upon the degree of depth-interpretation of the historical experience of the nation, and the symbolic ability to transform this fundamental experience into a multi-faceted symbol, not only for our condition in the world (concerning which there was no doubt), but of the condition of the world itself. The yoke of the nations and the humiliation, abandonment or diminution of the divine image within us were among the substantive signs of our experience as a nation in exile. And if here and there the yoke was lightened, the abandonment was restrained, and the sense of dignity was restored, this was insufficient to foster any illusions as to the true face of the exile. There was a profound reason for this: in our own consciousness the essence of exile had been defined in biblical prophecy even before it entered the world as a historical reality. It does not at all matter whether this perception of what was earlier and what was later, based upon the chapters of rebuke found in the Torah, was correct. What is important is that, through these chapters of prophecy, the horrors of exile were connected in our consciousness with the sources of revelation from which derived our religious consciousness. Therefore, by virtue of these chapters, it had the special capability to attach itself to our historical consciousness and to vary it with shades and nuances of its own.

The religious status of the understanding of exile was not diminished as a result of the terrors of historical experience. On the contrary: it shed a mysterious light coming from afar even upon our miserable situation, upon our degeneration and humiliation. And it was not for naught (and not only rhetorically) that the concepts of exile and redemption were joined together into a pair of concepts carrying weighty religious significance: the realm upon which one concept drew was identified with that upon which the other drew as well, so that bitter experience and dizzying utopia coexisted in the same framework and reinforced one another.

This unity, through which, in the approach of our forebears, all aspects of exile were united, has been challenged in recent generations, and the Zionist movement has not succeeded in restoring it. In the eyes of an ever-increasing sector of our nation, the concept of exile has lost its religious coloration. The objective and subjective factors have been detached from one another, so as to no longer overlap. There are cases in which the non-Jews still perceive us as a nation in exile, but we deny it: there is neither nation nor exile. Zionism came along and stated, in light of bitter and literally archetypal historical experiences, the simple and great truth that, whether we like it or not, we are a nation and there is an exile. Then came the Holocaust, with everything it implied, to reveal to anyone who had eyes to see that nothing has changed in the fundamental historical experience of the Jewish nation, even though a great deal has changed in the interpretation of that experience. The revolutionary will of those who built the new Land of Israel combined with the bad conscience of the Christian nations to lay the foundations for the creation of the State of Israel. At this point, with the formal realization of the goal of the Zionist movement, the dialectic involved in victory was revealed, justifying the prophetic words of Theodor Herzl, which were not always pleasant for Zionists to hear: that though Zionism had come to end the exile through the ingathering of exiles, in so doing it strengthened in many places the opposite tendency, which was set toward the destruction of the Jews as a nation. As has been stated quite correctly by the moderator of the present discussion: "Instead of the exile, it eliminated the consciousness of exile."

This process was facilitated by a change in perspective brought about by Zionism: the exile was given a national and social interpretation, beyond the religious conception which had accompanied it until then. In the eyes of those generations which preceded Zionism, the concept of exile was not merely the absence of a homeland or the lack of a natural social structure. The metaphysical dimension gave an additional (and possibly more fundamental, deeply rooted) meaning to the exile. When the analysis of exile and of our status therein was reduced to essentially sociological categories, such as nation, natural structure, and the like, the basis for evaluating the phenomenon was itself changed. Once a national society with a natural social structure was set up in the Land of Israel (even if only in part of it), one could argue that this was tantamount to the destruction of the exile.

The question as to whether, for those who live in the Diaspora, the exile continues to exist, has come to depend upon subjective decisions, insofar as people were given the permission and freedom to make such decisions. The individual, or even a public composed of individuals, is free to aspire to other forms of existence for itself, even if it sees in a positive light the creation of the state of the Jews for those who wish it, or assist it. It accepts the social critique of Zionism, but derives therefrom different conclusions regarding itself. It is even able, precisely by virtue of our presence in the Land, to strive toward partial assimilation or acculturation.

In my humble opinion, it is an error to assign the State of Israel the function of reviving the consciousness of exile in the Diaspora. It cannot fulfill this function as a state, so long as it has reneged upon those religious and metaphysical distinctions which alone lend it that type of charisma and influence. Under the circumstances of our generation, the consciousness of exile is sustained or vitalized, not by the State of Israel, but by one of two factors: (a) the personal decision of an individual having a certain Jewish consciousness, affirming not only the continuity of our history, but the continuity of the interpretation given to this history over the past two millennia (and how many such individuals are likely to be found outside of the circles of pious Jewry?); or (b) the decision of the non-Jewish environment, upon which the matter depends, no less than upon the decision of the individual or the Jewish public. There are some cases in which these two decisions still occasionally overlap. But the main difficulty arises in those cases where the contradictions between them are manifested. The present historical situation, in which there are nations which do not consider the Jews who dwell among them as members of another people, while the Jews themselves have eradicated their national identity, cannot be altered by the State of Israel. Such an exile will be eliminated, together with its Jews, without an outcry and without Zionism.

If change is to take place at all, it will only come about as the result of forces which are not dependent upon us, such as far-reaching economic changes, or changes in the attitude of the non-Jewish society to the assumption of leadership positions or excessively prominent striking cultural accomplishments by Jews. (In this respect, many of us are doubtless astonished at the results of the striking success of Jews in American literature, which began in our generation with far greater energy than the corresponding accomplishments by German Jews in their day). But there is no clear solution to the problem of those Diasporas in which the objective and subjective factors do not overlap, and there are endless different stages in the manifestation of this contradiction, as has been revealed today in the various countries of Western Europe (France, Switzerland, England) or in the United States. Most of the Jews in those countries have lost the consciousness of exile, as a result of personal feeling or an act of personal will; even the government and certain levels of the public see this decision favorably, albeit most of the non-Jewish public continues to maintain a feeling of alienness regarding its Jews. There are those cases (such as Switzerland or England) in which their Jewish feeling has been strengthened by the State of Israel—often, because non-Jews have begun to look at them with a new respect to which these Jews were not accustomed. However, this has in no way strengthened the consciousness of exile (in a small country with a very cohesive social structure, such as Switzerland, about which I happen to know quite a bit, this is very strongly felt!).

Moreover: I believe that anyone who visits New York and observes what goes on there will come to the conclusion that what exists there is exile—but an exile whose inhabitants deny its very existence. They ignore it and it ignores them, as in the verse, "I will surely hide my face . . ." (Deut. 31:18)—

that the very fact of its hiding is hidden from them; and perhaps the Ḥasidic preacher who said that this is the most difficult hiding of all was correct. This Diaspora, which is an exile denying its own nature and its obvious public existence, is itself a fundamental phenomenon of Jewish self-under-standing in our generation—but woe be to anyone who dares to mention its symptoms. Many years ago, Aḥad Ha-Am wrote the famous essay, "Slavery Within Freedom,"[1] directed against the assimilationists of Germany, France, and England. What would he say today about the second and third gener-ation of Russian Jews, etc., who went into exile in the United States, inter-preting their distinguished historical experience as they did, for their own reasons, coming up with a hundred reasons for purifying Gentile soil and eliminating the consciousness of exile—and we are still only at the very be-ginning of this path! The subject of exile has become so complicated that there is no longer a clear and coherent answer to whatever pertains to it. There are substantial portions of our people whose organs of perception have become dulled regarding this point. Their correction does not depend upon us or upon our historical logic, but rather upon the very air which they breathe.

Finally, there is one question which needs to be placed at the head of our concerns: it has come about, possibly unwittingly, that the best of the builders of our renewed land have emptied the concept of exile from the seeds of redemption which were always present within it, precisely at the decisive moment of awakening. This may perhaps be understood in terms of the needs of the time—that our most urgent problems have been con-cerned with the world of action. We have had to struggle for bread and security, for the conquest of the land and the conquest of labor, and for our very physical existence. In putting all their energies into rebellion, they have at times trodden down, together with the chains of exile, the state of redemption that was hidden in its throwing off. They thereby brought the problem of exile into an entirely different, but no less fright-ening, manifestation—into the fields of the homeland, thereby bringing about within Israel itself a fundamental imbalance which yet remains to be corrected.

Chapter Six

A Lecture About Israel (1967)*

I speak to you as one who has lived in Israel for the past forty-five years, and whose life has been bound up with the renaissance of the Jewish people in its old-new homeland in the Land of Israel. During this time (which I don't know whether to describe as long or short) a great deal has happened to us, and each of us has managed to make for himself an accounting of what he expected from this land and from our people in this land, and what of all this has been fulfilled.

Many different reasons have been given for the fact that over the last few generations people have dedicated themselves to Zionism, and these few moments are not intended as an occasion on which to present all of the reasons. The Jewish question is infinitely complex, and yet nevertheless seems also infinitely simple. If I may speak in my own name and that of many others like myself who were in a similar situation following the First World War: for us, the Jews of central Europe who were moved in their youth by the summons of the Jewish people and the voice calling for its revival, this was not so much a political as an ethical decision.

We felt an obligation to identify, with all our soul and through the decisions regarding our personal lives, with a concern which we came to know to be vital for the Jewish people. We could not know whether this concern would be blessed with success. None of us had any illusions as to the difficulties and obstacles which needed to be overcome. Many of us,

* Based upon a lecture given in Zurich following the Six Day War. Published in *Shedemot* 53 (Winter 1974). Reprinted in *Devarim be-go*, 128–32.

perhaps most of us, certainly hoped that this success might be obtained through peaceful contact, through the constructive labor of those who love peace, and without conflict or bloodshed.

What was the struggle about at that time, and what was the decisive factor which thereafter, under the impression of the horrible experience and nightmarish vision of the Jewish people in Europe over the past generation, became increasingly dominant? It was none other than the decision to return to ourselves, to become fully and consciously involved with the flow of Jewish history and to take into our own hands the responsibility for our lives as participants in all areas—both the secular and the sacred or religious—as Jews, and as Jews alone.

There are many people who believe that Jews are Jews because anti-Semites have made them Jews. Certainly, there were and are not a few Jews of this type; external pressure elicits an internal counter-pressure and cohesion. But more important and more decisive were those who wished to be Jews because they pondered within their own souls, where they discovered a relationship to their past, and no less to their future. One may argue about the essence of Judaism, of the historical image by which this people presented itself in world history: whether its nature is fixed and whole and not subject to change, or whether it lives and changes. I am numbered among those who think that Judaism is filled with an abundance of vitality, and that with all its rich past, it still has a rich future, stretching unto eternity; that it is a phenomenon in which the not-yet-revealed, the hidden, and the anticipated, flowing like the remnants of the riches of the past, are still present. In the words of the great German liturgical poet: "Master of our future—He who is capable of change."

The Jewish people has had a unique history, and it would be pointless to argue as to whether there apply to it in fact all those characteristics which constitute the definition of a people, or not. There are those who have long since made their decision—they have taken into their own hands the cause of Israel, fighting its battles with dedication and self-sacrifice. It was they who wished to take hold of their Jewish heritage with renewed creative powers—much as this tradition has changed in the present, and much as it will take on new forms—and who have decided to build a living society of Jews as a people.

The task of rebuilding the land of the Bible and of establishing the State of Israel constitutes a utopian return of the Jews to their own history, if I may use such a daring formulation. There are many nations who once lived in lands which they have long since abandoned, of which they have preserved no memory, or only in an extremely vague way. But the Jews never forgot from whence they came and where their roots are. Many years

ago, when asked by a British government commission about the source of
the Jews' right to this land, Dr. Weizmann, the first President of the State of
Israel, said: "He who remembers—has a right!" Memory has been a powerful force in the life of the Jews. To it, there has been added now the
tremendous impulse for the reconstruction and restoration of our land.

The Jews have undergone indescribable sufferings, yet over the past few
generations they have produced and performed an incredible amount for
the development of culture and civilization in all the lands of their dispersion. They have contributed their share—and more. Indeed, only rarely
has this been counted to our favor; on the contrary, more than once it has
upset the balance against us. In Israel, the Jews have decided to dedicate
their strength and vitality, their abilities and their hopes, to a common
future, to one in which we will be prepared to carry full responsibility before man and God for our acts and for our failures, for our accomplishments and—perhaps for our failures. This, in the final analysis, is the
significance of Israel for us.

True, the act of leaving the confessional realm (which too often became
completely confused) for the bright light of world history involved a certain challenge which also entailed dangers, as we ourselves have known
and experienced. It demanded the ethical courage to undertake dangers—
from within the context of a living heritage. The external events of a people's history are not determined by itself only. *"Es kann der Frömmste nicht
in Frieden leben, wenn es dem bösen Nachbarn nicht gefällt"* ("The most pious
person will seek in vain a peaceful life, if peace is not to his neighbor's liking"). In the eyes of a nation which has undergone the terrors of the Hitler
years and paid the price in its own blood, such dangers are nevertheless a
small thing compared with that which will decide the balance in the life of
the Jewish people for good or evil. We require the external conditions, for
which we will need to struggle in the political arena, in order to fix the
inner lot of our nation—and for that, we alone are responsible.

At moments of crisis and threat to all, such as we have experienced a
number of times, we have no choice: we must hold firm. But beyond that,
we need to shape and activate those forces which will act on behalf of the
building of a better future, on behalf of self-responsibility, of calmness,
clarity, and peaceful co-existence in human life. The Jews of Israel will not
and cannot avoid this task. Even during the present crisis, we have remained aware of it and it cannot be displaced. Our people has proven that
it knows how to fight. How sad the state of a world in which such a proof
has brought us more respect and prestige than the application of those
peaceful qualities for the sake of whose cultivation the Jewish state was
founded and intended.

We in Israel have no doubt that in the final analysis the positive attributes of peace are more important and more decisive than those which we
have had to display in the struggle that has been forced upon us. Or shall
we say that all of these positive qualities are essentially the same, albeit in
different concentrations and combinations. Israel has proven that it is prepared to stand up for its interests; would that we would be able to assure
the continuation of its building in peace, and not in war.

The building of the new society toward which we strive requires the
participation of people from many different lands and traditions, united
by a common memory and a common hope. Much has been said of the
tensions which result from the differences among the various groups living in Israel, particularly those between Jews of European origin and from
Oriental communities. People even speak of "Two Israels," between which
there is, so to speak, an ever-deepening gap. The events of recent days
have shown that there is no basis for these fears. Certainly, Israel is a country of many tensions, but in principle (and at critical moments) the unity
upon which these tensions are based wins out and is victorious. Today,
most of Israel's army would seem to belong to the "Second Israel." Evidently, the situation of war and of common conscription has contributed
more to creating bonds among people and the communities which they
represent than years of social activity and joined work. In terms of its socialist character as well, Israel will not be the same country after the war as
it was before it. The tremendous pressure of these decisive days will have
their impact in the social and ethical realms. Moreover, the connection
between Israel and Diaspora Jewry will also be filled with a new vitality
and greater responsibility, to a degree whose like has hardly ever been
known. We shall discover quite clearly the significance of Israel for the
Jews of the exile and how vital it is for all of them—a lesson that is too easily forgotten.

Much has been said about the failure of the dialogue between Israel and
Diaspora Jewry. I think that this dialogue has reached a new and productive
stage, in which it is seen that the Jews of the State of Israel have acted not
only for themselves, but for the sake of all. We wished to create a new and
freer relationship of Jews to themselves and to their environment, and to
heal the distortions which have dominated these relations in many respects. Regarding this matter, I believe that every Jew who dedicates himself
is a partner. Moreover, even beyond the framework of the Jewish people,
every human being who values freedom and devotion can know and understand the significance of the State of the Jews and of the great project of
renaissance which underlies it. There are times when simple words, which
have been distorted and profaned again and again, regain their original sig-

nificance—beyond all dialectics and confusions of human relations. During this time, all of us have been privileged to witness such hours.

In conclusion, allow me to say a word about our relationship to the Arabs. During my many years of living in Israel, I have hardly ever found any hatred toward our neighbors. Attempts to establish positive relations in all kinds of areas—from the explicitly political to the private and personal—and to act on behalf of mutual understanding have never ceased. I myself, within the framework of *Berit-Shalom,* have participated in such an attempt over the course of several years. One of the tragedies of our enterprise was that every one of the voices which reached us here and there from the Arab side, and with whom there seemed to be a productive conversation, was silenced by blatant terror; or, to put it more bluntly, by murder. Those now speaking in the Arab countries are captive to their own bloodthirsty, extreme, but empty rhetoric. We are convinced that, alongside the slogans of hatred and destruction uttered against us daily, there exist other forces. It will not be easy to activate them, to build a bridge toward them. But it will be our task to attempt to do so anew every day, because we believe that we not only need to live with one another due to force of circumstances, but that we also wish to do so and are capable of doing so.

The people of Israel has known through its own long history the meaning of being counted among the defeated. Over the past twenty years, it has come for the first time to know, through the experience of three wars which it did not seek, what it means to be the victor. Through our historical experience, both long term and immediate (and fresh)—the memory of the situation of the defeated, as well as the living, human feeling of the victor—we should be able to attain some balance in our experience. Peace for Israel will automatically also mean peace for the Arabs.

In ancient times, alchemists used to sit in hidden chambers, where they attempted to find and to utilize those forces which change and transform one element into another. The great enterprise of the Land of Israel in which the Jews have proven themselves, casting off one form and taking on another, is also a great experiment in human alchemy, one which shall in the future change hatred and animosity to understanding and respect. To friendship—that is our hope!

Chapter Seven

Our Historical Debt to Russian Jewry (1971)*

W̵e are gathered to raise our voice for the inalienable rights of the Jewish people in Russia to live their own lives as Jews. Let me dwell for a moment on the role Russian Jewry has played in our past and present, as perhaps the greatest and inexhaustible treasure-house and wellspring of pulsating and vigorous life. Russian Jewry is, of course, only one of the tribes constituting the Jewish people, each one of which has had its place and contributed to what we are, for better or worse. But few, if any, can compete with the depth, the intensity and vitality that Russian Jewry has brought to all dimensions of Jewish life, Jewish society, and Jewish spirituality.

What we call Russian Jewry is not that part of our people living within the present boundaries of the Soviet Union alone. During the period when it became most important in Jewish history, there was little if any difference between Polish and Russian Jewry which, seen in a wider perspective, formed one large unit—not only because, for many generations, they were included within the boundaries of the Russian Empire and shared a common fate, but also because they led a distinctive Jewish life of their own, quite unlike the Jewish communities of central and Western Europe. For, to a far greater extent than among those parts of the people, the non-

* An address delivered at the World Conference of Jewish Communities on Soviet Jewry, held in Brussels, February 1971. Published in Hebrew in *Devarim be-go*, 123–27.

40

Jewish society among which they lived was unwilling to accept Russian Jewry into its ranks, even to those of its elements that were prepared to pay the price of assimilation. The enlightened and the Orthodox, the so-called obscurant Jews, were all in the same boat and were never allowed to forget it. Thus, both the inner resources of this Jewry and the tremendous pressure from outside contributed to the vitality and dynamism which characterized Russian Jewry through all its vicissitudes. Russia—for long that meant also the Baltic provinces and states, Poland, Lithuania, Volhynia, Ukraine, and Bessarabia; even ignoring Poland proper, such places as Riga, Minsk, Vilna, Kovno, Grodno, Bialystok, Lubavitch, Mohilev, Berdichev, Zhitomir, Chernobyl, Bratislava, Medzibozh, Odessa, and Kishinev—these and a hundred others are unforgettable names, reverberating through the spiritual world of Judaism.

Of course, these and innumerable larger and lesser towns and villages had their common share of material hardship and persecution, of suffering and bitter internal social conflict. But despite all these, or perhaps because of them, there arose an infinite fertility of mind, a boundless idealistic enthusiasm, an imagination and sensitivity. The figure of the Russian Jew as it is imprinted on our mind is at the same time characterized by traits possibly reflecting some of the general influences of the surrounding Russian atmosphere, albeit transformed by the particular Jewish situation. I have in mind a certain generosity and spontaneity, a bent to disregard bourgeois considerations, a capacity for endless discussion, and last but not least a Jewish variant of the Russian Nitchevo.[1]

The Jews of Russia have produced many of the decisive phenomena of later and modern Jewish life, in widely different spheres. All these phenomena bear the unmistakable mark of the group that created them. Let me mention some of the outstanding ones.

Within the framework of traditional talmudic culture, they not only produced a long chain of great rabbis, scholars, and protagonists of rabbinic tradition, but in the archetypal figure of Rabbi Elijah, the Gaon of Vilna, gave to large parts of Jewry the ideal image of what Jewish learning and devotion should represent. His name has been a household word throughout Ashkenazic Jewry for two hundred years. This ascetic recluse, who spent most of his years in a little room immersed in all branches of Jewish tradition and only once, when he set out to do battle against Ḥasidism, descended into the public arena, captured the imagination of the Jewish people. His pupils, who founded the great yeshivot in Russia—Volozhin, Mir, and their successors—forged an instrument of Jewish education for which the Vilna Gaon became the guiding star. One can hardly overrate the importance of this institution, which for more than one hundred years provided Russian Jewry not only with a rabbinical elite, but also with many great minds who broke away and found their own path to Jewish activism.

In marked contrast to this contribution, Ḥasidism is essentially a creation of Russian Jewry in the sphere of intimate religious and emotional life, beginning with the mystical experiences of Israel Ba'al Shem and the revivalist and inspired preaching of his pupils, and branching out into ever wider circles. It presented the masses of Polish-Russian Jewry with an unprecedented galaxy of Jewish saints, who became the living heart for thousands of followers. An emotional upheaval of tremendous power found its expression in a new way of life which, after violent clashes with unreconstructed Orthodoxy, managed to reach an uneasy compromise, leaving Ḥasidism as the dominant factor in large areas of Russia, such as Ukraine, Podolia, Volhynia, and Russian Poland.

On the other hand, in Lithuania there originated the *Musar* movement, which stressed a radical way of life, acting under strong ethical inspiration and equally strong anti-bourgeois tendencies. The yeshivot of this movement, Novogrodek, Slobodka, and others, became the center of what might be called a radical youth movement within the confines of talmudic culture. Like Ḥasidism, it had wide repercussions beyond the Russian Pale. Its uncompromising attitude to standards of personal life and behavior formed a new ideal type of unconventional Jew that impressed and attracted many of the most remarkable minds during the end of the nineteenth and the first third of the twentieth centuries. Both Ḥasidism and *Musar,* each in its own way, have cultivated the ideal of the strong religious and ethical personality.

But all this was only one side of the picture. There was also the deep unrest connected with the crisis of Jewish tradition in the wake of its encounter with the modern world. The Haskalah movement, the Jewish Enlightenment, which became a strong factor in Russian Jewish life, sprang from dissatisfaction with and criticism of tradition, from the feeling that a new era had set in and demanded new answers. True, its advocates deluded themselves, like so many others, about the march of progress, about the chances of integration into Russian society, and their rosy visions were shattered when they came face to face with the bitter reality of the Russian pogroms and the intensification of persecution. But their unrelenting criticism of Jewish society and its depressing realities, often to the point of despair, did much to instill life into stagnation, to ask questions which these other movements had tried to evade. Their activities blended rational analysis and romantic longings. They were the first who, however dimly, faced the problem of secularization in Jewish life, which has never left us since. It was from their radical wing that, with Morris Vinchevsky and Aaron Liebermann, the first stirrings of Jewish socialism arose.

The Jewish Haskalah was unsure of its steps, but its two great off-springs—albeit offspring only in a dialectical sense—took a firm stand vis-à-vis their Jewish identification. I speak of modern Yiddish and Hebrew literature, and of the national and social movements which carried them, nursed them, and were in return immensely enriched by them. The creation of Yiddish and Hebrew prose and poetry is one of the outstanding contributions which we owe to Russian Jewry. Through these two avenues of expression, the wellsprings of Jewish vitality opened up. We all remember Khrushchev's saying, which gained wide currency some years ago, that there were too many Abramowitzes and Rabinowitzes around in Russia. We have every reason to affirm our debt of gratitude to them, symbolized by the great names of Sholem Jakob Abramowitz, known throughout the Jewish world as Mendele Mokher Seforim, the *Zaide,* the grandfather of both Yiddish and Hebrew literary prose, and Shlomo Rabinowitz, known as Shalom Aleichem. They stand for an unending line of great masters, as well as gifted and industrious contributors to these fields. For two generations before 1920, the life of Russian Jewry was expressed and fructified by these literatures, by Aḥad Ha-Am and Bialik, by Berdichevsky and Brenner, by Peretz and Shalom Asch. They radiated far beyond Russia, and their struggles, discussions, and achievements are enduring testimony to the prodigious creative power of Russian Jewry when it became aware of its national identity, whether of a traditional or a secular coloring.

Of course, the different branches of the national movement that sprang up after 1880 fought each other vehemently. There was *Galut* nationalism, represented in different shades by Dubnow or by the socialist Bund and the Yiddishists. There was Zionism in all its factions, from Pinsker to Syrkin and Borochov. But all of them were united in one basic proposition: that the Jews had a natural right to live the life of a national minority, to choose for themselves how to live their Judaism or Jewishness, and to convey their national culture and tradition through education. They fought for full rights as citizens, not only as individuals, as in the West, but as a national group. When the Russian Revolution came in 1917, almost every Jewish party included in its platform the demand for national autonomy for Russian Jewry. They had become conscious of their national existence and paid no heed to those isolated figures who demanded that they forgo their national rights. During those years, there was an immense upsurge of great expectations for a Jewish future in a progressive and socialist Russia, much of which flowed over into the building up of the new

life in Israel to which Russian Jewry has made such an outstanding contribution.

Much of the foundation of what is now the State of Israel was laid by
the untiring and selfless pioneering work and sacrifice of Russian Jews,
from the Bilus on. The idea of self-defense, first put forward by Jews in
Russia after the Kishinev pogrom in 1903, gave birth to the concept and
practice of the Haganah, to the recognition that Jews must if necessary
stand up and fight for themselves. On another plane, the idea of the kib-
butz was first conceived and realized by Russian Jews, and A. D. Gordon,
from a village in Podolia, became the prophet of a moral rebirth of the
Jewish people through work. There can hardly be a place in the world outside of Russia in which the ideas of Tolstoy have had a more profound impact than in Israel. Rabbi Kook, Jabotinsky, Chaim Weizmann, Berl
Katznelson and, to name only one among the living [as of 1971—Ed.],
David Ben-Gurion, were among the great figures who have shaped the
spiritual, social, and political growth of Israel—all Russian Jews. It is hardly
an accident that the three Presidents of the State of Israel who have served
until now, the four Prime Ministers, and the first four Speakers of the
Knesset have all been Russian Jews. They symbolize our debt to Russian
Jewry, but also our continuing obligation to our people in Russia. They
have done so much for us.

Chapter Eight

Understanding the Internal Processes (1977)*

It is my great pleasure to express my gratitude to those who have honored me with the Bialik Prize for my work in the field of Jewish studies, or, to be more precise: for my efforts in the study of the mystical teachings within Judaism, both their history and contents.

And how good it is that the poet Uri Tzvi Greenberg and myself have been brought together on this occasion! We have stood, and continue to stand, at opposite poles within the Zionist camp. Yet while our paths have not been at all similar, both of us are what our ancestors would have called masters of one trade—that is, we adhered to and continue to adhere to one goal, which each one has posed for himself.

My joy in this honor is double, being connected with the name of Ḥayyim Naḥman Bialik, whom I was privileged to know over a period of several years, and whose friendship and help I enjoyed at the beginning of my path in Kabbalah. I still remember my many hours of conversation with him and of listening to the conversation in his home and at the *Oneg Shabbat* gatherings which I attended whenever I visited Tel Aviv during his lifetime. The hours of spiritual elevation which I enjoyed thanks to his inspiration are unforgettable.

---

* Remarks made upon receiving the 1977 Bialik Prize. Published in *Ha-Aretz,* January 21, 1977; reprinted in *'Od Davar,* 43–46.

I first met Bialik in Berlin and in Hamburg, shortly after I had completed my studies and prior to my own *aliyah* to Israel, having been introduced to him by S. Y. Agnon. He was interested in the phenomenon of a young German Jew who had set his mind to studying, of all things, the neglected and seemingly obscure subject area of Kabbalah. He received me with good spirit and with more than a little curiosity, asking me why and for what reason I had chosen to descend to this locked garden, and whether and perhaps I had found the key to it.

When we met again following his own *aliyah,* he again greatly encouraged me. He was among those to whom I owe a debt of gratitude for my appointment to the faculty of the Hebrew University in the year in which it was opened, giving me the opportunity to devote all of my time to that selfsame enterprise for which I stand before you today. To this day, I am unable to read without excitement the exchange of letters between us during the summer of 1925, in which at his request I set out my research program, to which he responded enthusiastically and with great encouragement and support, as may be found in his collected letters.[1]

I would like to recall a small incident which occurred between us, which is not bereft of humor. One day Bialik came to Jerusalem, and I visited him. I had recently published a study in *Zohar* criticism about the data found in this book concerning the Land of Israel, in order to prove that the author of the *Sefer ha-Zohar* never saw the Land.[2] We were talking about this and that, when suddenly Bialik turned to me in mock anger and said: "You are such a *shegetz!* You know, you did a terrible thing!" I replied: "But Mr. Bialik, what have I done?" He said: "You wrote a terrible thing in your article!" "What did I write?" I asked. "You referred to 'the corpse *(peger)* of R. Simeon bar Yoḥai.' Heaven forbid! How could you write such a thing about the body of a *tzaddik?!*" Being unfamiliar with Yiddish, I answered with surprise: "But Mr. Bialik, it is written in the morning prayers, 'He who restores life to dead bodies' *(pegarim metim)!*" Bialik looked at me for a long while and said only one word: *Yekke!* [German Jew!; as if to say: What can someone like you understand of such nuances?—trans.]

Some twenty years later, this same error of mine in Hebrew usage elicited a rather different reaction. My research on the Sabbatian movement was not always to the liking of our Orthodox brethren, and I learned the hard way that the bitter taste of polemics was not only a thing of the past. I had innocently thought that the time had come to study the great chapter of Sabbatianism and those who adhered to it without prejudice and without partisan leanings—and I greatly erred. When, after profound examination and research into the depths of this painful chapter, I expressed my opinion that the great genius of *pilpul* (talmudic dialectics), Rabbi Jonathan Eibuschutz, was in fact a secret believer in Sabbatai Tzvi, I touched a raw nerve among many. They are not much perturbed by what a scholar may say regarding whether or not *Sefer ha-Zohar* was really written by R. Simeon bar Yoḥai, but when I publicly stated that the great genius of eighteenth century Polish *pilpul* was a Sabbatian—here I transgressed the permitted boundaries. If such a thing was possible, then anything was possible! I became the object of intense anger, and I was to be suitably punished. I was accused of lack of sympathy for traditional Judaism and people sought faults in my writings—and so, as conclusive proof of my enmity to rabbinic Judaism, they unearthed the selfsame unfortunate expression regarding R. Simeon bar Yoḥai. Such was the result of a single slip of the pen!

And now, allow me to say a few words about my specific academic interests. During the course of my studies, I have always swung between two poles of interest, which I must admit have not always been expressed with full subtlety and richness in my published work. The one pole—call it the exoteric side—was my scholarly interest in the literature of Jewish mysticism, in both its historical and philosophical-theoretical aspect. Of course, only gradually did I become fully aware of the tremendous dynamic in the development of this movement, in all its heights and depths, and of the powerful dialectical movement that arose within it from that historical moment, following the expulsion from Spain, when messianism entered it as a sweeping force. The understanding of these internal processes pertains to the multi-faceted functions played by Kabbalah as a public and historical factor. This entire complex fascinated me and stimulated my historical imagination, insofar as I had it. Much as it opened new perspectives to me, it also extended the realm of new and unresolved questions. I have attempted to formulate answers to several of them, many of which have remained open to debate or still requiring solutions, leaving room for others to innovate further—both my students and their students, no less than to my opponents, of whom, praise God, there have been and will be no lack. I plowed virgin soil, and insofar as it was fruitful, it may yield far more fruit.

The other pole of my attention has not been emphasized or recognized to the same degree in my numerous publications over the course of half a century, even though it was no less important to me—namely, as a person who saw and sees Judaism as a living organism, constantly renewing and changing, taking on one form and casting off others, without being subjected to any fixed or predetermined definition. I refer to my interest in the imaginative world of the mystics, from the Merkabah mystics of the talmudic period down to the various generations of Kabbalists, the Sabbatians, and the Ḥasidim. The pictures, images, and symbols which grew upon this soil or which fell upon these fields with abundance seemed to me to be filled with a poetic and lyrical significance, of equal worth to the theoretical meaning which I had set my mind to resolve.

The discovery of the tremendous poetic potential within Kabbalah, in its own unique language no less than in its poetry proper, which has also come down to us with great richness—all these constitute a realm which has hardly been examined and which holds the promise of great discoveries. Hillel Zeitlin, a great author who was killed in the Holocaust, but whose memory will never leave us, was, insofar as I know, the first one to sense this aspect of esoteric literature already seventy years ago, in his essays "Shekhinah" and "Supernal Beauty."[3] Later, Fischel Lachover commented on it in his essays on the Ramhal (Rabbi Ḥayyim David Luzzatto).[4] But a great deal remains to be done by literary scholars and those with a talent for aesthetic analysis. Luzzatto's Kabbalistic poetry has begun to arouse the interest of some scholars in our generation, but the tools have not yet been created for understanding the lyric plane within the language of the Kabbalists and the Ḥasidim. Without creating these tools, this question cannot be fully encompassed. My own secret longing to do so has not been fulfilled and remains unsatisfied. Thus, at the conclusion of my remarks, allow me to express the wish that we may look forward to someone who will remove the dust hiding the true face of such books as Sefer ha-Temunah, Berit Menuḥah, or Ḥemdat Yamim, to reveal the poetic depths in their imagery and that of many similar books.

The great wealth concealed here awaits those who shall toil to discover them, to their own benefit.

Part Three

The Existential Situation in Jewish Culture Today

Chapter Nine

Reflections on Modern Jewish Studies (1944)*

More than twenty years have passed since Bialik, in a letter to the editors of *Devir,* sounded his clarion call heralding the renewal of Judaic studies, returning to its own language from the alien Western vernacular. Twenty years have passed since the establishment, in the summer of 1924, of the Institute for Jewish Studies on Mount Scopus as the first seed of the Hebrew University, a sign of the renewal of Jewish studies[1] in its homeland. Fragmentary, lofty, and sublime words of vision were declaimed; from every hill and mountain the event, whose meaning seemed so clear and simple and far-reaching, was expounded. Would there not now commence a golden age of that selfsame Science of Judaism which had been exiled and beat about, which had contracted and shrunk into the four ells, not of the law, but, to cite Bialik's words of rebuke, of the grave? And would not the contact with the eternal soil of the nation give rise to a new vision, by means of the renewed contact with its eternal sources? Through the building of the present while raising up the past as a vital power? Who was not entranced by the dream, shared by elders and youngsters alike? The *Shekhinah,* the Divine Spirit of our nation, would cast off its garments of widowhood, and from Zion would go forth Torah—and we were satiated with words till the wee hours.

---

* Published in *Luaḥ Ha-Aretz, Shenat TSh"H, 1944/45* (Tel Aviv, 1944), 94–112. The heading to the essay reads: "An introduction to a lecture which will not take place."

Who then has clipped the wings of the dream? One generation has passed since then, and at times we look around in amazement: Was it this that we awaited? Is this the heritage and the goal? Where is the building which we were meant to erect, that building which was to go down to the roots of our existence, and which from the depths of its foundations would reach up to the heights? And if the building is not built—where is that whole stone with which we were meant to construct the building of Judaic studies? What is this task, and what are its arrangements? Has the hand of the builders weakened? Is there something wrong in the house of wisdom and science, so that one ought to think of repairing the house? Or did we perhaps err in our perception and blow the trumpet before the time, like those fools in Jerusalem as of old, while the spiritual air is still stagnant and there is no renewal, and we find ourselves declaring the birth of something which has not yet been born, of the redemption of Jewish studies which has not at all occurred? Perhaps there was nothing to acclaim, and therefore nothing to warn against?

Many of us who participate in the academic enterprise, as well as those who look on from aside and wish to learn from us, have asked questions of this sort, both from within and without, and are disappointed because our wells seem dry. Our best readers have publicly declared that they have not found what they sought among the scholars in this field, even among the sages of Mount Scopus. They have many complaints: we have not prepared the proper tools for their work, we have denied the great vision of building a true and solid structure, of gathering the heritage and shedding light upon its values. Instead, we have become cut off from our true destiny and our main task. There are those who fear that we have set ourselves up in an unreliable place and invested in sterile and unbeneficial studies, or that, in general, we have changed the gold of large interpretations and central problems for the small coin of the study of trivial details.

Such is the atmosphere and such are the questions. It is worthwhile to reflect somewhat upon the state of things, about the situation we have found and the situation which we have created—and indeed, there is much to reflect upon. There are many prejudices concerning the Science of Judaism and its functions, even among its practitioners, and certainly on the part of the public. But in this case appearances are likely to be deceiving. There are some problems which appear simple, and one does not realize how complex they truly are. On the other hand, there is also more than a little of the game of the scientific esoteric, who plays the cult of the nothing with unrivaled strictness and diligence. But what reason have we to be angry? Is it not stated that during the birthpangs of Messiah the hidden things will become revealed—and perhaps also by rights that the

revealed things shall become hidden? And whether this is said in praise
or in denigration—do not even the revealed things of the Science of Judaism also contain hidden elements?

II

In my opinion, one cannot understand the development of the Science
of Judaism except by taking note of the profound contradictions or, if you
will, the unique dialectical tensions present within it since its origins.
These contradictions left their impression upon its makeup, particularly
among the major and prominent figures of the nineteenth century. But
its function as an historical force in our history is connected with these
contradictions in its nature.

The Science of Judaism came into being in connection with the twi-
light of the Romantic movement in Germany, and its scholarly offshoots.[2]
The impressive scholarly attainments of the Romantic school in the historical, philological, and philosophical areas inspired the members of the
Verein für Kultur und Wissenschaft des Jüdentums, the living spirit of which
was Leopold Zunz (1794–1886). In the wake of romantic scholarship, a
tremendous change took place in the evaluation of the past and in the vision of the present: the moral to be learned from the world-view and studies of the practitioners of this science, which first appeared as an historical
force with a specific direction and a definite nationalist tendency, was a
certain relation to particular forces and their liberation in the life of the
nation. The practitioners of romantic scholarship in Germany severed
their connections with the Enlightenment, and the impressive manner in
which they formulated and elucidated problems in their own way forced
the advocates of Enlightenment within the scholarly world to defend
themselves, to introduce changes in their stance, and to accept some of
their slogans under the influence of the romantic attack. The political
function of this science was clear and striking. I do not mean to say that it
was not marred by contradictions of its own. On the contrary, there were
many such, as illustrated by the struggles between the reactionary and liberal tendencies within this camp. However, it was not these contradictions
that were to be important for the nascent Science of Judaism.

The Science of Judaism involves three inner contradictions, which became progressively deeper during the course of its classical development,
and which, with the change in the historical circumstances of the status of
the Jewish public, became obscured without achieving any fruitful solu-

tion. It was these contradictions which created the grotesque visage of this science—an aspect which even today people tend to ignore (insofar as the practitioners of this discipline bother to think about the history of their discipline at all). The contradictions in question are the following:

1. The contradiction between the repeated declarations of being a pure and objective science, which is no more than a branch of academic studies in general and which has no purpose outside of itself—and the striking fact of the political function which this discipline was intended to fulfill, sought to fulfill, and was accepted by public opinion in order to fulfill. How strange the image of those scholars, all of whose work indicates that they sought to create an effective tool in the struggle of the Jews for equal rights, and who made constant use of this tool in their polemics; and yet nevertheless closed their eyes so as not to see this primary goal too clearly, declaring repeatedly that they seek nothing but pure knowledge for its own sake. It was this blatant political aim which initially unbalanced the discussion of several major issues. There were some scholars who in truth never understood throughout their entire lives what their purpose was, and naively attempted to conduct their work on the basis of this declaration; others were well aware of what they were meant to do, all their high words about science that is free of any interest and does not serve any purpose outside of its own boundaries being mere lip service. Such objectivity did not and could not exist, and there were many documents, beginning with Rashi's *Seliḥah* (a certain genre of liturgical poem) concerning the slaughter of 1096, which were concealed for the sake of peace [i.e., not published so as to avoid negative response from the non-Jewish world]. There were other scholars who perceived this contradiction and attempted to obfuscate it, comforting themselves by saying that the pursuit of scientific truth for its own sake brings in its wake, by some benign destiny, benefit to the status of Jews in society. And because they were naive, it seemed to them that their teaching was realized and their labor blessed. They were unaware of their own peculiar distortions, which astonish our own contemporaries when they happen to read such things.

2. More serious was the second contradiction, which already pertains to the depth of things and does not at all depend upon the will or viewpoint of men of science. I refer to the contradiction between the spiritual stature of most of the great figures of this science, and those ideals which they inscribed upon their banner. These people were *Maskilim*—enlightened ones—and all of their human pathos was drawn from the school of rationalistic Enlightenment, whose outlook and rationalistic evaluations they were unable to deny by their own very nature. During that generation, all of the hopes of the Jewish people were pinned upon the victory of

those tendencies, and the entire House of Israel in the West followed them. The Romantic school of scholarship served an anti-Jewish function, giving the Jews excellent reason to fear it. Yet the program with which the founders of the Science of Judaism appeared before the public was a romantic one, albeit with a moderate and somewhat obscured formulation—but nevertheless it was romantic. A new relation to the past; the elevation of the aura and brilliance attached to the past by virtue of its being the past; the evaluation of sources in a unique light and taking into consideration popular forces; and, in general, an interest in the study of the folk and the nation (which is so striking in the original program of Zunz, which for good reason was never executed)—in all these there are reflected the basic lines of a romantic approach to scientific problems. Such a program might have been good had it been directed toward the building of the Jewish nation. Why then should it be surprising that there was a double conflict manifested here: a conflict within the tendencies of the scholars themselves, leading to instability within their approach, to vacillations and distortions, because they did not know at all where they stood, and whether they wished their labors to contribute to building the Jewish nation or its dismantling; as well as their conflicts with the powers guiding Jewish society in the West. The latter related to the entire program, which was completely alien to their spirit, with profound mistrust. The constant complaints of the great scholars regarding the utter apathy of the Jewish communal leadership toward their plans cries out for interpretation. It indicates the extent to which major communal forces, who were interested in the political battles of the Jews, had no trust in the romantic Science of Judaism or in the benefit to be extracted from it toward the realization of their own programs. These scholars put themselves forward as fighters and even as pioneers in the political battle, but their hypocrisy made them suspect to those who championed the obliteration of Judaism from the national viewpoint, and who hoped to attain their complete emancipation as a deistic sect within a deistic society. Perhaps these young doctors, who sought to engage in the study of midrashim and *piyyutim* and medieval philosophers and a thousand other forgotten things, hoped to shed light upon something which was better forgotten, and quickly? Perhaps their aim was not toward destruction alone?

3. And indeed—it is concerning this point that there emerges the profound and central contradiction in this entire great adventure called the Science of Judaism: that the conservative tendencies and destructive tendencies within this discipline are interwoven with one another. Historical criticism as a scientific method is by its very nature unable to avoid this dialectic. Its destructive function—and there is no doubt that its natural and

most striking function is its destructive one—can be completely turned about: to free all of those bodies of data or values which in one moment change the entire perspective, a liberation which may unintentionally transform all of the remnants of the past into marvelous symbols of life. The historical critic must at every moment consider the possibility that he will turn out to be a conservative at the next turn of the road. And this is precisely what gave the great scholars of the Romantic school their greatness: this profound understanding of the duality inherent in their path, "the path that is wiser than those who walk it," in the words of the poet. For them, there is nothing wrong in this ambivalence: they, who saw themselves oriented toward the building of the people, did not feel themselves to be gravediggers. They dwelt among their own people, and historical criticism was for them the dialectical approach to all true construction. How strange is the stance of the Science of Judaism toward this dialectic, and how terrible the paradox: their historical consciousness did not leave its practitioners the positive use inherent in their approach, while romantic science and its methods appeared to them as a hasty burial.

Particularly interesting is the exceptional case of Rabbi Naḥman Krochmal (1785–1840). How mistaken those contemporary authors who write as if Krochmal in fact exerted any tangible, real influence upon the development of the Science of Judaism! In fact, he did not affect the method of research during the generation which followed him, and one seeks in vain his impact upon those engaged in scientific work. Who would believe today that the greatest study of Rabbi Abraham Ibn Ezra does not even mention the existence of a chapter entitled "the wisdom of the unfortunate one" in Krochmal,[3] and not necessarily out of bad will. Among those Eastern European *Maskilim* who enjoyed his book, only the smallest minority participated in the actual work being done; had his *Guide to the Perplexed of Our Times*[4] never been published, nothing in the course of the development of the Science of Judaism over the course of the nineteenth century would have been different. This is a fact which is not accepted today, because there is a great tendency toward sentimental obfuscation, but one may perhaps for once be allowed to state this simple truth. In his own day, Rabbi Naḥman Krochmal did not influence anyone because his brilliant book was not at all suitable to the needs of the Science of Judaism during those generations, at least in several of its basic features, and only after a change in atmosphere did the brilliance of the hidden treasure suddenly emerge.

In recent times we have occasionally tended to ignore too much the tendencies toward historical suicide, of destruction and dismantling, which were operative within the Jewish Haskalah. The demon of destruction assumed a dozen different shapes among the nations of the West, both hidden and revealed. We tend to forget that the Science of Judaism also played a great role in the tendency toward destruction, and that it was primarily in this role that its practitioners became accepted by those forces which stood at the head of the community. True, these lines of conflict were not always clear. Romanticism took its revenge upon those *Maskilim* who spoke in its name, driving them crazy. All kinds of confusions came into existence here. There were some scholars, such as Moritz Steinschneider (1816–1907), to whom it was clear what they were doing, and who labored toward the destruction, celebrating the burial ceremony in thought, speech, and action. There were others, such as Zunz, who suffered the contradiction within their souls and were torn apart by inner tension. All of the great slogans reveal here a double face, pointed toward both life and death. There is no more striking example of this than the spiritualization of Jewish history (i.e., the changing of the history of the Jews into the history of Judaism), whose double-facedness is well expressed by Krochmal, on the one hand, and by Geiger, on the other. The disembodied spirits sought spirituality in order to justify themselves—but they did not always wish to justify themselves. It is the nature of disembodied spirits to seek rest, whether in an alien body or in the grave. And many agreed then to remove themselves, turning toward death. The well-known optimism in their opinions is a lying mask; something coming from the Other Side, a completely other side, is revealed in their deeds.

One might say that there is something frightening in the metaphysical platform of the Science of Judaism. Spirits which have been uprooted from their bodies and made abstract wander about in desolation. They dwell next to the fields of the living and gaze at the world with longing eyes. How they would wish to walk there too, and how weary they are of the wanderings of generations, wanting only to rest. Many have eaten their fill of contempt and were rejected by both the gates of life and the gates of death, longing for both, to be freed of their in-between state, from the unique hell of the Jew described by Heinrich Heine. But how can they move, when a generations-old curse rests upon them, a kind of charm or magic which in order to either live or die must be negated: bits of a burdensome and dangerous past are attached to them. Fragments of the past are scattered about, and these monsters have a charmed tongue of their own. The Jew wishes to be freed of himself, and the Science of Judaism serves him both as burial ceremony and liberation from the yoke that hovers over him. And it leaves room for the coming generations, when the awful game will be completed, the shells that separate him from life will be abjured, and the past embalmed and buried. There are times when you stand entranced by this diligence, which lifts up the phenomena and removes the facts from the thicket of their mutual interrelations, clarifying and cleansing the past from the dust of generations and from the contamination of lies and the beautiful falsehood of the legends—all for the sake of its final burial.

III

This chthonian aspect of the behavior of the great scholars of the Science of Judaism emerges with frightening power in three figures, whose demonic side has not been properly evaluated: Zunz, Steinschneider, and Geiger. Hence, the latent animosity between them and Heinrich Graetz (1817–1891), the romantic *Maskil* who remained loyal to the principles of Romantic scholarship, from which he derived the natural conclusion in the constructive sense as well, is not surprising.

I must admit that the images of Zunz and Steinschneider have always attracted me. However, nothing serious has ever been written about them. Whatever has been written, has been written by people of small spirit, and is filled with infinite prattle. It is my hope that some day, someone with open eyes will take it upon himself to portray the true picture of these princes of wisdom: a psychological history of souls from the shell of dark brilliance.

I do not believe that their like exists in the Science of Judaism: neither in terms of the breadth of their knowledge, which is world-embracing— and perhaps it was this very breadth which prevented them from seeing in depth—and certainly not in terms of the power of their presentation, which was totally lacking. Jokesters used to say that Steinschneider never wrote a sentence with a noun, a verb, and an orderly sentence structure. Instead, he used to write five hundred pages of notes, and call it a book. Zunz's baroque style during the second half of his life is widely known among those familiar with this period, and is best passed over in silence! However, one finds something in these two scholars that is not to be found among any other scholars, neither in their contemporaries nor in those that followed them: namely, that they are truly demonic figures. These sober figures are unique in their generation in their total lack of sentimentality in the approach to the past. They do not serve up their novellas with a stew of empty or mediocre sentiments or empty enthusiasm; they speak to the point and only to the point, and this zealously matter-of-fact approach seems marvelous to us: at times annoying and cold, and at times refreshing and restraining. One finds in them the full measure of that spiritual asceticism which is demanded of the ideal scholar, and whose absence is so strongly felt in the generation of gushers which followed them. How much coolness there is in these temples of science. But they also have an intense Other Side. Suddenly, while reading their words, you feel as if you are gazing into the face of the Medusa, as if from among the half sentences and side comments something completely non-human gazes back at you and freezes your heart—a hatred which is not of this world, a grandiose cynicism. And then the stage changes, and you see before you giants who, for reasons best known to themselves, have turned themselves into gravediggers and embalmers, and even eulogizers. And now they are disguised as midgets, gathering grasses in the fields of the past, drying them out so that there not remain in them any of the juice of life, and putting them in something which one does not know whether to call a book or a grave. The embalmed facts are spread out in the graves, line after line, marked by plot number, as if they were not merely notes. The monuments which are upon the graves, the text, is also so to speak sunken into the earth, and the letters have become faint and the language rubbed out—until here and there you encounter the anger of those who engage in this frightening work, who tell you that they are not so innocent and that they still have passions, and they know how to love and to hate. Their books, the classical works of the Science of Judaism, are a kind of procession around the dead, although at times it seems that the authors themselves are the ghosts of Old Israel, seeking their salvation while dancing among the graves. These are sparks of very great souls from the unredeemed shell of brilliance, from a world in which life and death are jumbled together.

Abraham Geiger (1810–74) was made of rougher stuff—he was without any doubt the most talented among the scholars of destruction, insofar as anyone can measure his talents. He was the only one who knew how to build a tremendous structure of chaos in this changing world, to perform the dissection into a scientific construction, which the lie of pure spirituality makes out to be a kind of reflection of reality. But here, notwithstanding his striking success and the flow of language which heralds great things, everything takes place ten degrees below the place of Zunz and Steinschneider. In the case of these two, the tendency to destruction is entirely inward; their hidden nihilism contains a certain measure of nobility, which functioned within them as a kind of creative despair. How can one read the letters of Zunz or the introductions/last testaments of the elderly Steinschneider without a sense of shock? They have an incredible inner freedom, and there is nothing more distant from their mood than adjustment to the bourgeois world. One feels in them something of the stubbornness of the democrat of 1848. How different the level of Geiger! Here there dance spirits from other spheres. In his words, one can smell priestly hypocrisy, clerical pride, and the ambition of an archbishop. His talent for refining and purifying is impressive, and he has that sovereign ability, which makes for the great historian, to rape the facts for the sake of his construction, and to clarify the contexts through historical intuition, a dangerous and creative power possessed also by Graetz—and one completely lacking in Zunz and Steinschneider, neither one of whom sold their soul for the price of an historical axiom with wings. But from what lowly and gross sphere does this intuition come; how gross the liberalism which is not liberal at all, but a kind of deistic papism, and woe to Jewish history at the hands of such a priestly-liberal philosophy of history.

There is more than a little settling of accounts with the Gentiles behind their tremendous enterprise. These three were in no sense enamored of Christianity, and it is not it that they are addressing when they speak of removing the dividing walls and stressing that which is common to all human beings. The utopia of Graetz and Geiger, with all the profound differences therein between destruction and preservation, is liberal but anti-Christian. But it never occurred to any of these three that their enterprise would serve to plant enthusiasm for Jewish national values that were discovered by them unawares, and no one would be more surprised than Zunz or Steinschneider to hear that these dead men came out of their graves and came back to life. One of Steinschneider's last students related how he, as a young Zionist, was astounded upon seeing his library, and began to lecture his master about the renaissance of the people, its hidden values, and so on. To which the hoary nonagenarian answered: "Please, sir; we have no other task but to conduct a 'proper funeral' for all that."

IV

Hence, I wish to say that this whole business of the Science of Judaism is not so simple. It involves complications embedded in the circumstances of its creation, complications reflecting the contradictions of Jewish reality itself in that generation. Not everything took place on the revealed level. There is also a secret history of this discipline, and the famous Book of Zunz—sealed and hidden away in one of the storehouses of Jerusalem—is not the only hidden book in its treasuries. Many of the most illuminating and vital works in our literature have become, from the perspective of the Science of Judaism, hidden works. Romantic philology and philosophy were as a magic wand which they used to awaken and bring back to life the subjects of its research. But in very extensive areas, this magic wand has been transformed by the Science of Judaism into a wrecker's rod. The old books, once they came close to them, had their brilliance taken away, and that which was translucent and shining became opaque and cold.

The dangerous tension in the above-mentioned tendencies was released by what may be called, if the sages will forgive us, an orgy of mediocrity. Mediocrity of measure, not of stature—although this too as a rule went on to conquer position after position, and the intermediate (or mediocre) track (in the formula of Breslau and its offshoots) took shape. Many people praise this scientific school even today—for did they not in fact leave an inheritance to the later generations, a rich heritage of facts and explanations, studies and research, which will remain in our treasure houses even after the house itself has collapsed. But as for a list of its shortcomings and sins—who remembers those? This intermediate track appeared as the safest line of retreat for positive historical science against the depredations of those contradictory tendencies which shatter it, as the line of retreat of the Science of Judaism which attempts to alienate itself from the dialectic movement in its veins, while forgetting it and obscuring it. It is worthy of note that, with the absolute victory of the *juste milieu* in Western Jewish society, the scientific representatives of blatant reform also continued of necessity on this mediocre track, and their stature became gradually weakened, until there was eventually no difference whatsoever between the radicals and the most proper among the reformers in terms of their scientific approach.

V

The contradiction of which I spoke above created the role of the Science of Judaism as an independent force which for its part sought to influence the course of events within our people. These contradictions likewise explain the fact—I say fact, even though it has not at all been recognized as such by historians—that the historical power therein, which was crushed between the tendencies of building the House of Israel and its destruction from within, was much smaller than is generally thought, and than Graetz and those who followed him would wish us to believe. Insofar as it enjoyed such influence at all, this came about through its ideological retreat

to the path of mediocrity, through its transformation into the spokesman
of a certain polite self-satisfaction which was angered equally by definite
slogans of building and of destruction, because it wished to sleep (at least
within the realm of its Jewish activity). This sleep is referred to by various
names: moderate progressivism, conservation through correction, and the
like. The refuse of romantic pathos—that is, sentimentality and obfuscation—laid waste to the souls of this generation and was pleasing to their
eyes, no less than the refuse of humanistic and rationalistic pathos; that is:
the hopes of the refined faith in something divine (it is very difficult to
determine what this something is) while cutting it off from its earthly
foundations (whose interpretation was likely to be very different). Thus,
they consciously encouraged both of these directions, and it was not difficult for the scholars to bring together what was demanded of them. Spiritualization and sentimentalization ran amok. It follows that the Science
of Judaism won its (admittedly modest) place and influence with the
Western Jewish public insofar as it appeared in a bourgeois edition, and insofar as it served its purposes (which seem very strange to our eyes today).
Knowledge of the martyrs who were killed and the great scholars who
spread the light of Enlightenment satisfied the feeling of pride of a generation which did not expect to follow in their footsteps and which awaited
the liberal messiah.

    The ability of this Science of Judaism to change anything was nil. De-
spite Graetz's proud words concerning its function, its power to penetrate
into historical consciousness was necessarily limited by the framework of
the various prejudices entailed in the liberal historiography common to
all streams. The picture of Jewish history which was constructed by this
science and which came down thereafter is conveyed as a heritage to subsequent generations, carrying with it all the signs of the generation—and
how much more so the picture of Jewish thought as depicted here. Many
of these zealous workers seem to us like giants in terms of their knowledge
and like pygmies in terms of insights. But it would appear that this was
what that generation wanted.

    A high price was paid for these attainments. There broke forth the ten-
sion between the impulse toward destruction and the impulse of conservation, between destructive rebellion against the national past and the
romantic desire to uplift that same past clean and purified, and even between contempt for ourselves and contempt for the nations of the world.
"Whoever is greater than his neighbor, his evil impulse is greater than
him" (b. Sukkah 52a)—and the tension of the impulses was likewise diminished, and became mediocre and exhausted of strength once placed
upon the new basis of the intermediate track. How weak and fruitless the

tension between these new tendencies of sentimentalization and spiritualization. One found here neither rebelliousness nor greatness—there is no dialectic in self-satisfaction!

Such was the traditional face of the Science of Judaism, well-known to all (even though not all wished to recognize it!) until a generation ago. One cannot say that the radiance of the national spirit shone above its face. Bialik's remark that the original sin of the Science of Judaism was its alienation from the Hebrew language, and it was that which made its masters into "heretics of the spirit" and the teaching of Judaism into "ten Torahs," seems rather questionable. For the truth is that the Torah of Israel was never uniform or spoken in only one language, just as then, in days of yore, it was uttered in seventy tongues! Moreover, all of the negative features which we perceive today when we look at the Science of Judaism of our forebears are strikingly manifested, without any change, in the scientific literature written in Hebrew—which is not surprising, in light of the mood of the *Maskilim* who loved the Hebrew language. In principle, there is no difference between them and their colleagues in the West. Nothing was changed here by the language of the writers, unless we wish to say that perhaps the voice of rebellion is sounded with greater clarity on the part of some of those who wrote in Hebrew, as demonstrated by the case of *Ba'al he-Ḥalutz*.[5]

For what reason, therefore, do I take to task the Science of Judaism during this period of adjustment to becoming good bourgeoisie? The list of its sins is particularly annoying, as I said, among the men of the center, among those liberals who call themselves conservatives and those conservatives who call themselves liberal—including the vast majority of the men of science. The following are the main headings of the charge against it:

The removal of the pointedly irrational and of demonic enthusiasms from Jewish history, through an exaggerated emphasis upon the theological and the spiritual. This is the fundamental, original sin which outweighs all others. This awesome giant, our history, is called upon to render an accounting of itself—and this great creation, filled with explosive power, compounded of vitality, wickedness, and perfection, becomes limited and reduced in stature, and declares itself to be naught. The demonic giant is no more than an innocent fool who follows the practice of a progress-loving citizen, who may be greeted in the city square by any respectable householder, in the tidy market-place of the nineteenth century, so they need not be embarrassed when they speak of his lineage in the gates.

An idyll—the distortion of the past by obscuring its disturbing elements, which rebel and break out into history and thought. Nearly all of those who wrote histories of individuals, families, and communities were of course affected by this fault. In thousands of cases, what wonderful material, which has now completely disappeared, was still available to these scholars! And what destruction was wrought by its dilettantish use, concealing those things which are important to us and stressing the incidental; and if they did not completely conceal it—what poor judgment they exhibited in its evaluation and use!

Morose sentimentality—this first emerged among those who wrote in German in the 1830's and 1840's, but it was considerably augmented by the later Hebrew writers, in keeping with the destructive possibilities hidden in their rhetoric.

The founding of history upon martyrology, in isolation from its real bases.

Apologetics and self-justification—in the sense that "their fear (of the Gentiles . . .) precedes their wisdom." Who does not remember the confusion and panic over the literature concerning circles of Jewish bandits during the period of the French revolution, and the concealing of this issue by scholars, who preferred to close their eyes to the facts or to denounce them as antisemitic inventions. And there is no shortage of other examples. How much pandering to the wealthy and the powerful do we find here, and how much reluctance to render cruel accounts!

Trivialization, to the point of ignoring or even hiding all those phenomena which did not suit the doctrine of progress according to those formulae accepted in the previous century. There was thus created the illusion of a great historical line, exemplifying the doctrine of progress in general within Jewish history.

It was these things which gave the Science of Judaism the striking sense of being a diligent but lifeless discipline. Here and there one still finds in it real men of character, who are far removed from apologetics and who are forthright about saying that they hate something, people who are still able to derive militant conclusions from their general orientation. How precious and clear in our eyes seem such great haters as these (as Heinrich Graetz or Joshua Heschel Schorr) who exhibit their own strength—as opposed to that watery love which embraces all streams and draws a thread of grace over every community and every family and knows no boundaries in its enthusiasm over trivia, e.g., as in the pietistic sentimentality of David Kaufmann. And David Kaufmann was no journeyman or mere academic feuilletonist: to the contrary, he was a great talent, and there have been few to equal him in the world of scholarship in his or our own generation! And yet it is precisely in his work that one finds all these tendencies which are the bane of romantic science. In him, this science appears in its full conservative power (not in its constructive power, Heaven forbid!), as if he had already shaken off the nods made in the direction of destruction, going instead to the opposite extreme—to a pseudo-romantic caricature of Judaism.

We need not waste words on the theological emptiness of this Science of Judaism, on its barrenness in the religious sense (which stands out clearly in the excellent analysis by Max Wiener in his *Jewish Religion in the Period of the Emancipation*).[6] And this may be readily understood: the historical critique which is the living soul of the Science of Judaism could only fulfill its mission through a secular, essentially anti-theological mood. The great heretics who were its leading builders did a great service to the cause of faith: only a faith which had reached a crisis could reveal whether there were seeds of vitality still remaining within it. I do not believe that it would be an exaggeration to say that over the course of fifty years (1850–1900) there did not emerge from this circle so much as one authentic, living, non-petrified word concerning Jewish religion, one which did not stink of the rot of artificiality in its bones and which was not chewed up by the worm of apologetics.

Entire sets of problems remained here like unturned stones. The Halakhah, not as the history of its literature but as the study of problems, remained to a large extent completely outside of their ken. It did not appear at all as a religious problem. Try to learn something of its essence from the writings of Zechariah Frankel or Isaac Hirsch Weiss! As a religious problem, it is no less alien to them than is Kabbalah! In a certain sense, there is no difference in principle between the position of these scholars regarding the question of Jewish criminals and their stance regarding more aristocratic problems such as that of the Halakhah or the Kabbalah: the very existence of these problems and these facts was opposed in a real way to their sentimental and idyllic dismantling, making it impossible for them to derive from them much apologetic benefit. Whatever may have been said about these problems from a twisted perspective, their true significance could only be discovered following a fundamental change of historical and ideological perspective. There are many sterile problems in this Science of Judaism, and many major problems which do not find their place. The secret of the Science of Judaism during this period was exemplified and expressed by that preacher who wrote in a German pamphlet, the most famous of all the self-satisfied preachers: *"Unser Erzvater Jakob das Vorbild eines Stadtverordneten"* ("The Patriarch Jacob was a model citizen of the city"). The prince of the nation is seen in the model of a petit bourgeois; Israel and its problems are viewed from the unpolished viewpoint of those who sit on the fence.

VI

At this point there took place that fundamental change of perspective which accompanied the national movement. We found firm ground upon which to stand, a new center from which completely different and new horizons could be seen. We no longer saw our problems from without: neither in terms of dismantling or partial destruction, nor in terms of cowardly and pietistic conservatism, nor in terms of the small-mindedness of an apologetic whose accounts with the past are not smooth. The new slogan was: to see from within, to go from the center to the periphery without hesitation and without looking over one's shoulder! To rebuild the entire structure of knowledge in terms of the historical experience of the Jew who lives among his own people and has no other accounts to make than the perception of the problems, the events and the thoughts according to their true being, in the framework of their historical function within the people.

If we have placed ourselves within the chain of the generations without looking aside; if we have connected our own lot to the historic lot of the nation in every sense, be it secular or the sacred, this must necessarily lead to a tremendous change in values, to a true revolution in many areas. The living flow, which had become invisible to insensitive hearts, will be restored to the sources; there will be revealed the tremendous vitality, the turbulent dynamic through the course of history, with all its light and shadow. The powerful battles over the soul of the nation between the temporal and the eternal will no longer be hidden away. We will be required to discover the secret of our true stature.

Factors which had been emphasized and considered positive in terms of a world-view of assimilation and pietism need to be fundamentally reexamined in order to determine what their function was in fact within the development of the nation. Some factors, which had been despised, may reemerge from this perspective in a new and positive light. Others, which had been considered unworthy of the attention of serious scholars, have been rescued from the depths of obscurity. It may be that what was considered by them to be degeneration will be perceived by us as a revelation of light, while that which they saw as the delusions of the powerless will be revealed as living and powerful myth.

In brief: the stones that were rejected by the builders will become the cornerstone. There is no longer a need for castration of the truth, for idyllic recasting of the past, for enlightenment, small-mindedness, and for the adventures of illusions. The solution of questions regarding the Bible and

the Talmud, the problems of living Jewish society and its physical and spiritual world—in short, everything about everything—demand a basic revision, an intellectual stock-taking in light of our new understanding. A
general change of orientation will not suffice. The new perception must
penetrate into each and every detail: must examine it anew in light of the
sources, each problem unto itself; reconsider it and plunge into its depths.
In brief: the construction of a new critical structure and the creation of a
completely new image of our history in the broadest sense of the word—
that is the task imposed upon the Science of Judaism during the generation of the renaissance.

New concepts and new categories, new intuition and new daring, are
required here: a "critique of the critique," the dismantling of the dismantling, and the use without fear of both horns of historical criticism. From
now on, the creative destruction of scientific criticism which examines
hearts and innards via the documents of the past serves a different function: not the washing and embalming of the dead body, but the discovery
of its hidden life by removing the masks and curtains which had hidden
it, and the misleading inscriptions. Through its fruitful dialectic, through
a radical breakthrough to its turning point on its way, which are the points
of construction, historical criticism henceforth also serves as a productive
decoding of the secret writing of the past, of the great symbols of our life
within history.

The freeing of religious thought from the prison of a distorted ideology
which alienates itself from the sources of its vision, both heavenly and
earthly—this requires destruction of the enclosing wall that was constructed over the course of generations. A science which noted the falsehood of pure spirituality will also know how to reformulate the issue of
the interrelationships between the body and soul of the nation, and will
teach us to see the tremendous problem of the relations of Israel and the
nations in a sober way, without lachrymosity and without conceit. Such a
discipline will relate seriously to the original forms of creativity in Judaism: exegesis, Halakhah, Midrash, and the profound dialectical problems inherent in these forms, as anti-systematic categories of religious
thought. It will expose their metaphysics—but also the concrete ground
upon which they grew. But why do I need to enumerate the problems
which occur to anyone who reflects upon them? Are they not endless?
And all of them are filled with tremendous historical vitality and deep significance for us, and all have been developed here as legitimate problems
when we approach them from the proper place: the renewal of the nation
from within its tumultuous and tragic history.

VII

I have described the change in perspective and its implications in terms of the new formulation of the problems of the Science of Judaism, (or Judaic studies, as it has come to be called). This was a charged atmosphere, an atmosphere electrified by the powerful vision of a renewed discipline which would draw its power from the roots of the national renewal, from the Zionist awakening, and from the constant contact with the atmosphere of rebuilding a nation. How many plans were made then, when we were enthralled by unlimited yearning to struggle with the spirit of the past and with the prince of the nation—and thus we too were drawn to Judaic studies in our youth. When we decided to forge our path toward the wellsprings of wisdom which were revealed to us in a vision, we had something of both pride and of modesty: the pride of the captive prince, who awakens from his exile to realize from what place he was exiled and from what place he will be redeemed, and the modesty of a person who lovingly accepts upon himself even the most menial task. We were enthused by the great idea, we hated those who falsified it, and we were ready to take upon ourselves all its strictures; indeed, we yearned for the strict rules of academic discipline. When we looked around ourselves, we saw a small number of scholars with a lively and developed scientific conscience, who worked strictly with careful discipline. Alongside them, one found in the fields of research a large camp of dilettantes, well-intentioned but using wild methods, who were only partially trained in the work in which they were meant to engage, and were confused in their ideas. We therefore longed for a science that was cruel to its practitioners, in which there was no place for the kindness of a type of intellectual leniency which was widely used to cover up for all shortcomings, for lack of ability and talent, for lack of depth and lack of precision.

We sought to return to science, with all its strictness and without compromise, as we had found it in the words of Zunz or Steinschneider—but we wished to direct it toward construction and affirmation. We wished to immerse ourselves in the study of the finest detail. We were seized by a compulsion to deal with the dry details, the small things of the great things, so as to develop therein the closed well of turbulent vitality, for we knew that this was its place and there it was hidden, and that from there we could draw upon its waters and quench our thirst. We sought the great scientific idea which would illuminate the details like rays of the sun playing upon the surface of the water, yet we knew—and is there any serious man of science who has not experienced this eternal debate within his heart?—that it does not dwell save in the details themselves. We knew the power of the fact—and we knew that there is nothing more misleading than a fact, as the French proverb has it. Thus, we sought to draw the ideas out of the facts and from the facts. And we thereby became specialists, masters of one trade. And if we did not struggle with God, as in the words of the *aggadah*, we struggled with the Satan who danced among us. This was the Satan of irresponsible dilettantism, who does not know the secret of construction, because he does not know the secret of destruction. The same great and necessary surgery, the dismantling of the dismantling, the removal of the cancer from within the living body of the Science of Judaism, cannot be performed in an off-hand, distracted manner, without exact knowledge of the sources of the disease—that is to say: it requires an anti-dilettantish spirit.

We struggled. Did we win? We changed the perspective—but did we derive the detailed conclusions from this change with all strictness, with all cruelty? Did the critical orientation truly penetrate to every sinew of our work? We went to the details: did we indeed develop them and resolve them, creating new combinations and reading their secret language? Did we definitively abandon, in every concrete scientific examination, the paths and sins of which we accused the assimilationist scholars and their followers?

It is difficult to answer these questions with a simple yes or no. There is much calculation and much movement and anarchy. We have moved away from the static point from which we set out thirty or forty years ago on our new struggle. Why have we not yet won great victories? There can be no doubt that the atmosphere of scholarship in our generation has changed completely, the orientation of our perception has changed, and we have taken upon ourselves the strictures of the spiritual place in which we intend to build. There is no doubt that a great deal has been done. The awakening was not lacking in contents. But we are obliged to admit that we still remain stuck somewhere along the path between the vision and its realization.

We have not applied the critical knife to everything that was crooked, grotesque, and embarrassing in the heritage of the Science of Judaism which we set out to renew. We declared programs, but we were satisfied with generalizations. In practice, regarding innumerable details we accepted the same form of perception which we held in contempt in our earlier declarations. We came as rebels and found ourselves to be heirs.

We cannot say that we have already performed the profound surgery which was meant to uproot from our flesh the multi-colored plague that spread therein. We have not cut to the depths properly.

Have we destroyed sentimentality? It still walks among us, in new dress and in a new style, no less annoying than the original one. Have we destroyed the false idyll? It has reemerged in this generation in the form of orthodox science, that is constantly growing around us. Have we destroyed the Enlightenment ideology regarding its pre-judgment of religious phenomena, and attempted to truly understand them in depth? Observe what Dubnow attempted to do in his *History of Ḥasidism*. Have we destroyed dilettantism and its illusions that run amok in history, in philology, and in philosophy? Has it not slipped through our hands in ten new disguises? Have not a few souls from this world of chaos entered and sown confusion in the world of correction with which we have been engaged?

All of these ills have now assumed a national dress. From the frying pan into the fire: following the emptiness of assimilation there comes another type, that of the contentious nationalist phrase. Instead of religious homiletics and religious rhetoric, we have developed a national homiletics and a national rhetoric in science. And in both cases the true forces which operated in our world, the true demonics, have remained outside of the picture which we created.

We have commenced the work, we have tried to perform it faithfully, our eyes have been opened, and we have become sober. The problems which require attention are piled up on both right and left, and the summation shall not be quick to come. If our mind is set toward a fundamental revision of our heritage, we will require great courage and the daring to break through into many hitherto closed realms. In a number of different fields, historical criticism still has a long way to go before it reaches those mighty elements upon which the building may be constructed. Perhaps it is not mere chance that we do not to date have a scientific introduction to the Talmud. Woe to that discipline which forgoes the need for summary, but even more so to that science which engages in summary before it has completed the analysis, classification, and exhaustion of details. Unfortunately, there is a tendency for the renewed discipline of Jewish studies within our nation to feel both of these dangers. Gentiles whom we mocked as ignoramuses have written introductions (in the German sense of *Einleitung*) that embarrass us, because we have not found the strength to do so within ourselves; just as there are introductions written by our own scholars that would have been better never to have been written.

The time has not yet come to sing our own praises. The Science of Judaism requires repair both of its head and limbs. Who knows whether we shall manage to complete that which is imposed upon us, for we had hoped for healing, and received instead terror. In the total destruction of our people in Europe, there were also destroyed the majority of those fresh forces with which we had hoped to continue this enterprise. Or perhaps we do not at all realize the extent to which we are orphans and alone in our project. From this power of our being shall we build the last remnant? At times, it seemed that when we stand before the great vision of a renewed discipline of Judaic studies our stance is like that of the angels who were called upon to recite praises to God and did not manage to finish their chapter, for their power wore out and they were negated from their standing before the Creator, like the spark which is negated in the coals.

Chapter Ten

A New Spiritual Perspective on the Exegesis of Primary Sources (1959)*

Everyone agrees that the development of Judaism did not cease with the closing of the Talmud, but continued, each generation with its own tendencies and making its own interpretations. The Sages of Israel read and interpreted the primary sources, the Oral Torah and the Written Torah, on the basis of their own understanding and the circumstances of their generation, and were not afraid to deviate from the paths of their predecessors when they felt a vital need to do so. Thus, the gates of exegesis were never shut. Both Jewish philosophy and Kabbalah, each one with its own streams and offshoots, are attempts to interpret the primary sources in terms of a new spiritual perspective. The factors generating this never-ending development and adaptation to the problems raised in each generation may be perceived in the words of the sages.

Since the beginning of the Karaite period, with the criticism leveled by them against talmudic literature and midrashim, the *aggadah* has been at the center of renewed exegetical efforts by Jewish sages of all camps. The strident criticism launched against it by the Karaites, ridiculing the tal-

* This chapter is the introductory section of a longer textual study by Scholem, "New Information on Rabbi Joseph Ashkenazi, the Tanna from Safed" [Heb.], *Tarbitz* 28(1959), 59–89, 201–35, published in its present form in *'Od Davar,* 184–86.

mudic sages for the mythology and ways of thought expressed in the *ag-gadah*—all these forced the rabbis to rethink the nature and proper under-standing of the *aggadot* in many places. This in turn generated attempts to reinterpret much of the Talmud and midrashic *aggadah* in a non-literal manner, thereby adapting them to the religious views current in the Mid-dle Ages and saving them from the barbs of the "sectarians" [i.e., the Karaites]. Hence, the issue of the relationship to the *aggadah* became one of the major factors in the development of the spiritual world of Judaism during those generations.

There were very few expressions of opposition in principle to this process of "thawing" of the crystallized world of the *aggadah*. Such oppo-sition made the task of the Sages struggling to defend rabbinic Judaism more difficult, and was a disturbing and upsetting element for all of the positive tendencies operating at that time. It is therefore clear that, even from the viewpoint of the most Orthodox Talmudists and halakhists, such opponents were perceived as reactionaries, sowing confusion and diffi-culty by their uncompromising stance. Notwithstanding the scant writ-ten evidence for such a tendency, one may conjecture that the number of such reactionaries, who rejected in principle all efforts on the part of the rabbis to interpret peculiar *aggadot* and bizarre Midrashim in a non-literal way, was not inconsiderable. It may be that such expressions of opposi-tion, which did not please the contemporary rabbis, were censored. The aim of these innovative interpreters and exegetes was not to drive a chasm between themselves and the world of the Talmud. On the contrary: they had a considerable and very understandable interest in emphasizing the continuity and even identity between their own world and that of the Tal-mud. The position of their opponents, who argued on the basis of a sup-posedly pure Talmudist position, was cited as evidence of the distance they had taken from the mythological world of the *aggadah*. The consistency with which these "reactionaries" fought was likely to provide new tools for their critics, from both within and without. Because it was difficult to refute or negate their basic position within a talmudic world, and because it was likewise difficult to negate their authority, these sages generally speaking chose the path of silence.

We have become acquainted with the work of an outstanding, coura-geous, and articulate exponent of this reactionary position from the thir-teenth century—namely, Rabbi Moses Taku, author of the work *Ketem Tammim,* who shoots his barbs in every direction: against the philoso-phers, from Rabbi Saadiah Ga'on to Maimonides, as well as against the Ashkenazic Ḥasidim. In his book, only part of which is extant, he advo-cates an integral and uncompromising talmudic Judaism, which does not

seek out interpretations that are convenient for apologists and Enlighten-
ers. He was a strange and remarkable figure, the like of which was seemingly found nowhere else in the history of Judaism.

And yet, we have recently discovered such a fellow-spirit, who lived in
that selfsame Ashkenazic Jewry that Rabbi Taku strengthened, some three
hundred years later. During the age of deep ferment and turmoil undergone by Judaism during the sixteenth century, there once again emerged a
sage, who to this observer seems a spiritual rebirth of Rabbi Moses Taku.
Under new circumstances, and on the basis of new material, he waged the
same battle and presented the same arguments. Thanks to an interesting
discovery which I made a few years ago,[1] we now have rich material by
which to become acquainted with the spiritual mood of this militant
zealot.

Rabbi Joseph Ashkenazi (1525–1577) became known at the end of his
life, when he lived in Safed, as a critic of the text of the Mishnah. He corrected and interpreted the Mishnaic text with precision and scientific lit-
eralness, using for this purpose an ancient manuscript of the Mishnah
which he had found. This activity of Rabbi Joseph, who was referred to
by the people of Safed as "the divine *tanna*," was discussed by David Kaufmann (who gathered all the material known about him until the year
1898), and by J. N. Epstein in his *Introduction to the Text of the Mishnah*.[2]
Both of these scholars praised the sobriety of spirit and extreme care which
he exercised in his treatment of the Mishnah.

Chapter Eleven

What Others Rejected: Kabbalah and Historical Criticism (1962)*

It is both a great honor and a pleasure for me to speak here on behalf of this year's recipients of the Rothschild Prize, to express our feelings of gratitude and honor at having been found worthy to be singled out in recognition of our activity in various fields. There has thus been completed the first cycle of these prizes, and it is no small thing to be counted among the members of that cycle. My joy is mingled with pain at the fact that I am unable to understand or to explain the contributions and accomplishments of each one of us in his own respective field. But I can say one thing: I am doubly happy today that I recognized my limitations in time! My university studies were in the fields of mathematics and physics, and thereafter, in a kind of adventurous *salto mortale*, I switched to Semitic philology—and how fortunate it is that I did not attempt to compete with either Racah or Polotsky![1] Instead, while still young, I decided to pioneer a new field, which in those days was entirely my own, as no one else troubled to toil therein. It was in that manner that I accomplished what I did, and arrived at this distinguished position. And, if once I had a longing for chemistry, I have remained stuck in the period of alchemy, writing my

---

* Remarks made upon receiving one of the Rothschild Prizes at Zikhron Ya'akov. Published in *Molad* 20/164–65 (1962), 135–37; reprinted in *Devarim be-go,* 64–67.

first study in Israel on the subject of "Alchemy and Kabbalah,"[2] and I never looked back or tried to go beyond these limits. Hence, my authority to speak today in the name of the four prize recipients is somewhat questionable. But as the Sages said, necessity is not to be denounced.

I said that I was clever in the choice of my field of endeavor, but I must admit that this field, the study of Kabbalah and Jewish mysticism, drew me like a magnet, so that my involvement therein involved rather less wisdom or reflection and rather more enchantment, magic, and love. Allow me to relate something which happened to me at the beginning of my path, exactly forty years ago.

When I had completed writing my first book in the study of Kabbalah, I heard that there had moved to my native town the one and only of Heinrich Graetz's disciples who had studied this field, and who was considered the spokesman regarding matters of Kabbalah of this school of the previous generation. He was a distinguished *talmid ḥakham,* a liberal rabbi, sharing all the views of that liberal generation, an extremely elderly gentleman whose power was not diminished and was still full of juice.[3] I went to visit him and was received hospitably. He said to me: "You and I, we two are the only crazy ones," and proceeded to show me his home and his entire library of Kabbalistic works, being the only Jewish scholar in Germany who collected books and manuscripts belonging to this literature, to which no one else paid attention. I was overwhelmed by his collection, so that when he showed me a large manuscript from the Lurianic school, I exclaimed with youthful enthusiasm: "How wonderful it is that you have read and studied all of these sources!" The old man turned toward me and replied: *"Was? Den Quatsch soll ich auch noch lesen?"* ("What? I also need to read this junk?") At that moment, my heart suddenly opened up and I understood many basic things concerning the Science of Judaism. I understood that there was much work left for me to do, so as to cross the line from irresponsible amateurism to what might appropriately be designated as historical science, with all the problematics and misgivings associated with this concept by its very nature. And, if there is perhaps no science here, there is at least a struggle toward science.

Many years have passed since that day, and I have done what I have done. I may say that I feel myself to have been fortunate, and that I am happy to have succeeded in three things:

(a) I have pioneered what has proven to be an extremely rich field; (b) I have at least in part fulfilled the blessing of the sage who said, "Happy is one who corrects his own mistakes; woe to one whose mistakes are corrected by others"; and (c) I have managed to train a generation of good and honest students, who could be relied upon, not only to learn from what I had to give, but also how to fill in that which was missing and that in which I had erred, and to set off on their own paths.

This is not really the appropriate time to dwell at length upon my own mistakes, which primarily came about whenever I believed the words of my predecessors and did not engage myself (as was likely to happen) with all my strength in clarifying the subject in depth. But, truth be told, I learned far more than I can describe in words from my errors. For example, I attempted to prove, using methods of philological research, an assumption which had some following in my youth and which suited the scientific romanticism that dominated Hebrew literature at that time. Namely, that *Sefer ha-Zohar*, the outstanding work of the Kabbalah, was a creation of the national genius—that is, an anonymous work of many generations, forged in the creative crucible of the nation, just like the Talmud and the Midrash—rather than being the product of a daring individual genius, possessed by inspiration and a tumultuous spirit that imposed his vision upon the nation. I set out to prove this assumption, which seemed plausible, and which was accepted by many people without serious examination, but ended up refuting myself and proving the opposite of my original assumption. Such things have happened to me on more than one occasion.

But to return to the initial and more significant point: what was so special about the study of Kabbalah and everything associated with it that transformed it into a cornucopia for the historian and for those interested in Jewish thought throughout the generations? Why did this brick, which had been rejected by the builders of the Science of Judaism in both the East and West, become one of the cornerstones of its renewal? What was the focus of vitality therein which we were privileged to perceive, yet which people of the previous generations who were more whole and greater than ourselves failed to see?

The answer is essentially simple, and does not at all relate to the problem as to how we today are to evaluate the ideas and teachings preached by the various mystical movements in Judaism. We do not approach the world of mysticism as mystics (although admittedly we do so with trembling and awe): not as Merkabah mystics, nor as Kabbalists, nor as Sabbatians or as Ḥasidim (this last point perhaps requires emphasis!). Both their loves and their hates are long gone; and insofar as they have not passed into oblivion, either love or hatred would spoil the discussion, as may be seen by anyone who reads the writings of either their admirers-defenders or their haters-prosecutors. But one factor was central to the great turnabout that took place in the historical evaluation of those phenomena which are the content of my life's work; more than I brought about this turnabout through my own work, my own work was caused by it. What is this factor? I would define it as our willingness to acknowledge and to recognize all of those forces which vitalized and sustained the Jewish people as a living body throughout the peregrinations of our history.

I have said: all of the forces, as opposed to those who seek to limit these forces, and only to see those whose activity is for some reason convenient or acceptable to them. I have said: as a living body, as opposed to those who see in our history the embodiment of an idea alone—indeed, an idea that is permanently attached to the definition they have given it. I firmly believe that, if we do have here the embodiment of an idea, it is a utopian idea: that is, an idea which has not yet revealed all that is implied and contained therein, and which is not fully encompassed by historical and theological definitions relating to the past. The heroes of Kabbalah would say: the Torah has seventy faces! To which I would add: many of these faces have not been revealed, and woe to dogmatics as a criterion for the study of the history of our people!

This new desire to understand all aspects of our history, with God and the angels and the demons, with our upper worlds and lower worlds, in all the meanings of this word—has opened new wellsprings for inspiration and for perceiving the truth: *"Nihil Judaeum a me alienum puto"* ("Nothing Jewish is alien to me"). Such a perception assures a path to both the heights and the depths.

And indeed, in light of this, the long-abandoned field of Jewish mysticism was revealed as virgin soil, but as extremely fertile soil. It is true that some philosophers and ideologists, aesthetes and poets, have here and there expressed their opinion concerning the sparks of light which flicker from it, not knowing whether to see it as light out of the darkness or as misleading lights—not to mention the charlatans, who over the course of time have treated this field as their own personal property. But the actual substance of these phenomena as historical entities, or even more: as one living chain, as a continuous unit possessing historical significance—all this has remained hidden and obscured. Wherever you touch, it is as if you touch gold, if you but have eyes to see. There is opened up here a world of profound personal and human experience, combined with the historical experience of the nation. Daring ideas were formulated with great clarity or in allusive language; the very soul of an entire period speaks to us through these obscure and halting symbols, and through its strange customs and ways of life we have come to understand the terrors of life and death of pious Jews. Rather than isolated phenomena, understood neither in their connections with one another nor in their connections with the great historical processes of the Jewish and non-Jewish world, there was a possibility of seeing two thousand years of development in this realm as a unit bearing high vital tension and playing a role within the life of the people requiring definition and clarification. The labor of laying the depth foundations and of building the edifice by combining one stone with another has begun—and our hands are still stretched forth.

Many qualities were demanded of one who would seek to enter into this world and these studies, and I am doubtful whether I possess all of them. But I may testify that from the very outset there were two qualities which I did possess, which I trust I will not lack in the future as well: namely, courage and humility. That is, the courage to set forth and to ask far and wide-ranging questions, and humility in face of the facts and conclusions, whether these suited my theories or not: in brief, the willingness to take upon myself the strictures of historical criticism. Allow me to say one more word on this matter, before I conclude. Historical criticism is a modest tool, which tends not to exaggerate its own worth or to see itself as the be-all and end-all. It is not the key that opens all of the locked chambers. There are proofs that see further; there are intuitions and reflections that penetrate (or claim to penetrate) to the depths. In contrast to them, historical criticism is like a daughter of the petite bourgeoisie. Yet nevertheless—how great is its power, as it protects us from the illusions and self-deceits which we all love so much. This may not be much, but we have nothing better, and in a generation of self-aggrandizing and hollow existential analysis it is fitting for a scholar of humanities to stand up and to declare where he stands. Whoever denies the methods of historical criticism holds in contempt its conclusions or attempts to avoid them, builds his structure upon quicksand, and will in the end pay the price for his alienation. With all due respect to intuition and faith, historical science stands and falls upon historical criticism.

We have spoken at length, ladies and gentlemen, and I shall conclude. A door has been opened leading toward a hidden chamber, and we do not know what else is hidden there. May we not stumble in our teaching and may we not be found wanting, for the needs of this discipline are great.

Chapter Twelve

On Education for Judaism*
(1971)

The following credo, embodying the *Weltanschauung* of Professor Gershom Scholem, found expression in a talk he had with a group of teachers, one of a series of meetings these teachers had with leading thinkers in Israel, in which he explained the essence of his conception of this generation's problem in the area of Jewish education: historical truth. The discussion was opened by the Secretary of the Teacher's Union, Mr. Shalom Levin, who requested an elucidation of the nature and significance of the Jewish consciousness which teachers have been asked to foster. He had read Professor Scholem's book, *Sabbatai Ṣevi*, from which it emerged that one cannot define a particular phenomenon *a priori* as Jewish or non-Jewish, since rabbinic censorship had suppressed opposing views. Professor Scholem nevertheless spoke of the spark of Jewish life revealed even in such phenomena as Sabbatianism. If there was then no model that could be defined as Judaism, what then was the foundation upon which our Jewish education could be based? What was the kernel in Judaism?

Scholem: Your question can be divided into two: (a) What is needed for education from the practical viewpoint? (b) Is there more to Judaism than what has been crystallized in history so far? The first question may be an-

* Based upon a transcription of an open discussion with Israeli educators, published in *'Od Davar*, 105–119.

swered with certainty, but the second may only be answered on the basis of faith. I would say without hesitation that the teacher must explain to his pupils a tradition that has had a continuity of generations. The question is whether the educator would teach in a concrete manner or abstractly, dogmatically. Even if the educator has one conception or another, is it possible to define Judaism in a single, definitive way once and for all? Education rests upon history, and it is the educator's task to find a close tie with the actual past. That which is generally accepted is not good enough, since those who were opposed were killed, or left us no information about them. As a teacher of future teachers at the Hebrew University, I am not called upon to discuss whether there is still any utopian content that has yet to be discovered. In this context, my duty is to explain known or unknown phenomena. By means of research and reflection we can arrive at a conclusion as to which phenomena constitute Judaism from the historical point of view. I start with the assumption that all of us have a common attitude toward the past, but the teacher nevertheless makes a choice. I assume that teachers affiliated with *Hashomer Hatza'ir* will not select the same topics from that past to teach as do religious teachers, but they too choose concrete matters from the past which they regard as Judaism. I myself have doubts as to whether only certain phenomena are to be considered as Judaism. From my historical research I have learned to see things differently than did former generations. There is no doubt that the perspective of Jewish history has changed from what it was fifty years ago, from what it was in my youth to what it is today. I can imagine one teacher standing up and supporting certain phenomena, and another teacher others. Let me give an example from recent times. There are Jews who believe that Ḥasidism brought disaster to the Jewish people, and they support their view with evidence. But today the romanticists are on top. Through my research on Sabbatai Ṣevi, I learned that there is no universally accepted truth wherever views and opinions are concerned. It follows that the teacher must choose from the factual historical material that is meant to clarify the past as a living force. In this respect I can say right off that I have no doubts or problems.

As for the second question—What is Judaism?—that is something else. I have said that every generation interprets Judaism for itself, implying that what Judaism is not be defined once and for all. I said this as a blatantly anti-theological definition, and as opposed to dogmatic tendencies which I do not accept. Just because a certain type of Judaism existed or crystallized during a certain period, say between 500 and 1800, does not mean that we cannot assume some other type of Judaism. The criterion must be the living manifestations of the nation's strength that existed in each generation and which are destined to come to the fore in the future. What Judaism is has not been defined by religion, although such is the pretension of the religious. In general, I believe that an historical phenomenon can only be defined by history itself.

There is no uniform content here: What is there in common between the Judaism of the period of Abraham or Moses and that of the Ba'al Shem Tov? The phenomenon called Judaism does not end on a particular date, and I do not think it is likely to end so long as a living Judaism exists. If you are seeking a precisely formulated definition, I cannot satisfy you. That is something for God. Were it possible to define Judaism by using formulae, we would not have a comprehensive spiritual phenomenon but a body whose life is determined by definitions. I deny that view. I do not deny that in the totality of life, in the continuity of the generations, very different trends did evolve in Judaism. I believe that there will continue to be new expressions of this kind in the future. But there is something living that is beyond dogmatic definitions. In my opinion, Judaism includes utopian aspects that have not yet been discovered. It possesses a living force which I denote "utopian aspects." There are aspects that look backward to the Jewish people in the past. I do not think that everything in it has already been discovered. I believe that we shall still discover lofty things which no one can foretell. My faith in a living Judaism is based on this conception. There are manifestations that have already been discovered and have assumed historical form, and there are those who choose from among them only those things that appear to have a rich future. They forbid us to go beyond such manifestations—or even to select phenomena which, while they certainly did incorporate a manifestation of our historic character, were for some reason defeated in the battle of the generations. There are others which have been completely suppressed. I consider this approach inadmissible. We are not affiliated with the adherents of the conflicting trends, we are not for or against. Furthermore, it is certainly not for us to say, on the basis of the criteria of rabbinical tradition, that this side was right and the other side was wrong. Anyone today who reads the Dead Sea Scrolls knows that the reality of Judaism is not exhausted by the definitions of the halakhic scholars. Here too we find a living Judaism, even though it was hidden away. It is clear that these writings were written by men whose conception was very different from that of the rabbis of the Mishnah and the Talmud. Does the fact that they were suppressed bind us in judging their Jewish character? On the contrary, concealment of this type would stir us up! Those who hid them wanted nothing but their own version of Judaism to remain. Does that bind us? We are not a party to their dogmatic evaluation. The historical fact that certain conceptions of Judaism were defeated by others does not mean that the former were not "Jewish." Can one say that the Sadducees were not Jewish while the Pharisees were? That is basically incorrect. As to the future, I am certain that there are possible manifestations of Judaism as a spiritual-national phenomenon. If I were a teacher, I would teach history as one who believed in it as a living phenomenon. I would say that not all of its values have as yet been appreciated and that not all of its manifestations have ceased, just because in such-and-such a year the *Shulḥan 'Arukh* was published or the Basel Program formulated. That is what I mean by "utopian content." Much has been put right in the past, and will in the future. I am all in favor of this.

Question: You have taught us that at least a certain stream in Judaism does not content itself with the phenomenon of Revelation but also seeks personal spiritual elation in its time. Irrational questions are raised and an attempt made to provide a solution to a rational, existent situation. If I were to put the question, "What is left, and what is the connection with the past?" I would answer, "Torah and mitzvot." But how—if I myself don't observe the mitzvot? Of course, I assume that Judaism develops by evaluating itself in every generation. What is your opinion, taking a cross section of our time, in which the whole matter of the mitzvot is for us something utopian?

Scholem: The question is in what sense do we perceive a living reality in history as one that is binding each of us. What is the problem? You say: we do not have that foundation of faith that enables us to accept a rational definition of reality. Take, for example, Maimonides' Thirteen Articles of Faith—a rational definition of the reality of Judaism—in which I myself do not believe, or at most in only two or three of them. According to Maimonides I deny the existence of God . . . What then is the difficulty? It can be explained to any mature pupil that rational formulae do not exhaust historical continuity. Any such pupil will understand that no rational formulation is ever exhaustive until the phenomenon itself reaches its end. There are phenomena that do not lend themselves to rational extractions, such as the living individual. It is the teacher's power to awaken in the pupil a consciousness of a changing history that cannot be exhausted, and an awareness that an existential complex is not subject to definitions. What is true of the individual is true of the group: despite changing facts, it constitutes an entity embodying many things which will not be manifested until later on. This can be explained even to an elementary-school pupil.

We turn now to the fundamental question: What remains? My answer is: I don't know. It will become clear when the vital, creative force manifests itself. Even the most Orthodox are selective, just like the non-believers. Both suppress phenomena they find disagreeable and needs that are not in accord with their views. Sometimes, when I reflect upon how much suppression the selective Orthodox carry out, my hair stands on end. The dogmatic question, "What remains?" is no question. There always remains whatever remains as the heritage of the generations, which I treat with awe and dignity, for I find in it an expression of that creative life force that manifested itself and was handed down as the heritage of the generations. We are capable of evoking a positive attitude, a certain identification with that heritage. I go quite far in identifying myself with the past, with my forefathers, yet I nevertheless do not derive dogmatic conclusions from that. Today we have entered an anarchical situation. I cannot prophesy what will remain of all that has been crystallized from the battles of the past and down the generations. As an optimist I am confident, and I affirm that we must preserve Jewish consciousness. I agree with those who seek to foster it in our life, and I do not go along with its critics. We must arouse in the next generation a sense of understanding and of general identification with the great heritage of the generations. Each generation will have to take from it that which speaks to its heart. There was always suppression. Thousands of things were suppressed which were once of very great importance. For example: there used to be great interest in the belief in the Garden of Eden and *Gehinnom*. These subjects exercised heart and mind in that which is called Judaism—as testified to by thousands of books. The subject was not confined to some booklet but spread throughout the people. But go and see what has today become of the Garden of Eden and of *Gehinnom*, even among that group which favors a dogmatic conception. It is a fact that these concepts have disappeared almost completely. They are of no importance. No one can arouse interest in them even among ninety percent of the Orthodox. Yet tremendous imaginative powers were invested in the Garden of Eden and *Gehinnom*. Is it not amazing? Today's children do not even know that the subject exists. I have even found observant Jews throughout the world who never heard anything about it. There were even those who thought that these were Christian subjects! This is one glaring example.

Let us return to our initial point. Everyone engages in selection. There is subjective selection, based upon certain tendencies, and there is suppression, whether complete or partial, in many areas, including vital ones. In other words, what is true with regard to the proponents of traditional education is undoubtedly true with regard to those who reject the dogmatic way of life.

Question: If we accept the view that Judaism is a flowing stream, can we ignore the fact that two things must nevertheless be accepted: (a) belief in the Creator of the World—"I am the Lord thy God" and (b) observance of His commandments. If we accept the view of "development," the question is: What must be scrapped from Judaism? Furthermore, since it would seem that most adults today are non-believers out of scientific conviction because they are lacking in faith, the question arises: Do I have the right to plant in the child the lack of faith that nestles in the adult? Faith—because it comes to preserve the nation and its spiritual and national assets, and also because it guards against moral decline.

Scholem: I have no answer to the last question. If I were a teacher, like you, I would not plant lack of faith in the heart of the child, but say explicitly and with a clear mind that there is no answer to that. From the educational perspective, it would be more correct to say that there are many answers and it is impossible to decide among them. A teacher cannot say, "I do not believe, but I want you to believe—and may the Lord preserve us." I would act differently. In a generation of crisis, the teacher's activity cannot be reduced to a framework of dogmatic, positive formulations. That is out of the question. There can be education for reverence, to awaken a living feeling towards the past, but I don't know if there is only one possible stand, and if man can give an unequivocal answer. You ask whether there can be any Judaism without "I am the Lord thy God." We have been grappling with that problem for fifty years, ever since Zionism arose. If there is an atheistic Judaism or Judaism as a living body with a complex of phenomena, of experiences of tremendous historical significance, the question is rather whether a comprehensive theistic explanation can be plausible. Who, then, is a Jew? Only someone who gives a religious interpretation to the historical phenomena of Judaism? That is absurd. Cannot spiritual phenomena which have been given a mighty monotheistic, theological interpretation also be given to other interpretations, that will pit themselves against it? Perhaps they will have no lasting value and will disappear from the world. It may be that God will overcome even that. I myself believe in God, but I am a religious anarchist. I do not believe in the Torah of Moses from Sinai. If God really exists, then there is something sublime in the very wrestling over belief in Him. That was the situation when Zionism arose, and we know full well that there were also secular interpretations of the complex of problems of the Jewish people and Jewish history. I believe that an atheist can be a Jew and can give a correct or incorrect explanation of the manifestations of our history, and this is legitimate. It is a question of tendentiousness. Only the severance of the living tie with the heritage of the generations is, in my opinion, educational murder. I will admit that I am a thoroughgoing anti-Canaanite. Let me give one example. I do not agree with those who wish to skip over the *Galut*. We all know that there are those among us who preach that there is some inner bridge between those of us (here in Israel) and the biblical period, and that Diaspora is something that we negate. I do not share such views. The jump to the Bible is fictitious. The Bible is a reality that does not exist today. But there does exist an ideal which we call the world of the Bible and which we wish to promote today. That is certainly legitimate, even though I believe that this jump may cause an educational failure with regard to the continuity of the generations, which has bequeathed us strength and a powerful tradition which would be fostered, from which we would select, and which we would treat as a problem. In this sense, I am a religious anarchist, since I cannot judge one or another phenomenon of the past and decide who was right and who was wrong. But there is room for a struggle in the face of manifestations of ideas that demand their expression.

Question: Concerning the issue of severance from the Tradition: as a teacher, I frequently encounter the following question: How can we impart something of the heritage our forefathers have bequeathed us? Since you are an authority, tell us what to give young people between the ages of fourteen to eighteen from those areas to which you refer. More than once, when I have asked new pupils who have come from the elementary schools what they know about the views of Ha-Ari (Rabbi Isaac Luria) or even about Sabbatai Ṣevi, I have been shocked by their ignorance. Isn't a revolution called for in this respect? How are we to bring Jewish culture to the consciousness of the generation? I studied at the university, and when I tried to make use of what I learned in my teaching I discovered that these subjects were not included in the curriculum.

Scholem: As to ignorance, who am I to lay down the law on this subject? You teachers are experts in the difficulties which you confront. But we all agree that the extent of the ignorance is abysmal. I still cannot explain the cause of this to myself. I came to Eretz Yisra'el forty years ago, and the atmosphere in education was different then. I often wonder about the terrifying ignorance revealed by secondary school graduates when they enter the Hebrew University. You cannot imagine the students' lack of knowledge. Something has happened; I cannot explain how. One of the important tasks of the educator is to carry on a war against ignorance, but the school—perhaps because the complex of our education lacks a feeling of cultural tradition—only reflects one reality. It also depends upon the home, upon the atmosphere outside the home and the school. After all, does the main influence come from the school? The consciousness of culture is primarily acquired from the outside. I studied at a gymnasium in Berlin and there can be no question that most of what we learned did not come from the teacher but from reading books, forbidden and permitted, whether we were required to do so or not, whether we delved into our own sources or into other sources. Education for cultural consciousness is only found to a small degree within the walls of the school. The difficulty is the environment. Rather than being rich in the treasures of a living tradition, we have been emptied of it. The sixty or seventy percent of the knowledge which my classmates and I acquired outside of the school is a complete void. The content provided by the home is miserable. The environment has been emptied of its treasures, and the extent to which it can be filled with real content is a question that you are obliged to answer. But I know that there is no clear-cut answer. You will ask me: "Are the things that I am doing good for education?" That is another matter, one that depends on the spirit. They would not be coming to the university as ignoramuses, as we meet them today. They would know that there are many branches and directions among the People of the Torah, and while they cannot be expected to have a thorough knowledge of all of these, they would have some notion of them. But there are subjects beyond the comprehension of the child. He can grasp the world of the *aggadah*, but the study of the Kabbalah is beyond him. Let us assume, for example, that the Torah culture ascribes importance to *pilpul* (talmudic casuistry). Here, too, the child cannot grasp the value of *pilpul*. There is one world that is suited to children and another for adults. If in a world steeped in knowledge one can deal with these areas, in a world of ignorance it is our duty to fight it. I don't know how this should be done.

A whole series of questions was asked by religious and non-religious educators. One of them asked: "Which is to be preferred—imparting a consciousness of the past or of the future?" A religious teacher said that as far as he was concerned, his conception of Judaism was clear, whereas for the Professor, who said that each generation defines Judaism for itself, but on the other hand must preserve the continuity of the Tradition, the question arises, for example, as to whether the Sadducees are to be considered part of the Jewish tradition. As Naḥman Krochmal once said, there was a creative spirit in the nation which made the selection as to what was Judaism. Furthermore, while there were practical mitzvot which assumed different nuances in each generation in accordance with the needs of the time, there were also unchanging permanent values, such as the Sabbath. Could a teacher tell his pupils that since the Sabbath was something from the past, it was a primitive conception? How could this be ignored?

Scholem: Who said it could be ignored?

An Educator: The very fact that man is a thinking creature means there cannot be a contradiction between his thought and his action. To me it is clear that Judaism encompasses the entire tradition. Everyone is in favor of

Jewish consciousness, but which consciousness? Even here we must choose. In order for a pupil to identify himself with a value, I must guide him and tell him with which value he would identify himself. For example, do we identify ourselves with Zedekiah or with Jeremiah? With what and with whom do we identify ourselves? Is it a question of a certain period, or of a socio-economic stream? How was Rabbi Akiba regarded down the ages, and how is he regarded in Israel today? Or the image of Rabban Yoḥanan ben Zakkai? These things are not answered in accordance with historical periods, but in accordance with the stand that the teacher adopts for himself, under the historical conditions of his time. Thus, it is only natural that the identification cannot be the same for everyone.

Another teacher asked whether the aspirations, the exaltation, and the faith of individuals could inspire the entire nation. A woman educator revealed her confusion at the implication in the Professor's approach that there are no absolute values. She had always thought that there were absolute values, and it was these that had influenced her to continue working in education. Yet another teacher said he had been shocked by the term, "religious anarchist." Could one admit the existence of God without observing *mitzvot?* There was reverence for the tradition of the past, at the apex of which was *kiddush ha-Shem* (sanctification of God's name). Finally, the Professor was asked what educational principles he would set down for our generation on the basis of the Great Tradition.

There was silence. The Professor studied the questions he had jotted down, and it seemed as though he was classifying and selecting them. Then he said:

Scholem: I would first like to address myself to the question of the woman educator who asked about the existence of absolute values and their place in history. The question of Jewish education cannot be answered dogmatically. There are many questions in education that involve value judgments, even though we cannot speak of an absolute value as an agreed subject in education. Personally, as I believe in God, I believe in the existence of absolute values. The puzzlement is as to where to find the absolute values in our history. Certainly, there have appeared demands for absolute values in the past. To the degree that absolute values have been embodied in history, it is a history worthy of the name. We call that a legitimate, creative phenomenon. Certainly, the theological-dogmatic approach, insofar as it comes to embody supreme matters such as these, is also Judaism. But to declare that only one approach is Judaism while another is not seems to me basically unsound. I cannot discover the values themselves in history, but only the struggle over supreme values, and this struggle is measured by the degree of success or lack of success. True, the extent to which a particular culture or an age-old tradition has set certain values for itself and has fought for their realization is the measure of its historical value. If it did not succeed in the struggle, it gives rise to doubts and even disappointment and disgust. Yes, disgust. Every history arouses such feelings. I am more of an historian than a philosopher, to my regret, and I am not acquainted with any culture (I refer to cultures which I regard with respect) that has not disappointed me in this respect and even aroused disgust. Judaism, after all, has laid down tremendous demands, a heritage from what in the language of the Tradition is called *Ma'amad Har Sinai* (the revelation at Sinai)—which has validity even for one who does not believe in it literally. Our history is a mighty struggle over these demands, and this struggle has many worthy manifestations, not all of which are on the side of the rabbinic tradition. There is also much that is disappointing, and much that deserves to be called "the camp of Satan." True, our history has a great tradition. There were struggles over values that were placed in a socio-national-ideological framework, not as the soul might wish, but as they found expression in practical reality. For example, the Sabbath. The struggle over it fills the cultural tradition of generations.

You ask me what to do. If I were called upon to teach, I would try to show that Jewish history has been a struggle over great ideas. The question is to what extent we ought to be influenced by the degree of success achieved in that struggle by values that were formulated and defined in the Tradition, by the extent to which demands were achieved in reality. At the same time I would consider with my pupils the failures in history, matters having to do with violence, cruelty, and hypocrisy. You will find these abundantly in history, in every history. Jewish culture has set itself lofty ideals. Even one who does not believe in the existence of absolute values will admit this. This gives us a yardstick for success and a yardstick for failure: what was demanded with respect to *Yiḥud ha-Shem* (profession of the unity of God) and *kiddush ha-Shem,* with respect to the Sabbath, with respect to giving form to man's life by force of the law, and hence what was demanded of people which they were not strong enough to fulfill. This is the way history should be taught. Yes—even by making value judgments, for without value judgments it is difficult to teach young people. Value judgments inform us whether a particular culture has done its job within the framework it set for itself, or whether it failed in that task. No doubt we have succeeded greatly. A consistent socialist will judge Jewish history with more reservations than will a thoroughly religious person, for whom the social question is of secondary importance. This is an endless debate. I believe that the pupils in the Hebrew school can be confronted with great matters which people regarded as supreme values and for which people

gave their lives, such as *kiddush ha-Shem* (though not everyone in the past
died for *Kiddush ha-Shem* nor does everyone today do so). The question is:
for what is a man prepared to give his life? There is obviously great educational value to such points in Jewish history. Another question is the vitality of a body that has set ideals for itself. The Jewish people is of course
such a living body, whether there was Divine Revelation according to the
religious conception or whether we define it in other and perhaps quite
complicated concepts. In any case, here we have something—the secret
of the people's being, the secret of the people's existence. From this point
of view, any teacher worthy of the name must be prepared to explain to
his pupils this phenomenon, this riddle we find so fantastic: How did it
happen that this living body held its ground in circumstances where other
peoples succumbed? What difficulty is there in teaching this? I believe it is
easy to instill in the child a sense of the greatness of this riddle. The secret
of the existence and survival of the Jewish people for three thousand years,
with all their strata and classes, is not subject to rational analysis, for there
is no end to the secret of this existence. Just as there is no end to the existence of man as an individual, so I know of no end to the secret of the existence of this people as a living individual body. Why would it be difficult
to implant a consciousness of this infinity in our pupils? There is an infinite wealth that has not yet reached the end of its full manifestations. This
is the utopian side of Judaism. I do not despair of accomplishing this mission, even though I do not believe in Revelation at Sinai as an historical
fact. Some hidden laws govern Judaism, and we are trying to get to the
root of it, as it has been transmitted to us with all its splendor and greatness, but also with the glut of lies and distortions in that transmission.

I would likewise discuss manifestations of Judaism that did not succeed.
The fact that things were suppressed is a basic fact of our existence. There
are many societies (not only Russia) that do not permit the teacher to impart his own value judgments. There a person is not allowed to transmit
his own value judgments, but only those laid down by some other authority. I do not know whether Napoleon was a positive or a negative phenomenon, destructive or progressive. In my opinion, value judgments can
tend to the positive or negative side, whereas nations transmit value judgments in accordance with their own benefit and interest. In this respect,
there has been anarchy in our country ever since the foundations of the
educational system were laid. The problem is that the crystallized religious
tradition has disintegrated and we have been thrown into a no-man's-
land, in which each educator is obliged to decide for himself. However,
the teacher has tremendous opportunities to impart a certain picture from
the heritage and tradition of the past that can stir and gladden the hearts

of the young and of every Jew, and he would link them to this heritage without being false to the view that he works out for himself. It is the obligation of the educator to show the forms assumed by these traditions and this heritage. The teacher is not merely a social functionary. He cannot do that which he is precluded from achieving by the society as a whole. But the teacher can transmit the great happenings of this living and dynamic body that is the people of Israel. To be sure, there must be selection and variety—all in accordance with the experience from the past, and the good taste of the teacher. If this is not being done, it may be because many teachers do not have any real feeling for Jewish history. I admit that it would be very difficult for a Canaanite, who repudiates the living body and its hidden, inner laws, to teach history. But when it comes to one who does not repudiate these, to one who retains that utopian stuff on which all our hope is based, I do not see that his subjective choice leads to social disaster.

Question: Is the Sabbath Judaism?

Scholem: Without question.

Question: Which means that there are certain things, absolute values, that link us as Jews.

Scholem: That is not the sort of thing we are discussing. The problem begins beyond the things that have crystallized in the Tradition. I said that we must change our evaluation of the past and that we must not regard certain phenomena as negative manifestations and judge them with anger simply because they are not in accord with the Orthodox conception. I was asked if we should choose between Pharisees and Sadducees. I am not sure which I ought to choose. The success of the Pharisees, who suppressed the views of their opponents, should not influence my judgment. My judgment of Sabbatai Ṣevi, which had been based upon reading only what his opponents had to say, changed after I discovered documents of his followers. One exceptional phenomenon explains and throws light on another, if we are wise enough to penetrate it to the core. Who knows if our judgment about the Sadducees might not be different if we knew more about them? The same goes for the Dead Sea sect or the Karaites, whom I regard as Jews.

As for the question whether it is better to teach the past or the future: I said that education means transmitting a tradition. Anything else is liable to distort education. That is the essential thing in education: past and present. That is the essential task imposed on education in Israel: to foster the feeling for tradition. A people that destroys its living feeling that it is bound up with the continuity of its existence and its historical reality, the heritage of the generations—such a people will disappear. I believe in the fu-

ture of our people. However, a future built upon a severance from this tradition is tantamount to handing down a death sentence on the people.

As for taking the side of Jeremiah or Zedekiah: It is Jeremiah of whom
Judaism is so proud. Yet he was a negative phenomenon from the viewpoint of the interests of society. Had the Jeremiah of whom we are so
proud lived in the State of Israel, he might well have ended his days in
jail. Statehood and prophecy don't go together, and there is something
hypocritical about praising both of them simultaneously. For Zedekiah,
Jeremiah was a man harming the interests of society. There was a conflict
of ideals here. Here one must reflect and lay bare the heritage of Judaism
in this area. There is the value called prophecy, a phenomenon in which
people demanded something in the name of an ideal and would not yield.
If such a Jew were to appear today in the name of Truth, he certainly
would not have an easy time. The teacher must get his pupils to understand that there necessarily arise conflicts of interest in history. A person
who embarks on a supreme mission and comes into conflict with the
rulers of society can suffer in the State of Israel what Jeremiah suffered.
The question of prophecy, and its implications for patriotic conformism, is
truly a big subject in education and is filled with far greater vital tension
than our excitement over archaeological findings.

Chapter Thirteen

Who Is a Jew? (1970)*

In approaching the subject of "Who is a Jew?" I do not speak as a statesman or a politician. I am not a lawyer, nor am I a rabbi. I speak as an historian. And I think that this question is not only a purely philosophical one but an historical one, or, if you wish, an historio-sophical one. I speak as a Jew who believes that Judaism is a spiritual phenomenon, a living organism.

It is clear that in the eyes of many people, even some scholars, Judaism is a closed system of definite concepts, but in my opinion this view no longer holds true. With the return of the Jewish people to its own history and to its own land, Judaism has for the majority of us become an open, living, and undefined organism. It is a phenomenon which changes and is transformed in the course of its own history. The scholarly work of our generation has discovered new dimensions of depth and of living movement in what we call Judaism or Jewishness.

The complete identity between being a Jew and being a religious Jew of a certain persuasion, which the defenders of traditional Judaism talk about, was an historical phenomenon, the outcome of historical developments, and subject to historical change. It was crystallized in its main lines

* A lecture given at the eighty-first annual convention of the Central Conference of American Rabbis, held in Jerusalem, March 6–10, 1970, in the wake of the controversy surrounding the proposed "Who Is a Jew" bill placed before the Knesset at that time. Published in *Devarim be-go,* 591–98.

after the destruction of the Temple and prevailed in the *Galut* before the era of Emancipation.

A point widely overlooked today, especially by defenders of this identity, is that conformity to halakhic norms could be, and was, forced upon the community by the *Ḥerem* (ban or excommunication), a very powerful weapon, which put before the people the choice to either conform to certain norms or to leave the fold. When the rabbinical power of the *Ḥerem* broke down, as it did at the end of the eighteenth century, diversity set in. And we may ask today whether this power of excommunication, apart from its positive side of enforcing conformity, did not also have quite disastrous consequences and was not one of the most sorrowful aspects of our history.

With the era of Emancipation a new process set in under the impact of internal and external forces. Externally, in order to gain emancipation, Jews and Gentiles sought to separate Judaism as a religion from its ethnic character, disrupting the unified ethno-religious view of Judaism which all Jews—even in the West—had held before 1820. Internally, by the efforts of groups within Judaism to find legitimate expression for various heterodoxies.

The official spokesmen of Judaism—Orthodox and Reform alike—stressed religious definitions exclusively. Those who insisted on a unitary concept of people and religion were marginal and were as much of an embarrassment to the Orthodox as they were to the liberal and assimilationist Jews. The fight against existing rabbinical authority of whatever persuasion, by those who ought to restore our national identity and dignity as a people, was carried on by forces for which the problem of Jewish identity as defined by the Orthodox did not exist. Those who strove for the regeneration and renaissance of the Jewish people and were the main carriers of the message of Zionism were not interested in the definitions of the rabbis. They simply did not care.

During the last hundred years, following the full achievement of emancipation in the Western world around 1860, there has set in a new historical process which has profoundly changed our self-definition as against that of the Halakhah. Up to that time halakhic definitions of Jewish identity were accepted. This was so for a very simple reason. In former times mixed marriages were a very rare phenomenon. Those who thought of contracting a mixed marriage, or for that matter of going over to another religion, were those who wanted to leave the Jewish camp, and who did not care what was said about them. Nobody asked questions about such marginal cases; the problem of their relationship to other Jews hardly existed.

The problem arose around 1870, when many such people sought to maintain some sort of connection with the Jewish community. The question is whether the definitions found in sacred books are really decisive for most Jews in the determination of a personal affiliation to the Jewish group. In my opinion they no longer are so, except for the really Orthodox, with whom we have no quarrel because they have a fixed idea about what they believe to be the essence of Judaism and its laws, unchangeable and beyond time, and in categories other than those employed by historians. The problem is what those who do not share the views of the Orthodox and who perhaps form the great majority of Jews today think of their own Jewish consciousness and its definition.

Among those who have had the greatest share in the building up of Israel, only a very small minority adhered to the old definitions of Jewish identity. Most people who came here out of Zionist motives did not care about the Halakhah. They expected their community to be run by laws enacted in a free country for a free people, who could make their own decisions, staying within the confines of the historical consciousness of this people.

In former times, if a person found himself in disagreement with the rabbinical authority, he left Judaism. He had no choice! He had either to conform or to leave. Later, during the period of Emancipation, he took the way out by assimilation. But slowly, the phenomenon of people within the community marrying outside the fold became widespread.

The traditionalists' definition of Jewish law, which maintained that since ancient times Jewish society was constructed on a patriarchal basis, paradoxically uses a matriarchal criterion in defining Jewish identity. For myself and for innumerable people who live in this country, this halakhic definition, which has been for a long time, has lost its meaning and its psychological relevance.

In the case of a mixed marriage, we are much more inclined to regard the son of a Jewish father and a non-Jewish mother as Jewish rather than the contrary. In general, I would say that the rabbinical definition no longer has much relevance for the great mass of Jews in Europe or America. Certainly, during the last forty years [writing in 1970—Ed.], if the son of a Jew wanted to be identified as a Jew, whether by religion or nationality, he was accepted as such by general consent. No one would even ask questions. Thus, when the daughter of my brother, who married a Gentile, went to the Jewish community in Berlin after the Holocaust and said: "I want to be a member of the Jewish community," she was not refused. They took her in. She was the daughter of a well-known Jew, and they ignored halakhic complications.

It is not only a question of joining synagogues or communities. It is a question of general public reaction, and I can discover no sign that we prefer or that we insist upon the old rabbinical definition of Judaism. There has been a great change in psychological outlook, and this determines the situation in which we find ourselves today. Formerly, ninety-five percent or even more of people who intermarried or were the offspring of mixed marriages were not interested in retaining their Jewish identity, let alone insisting on it. During the last forty years there has been a complete reversal. Through the vicissitudes of history, through the tragic fate that befell our people, they decided and insisted on being counted. And when such people said: "I want to be counted as a Jew," everyone was glad to have them counted, and nobody said: "You are not one of us." To my mind, it is very important that we take cognizance of such historical and psychological facts.

The process of emancipation and later on the struggle to, and the necessity for, rebuilding a national life of our own brought about this change of attitude, which was no longer dependent upon categories of the Halakhah. There is a public consensus which considers as Jews certain individuals who are not recognized as Jews by the rabbinical law. This certainly holds true for people who have come to Israel to live here as Jews.

In our time, Jewish consciousness has undergone a definite split, whose existence we ought to recognize: namely, the split between a religious view of Judaism and a secular view. Zionism welcomed both in its midst. People were free to decide whether they wanted a secular identification with the Jewish people, a religious one, or both. There was a struggle of ideas, a struggle of organization, but nobody said that you cannot come here unless you undertook halakhic obligations.

This is one part of the picture. The other part is that some people retained certain religious opinions with passionate conviction—which is a legitimate right. We cannot speak of Judaism as a one-sided phenomenon only in light of the history of nineteenth- and twentieth-century Jews.

Both secular and religious definitions exist, which may and should develop. I say so as an historian. I say so also as a Jew who identifies with the whole of Judaism as an historical phenomenon, a phenomenon which might develop to a new religious level, to a new inspiration, into something which we cannot yet define. We have invited people to a creative enterprise in this land, which is not defined by books of law but by a living historical experience—and this living historical experience should be decisive.

There was a time when, for people of doubtful identity in the halakhic sense, Judaism was a burden and not a privilege. It was easy, and sometimes it is so even today, to throw off this burden. There are now many people who want to share the Jewish destiny and who wish to be counted. This is a phenomenon of which we are all aware, and we should not make light of it.

There are many definitions of a Jew which make sense. There is the Orthodox one, which for an Orthodox community is fully relevant and important. There is the definition that a Jew is a person who is considered a Jew by others. We don't think that this very fashionable definition is a good one for us, since we want more than people who are forced upon us merely because other people regard them as Jews. Neither do we think that this is the most desirable type of Jew, nor do I think we should make a case for such Jews.

There are people who think that a Jew is anyone who considers himself a Jew. And there is the definition that a Jew is one who is born of a Jewish parent and considers himself a Jew by taking upon himself the burden and privilege of being a Jew. This is the definition to which I would adhere, and which is in my opinion the view taken by most Jews of European or American descent.

There are famous instances which point up the paradox of traditional definitions. Mr. Bloom, the hero of James Joyce's *Ulysses,* is considered a Jew by the author, by himself, and by everybody else except the Halakhah.

There are examples of the offspring of mixed marriages. I remember the case of a famous physicist. In his later years he underwent a violent storm of conscience and discovered his Jewish background. He was the son of a Jewish father and a Gentile mother. He looked like twenty-eight Jews and behaved like two thousand. He had the mind of a Jew. His way of thinking was that of a talmudic rabbi. Yet he was not halakhically a Jew and was completely confused. He used to ask Mrs. Scholem and myself: "What am I?" One could have said to him: "You are nothing; you have discovered you are not a German, you are not an Austrian, you think of yourself as a Jew yet you are not a religious Jew in the sense of the Halakhah, since your mother is Gentile and you yourself have been baptized." Such cases are legion in our time. Should such people be excluded?

I do not think that Jewish descent is the only element. Proselytizing will always be, and should be, a marginal phenomenon. If people want to identify with us by a ritual act, I don't see any objection to that. If they have qualms about it, they should not identify with us. We have been critical of Jews who underwent baptism for the sake of their careers; we said it was hypocrisy. We should be honest enough to say that the same thing applies in our own case, and should not force people to do something which they consider hypocritical.

I think that the threat of dividing the Jewish people, of which we hear so much, is greatly exaggerated. It may even be the other way around: that the divisiveness may come from the other party. In nineteenth century Hungary there were two different kinds of officially recognized Judaism—Reform [or Neolog] Judaism and Orthodox Judaism. I advise everybody to read the sorrowful history of the Hungarian schism, which was brought about by the Orthodox, who said they did not consider the Reform Jews to be Jews.

I consider it a grievous and unfortunate error of judgment on the part of the government of Israel to have brought the present proposed law before the Parliament. I think it is unfortunate, because they are trying to impose conditions which are rejected by public opinion. This is a step which I deeply deplore, and which can only have deplorable consequences for the whole community. I would say that Mr. Ben-Gurion bears a great deal of the responsibility for having given the power to the rabbis several years ago, for reasons of expediency. It is not Golda Meir's government which committed this original sin, but that of Ben-Gurion, which should never have agreed in the first place to place a bill before the Knesset forcing rabbinical law on those Jews who do not want it, creating, in a democratic state like Israel, a condition which does not allow civil marriage or which does not acknowledge that marriages of Jews may be performed by non-Orthodox rabbis.

I do not think that considerations of what some call statesmanship and what I would call political expediency should be a decisive factor in matters of such great importance. I do not think that the State of Israel or any other great Jewish body anywhere in the world has any quarrel with Orthodox Jews who take their tradition seriously as a sacred heritage and wish to adhere to it; by all means let them do so. No steps can be envisaged by the Jewish people, here or elsewhere, that would in any way force on them something against their will. But I cannot understand why the majority of our people should be subject to a law which has no root in our historical and Jewish conscience.

Finally, if you ask me what advice I can offer, it is this: to keep our hearts and minds open to the new forces that seek expression in our history; as a Jewish people to be aware of the transient character of all present metamorphoses of Jewish life; and to hearken to the voice that might be forming and seeking articulation—that voice in which, if we believe in God as I do, we might recognize the continuity of what we call the voice from Sinai.

I define Zionism as a utopian return of the Jews to their own history. With the realization of Zionism, the fountains of the great deep of our historical being have welled up, releasing new forces within us. Our acceptance of our own history as a realm within which our roots grow is permeated with the conviction that the Jews, following the shattering catastrophe of our times, are entitled to define themselves according to their own needs and impulses; and that Jewish identity is not a fixed and static but a dynamic and even dialectical thing, because in its spiritual, no less than in its social and political aspects, it involves a living and creative body of people who call themselves Jews.

Chapter Fourteen

Secularism and Its "Dialectical Transformation" (1976)*

Jerusalem

February 1, 1976

Dear Mr. Ben-Ezer,

Many thanks for your letter of ten days ago. I have not yet seen your review [of *Devarim be-go*], and so do not know what you said there. In the final analysis, it was not my intention in publishing a collection of different essays to stir up controversy concerning any specific views which I expressed, but to give my readers (most of whom know nothing about me) the opportunity to form for themselves some overall impression of what I have dealt with beyond my philological work, and the sources upon which I drew. I would be most surprised if anyone will pay attention to this aspect of the book.

As for what you wrote concerning symbols which would express the crisis of our period in the history of the Jewish people—you are certainly

---

* The above comments appeared in a letter addressed to the writer and intellectual Ehud Ben-Ezer, dated February 1, 1976, in response to a letter by the latter raising various questions and thoughts elicited upon reading Scholem's collection of essays, *Devarim be-go*. Both Ben-Ezer's letter and Scholem's response were published in Ben-Ezer's introduction to his collection of "Conversations on the Price of Zionism" with various thinkers, *Ein Sha'ananut be-Tzion* (Tel Aviv: Am Oved, 1986), 25–28; reprinted in *'Od Davar*, 124.

correct in stating that there is no chance of the emergence of something like the Lurianic Kabbalah, and I never dreamt of such a thing. I gave my reasons for the absence of such a possibility in one of my articles, where I state that there is no longer a common authority obligating the public from which there might emerge symbols that would be accepted by all in the religious realm. I do not deny that this might change under new historical circumstances, but with the decline of belief in the Divine origin of the Torah there has been removed the authority and common basis that gave birth to new symbols. The local Jewish experience in the Land of Israel is not such a basis, and it is liable, as all of our controversies indicate, to be interpreted in diametrically opposed manners.

I never stated that the transition via secularism fascinates me! Indeed, it may be that it frightens not only you, but also myself. The question is whether any other way will be found. I believe that there is a greater chance that total secularism will bring in its wake a dialectical transformation, leading to the emergence of more men of truth and faith than the enclosed world of the tradition. On the other hand, it must be said that your statement that the vast majority of the Jewish creativity in our period is the product of secular people is not as correct as it perhaps ought to be! I have found much "wondering, thinking, and renewing" in what is known as the religious camp as well.

Chapter Fifteen

Messianism—A Never-Ending Quest (1977)*

I would like to express my appreciation to all of the institutions—the Israel Academy of Sciences and Humanities and the Hebrew University—which made this one-day seminar, which was filled to the brim, possible. I must admit that I did not initially intend to study the subject of messianism, specifically, in depth. Exactly fifty years ago, while sitting in Oxford studying some of the Kabbalistic manuscripts found there in abundance, I came across a tract entitled *Iggeret Magen Avraham* (The Letter of the Shield of Abraham) by Abraham Michael Cordozo, one of the great believers in Sabbatai Ṣevi, To my surprise, I discovered that the arguments of the followers of Sabbatai Ṣevi were not without interest, and this prompted me for the first time to reflect upon this complex and involved issue, thoughts which have since not left my heart.

I am very grateful to all of our colleagues who spoke here, who have taught us a great deal. I too found much to think about and to learn from their teaching. I had been told that today the young of the flock or my young disciples would speak, and I was somewhat surprised by this con-

* This paper is composed of Scholem's concluding remarks at a study conference on the subject of "The Messianic Idea in Jewish Thought," held in honor of his eightieth birthday at the Israel Academy of Sciences and Humanities on December 4–5, 1977. The papers were published in the volume entitled *Ha-Ra'ayon ha-Meshiḥi be-Yisra'el* (Jerusalem, 1982) [below: The Messianic Idea], Scholem's remarks appearing on pp. 255–62 of that volume; reprinted in *'Od Davar*, 263–74.

cept, because more than being young in years they are young in spirit, and their words speak both of themselves and of the freshness of their spirit.

On the basis of what I heard, I have set down some impromptu thoughts concerning a few major topics which seem to me to be important regarding the issue of messianism—that same chapter which has no end. I would like to relate to these in terms of what I understood, both in terms of what has been said here at length and with great precision, and in terms of those things I have thought about previously or in response to what was said here by the various lecturers.

The first characteristic which, in my opinion, marks Jewish messianism, the history of the messianic idea and the history of messianic movements, is that of continuity. This is admittedly a dialectical continuity, but it is a living dialectic, one testifying to the tremendous vitality present in the heart of the people and expressed in the very different forms assumed by the messianic idea over a period of more than fifteen hundred years. The earliest roots of this dialectical continuity lie in the Bible, as we were shown today in an excellent and praiseworthy manner by our colleague Ya'ir Zakovitch.[1]

The sources of the second characteristic of Jewish messianism—its paradoxality—are likewise found in the Bible. The paradoxical nature of messianism did not begin, as we might be inclined to think, at some later point in our history, in those disappointments which were our lot in later history. The basic paradox inherent in the messianic idea has its sources in the biblical verse concerning the poor man riding on a donkey, the righteous man who is also a ruler, and in those obvious contradictions whose source evidently lies in those contradictory verses which were expounded by the ancients pertaining to the messianic realm during the period when the body of the Bible was taking shape. These verses, which were initially very few in number, and which were gradually added to, originally included entirely contradictory elements: the idea of the Davidic king who would rule in the future; the idea of the servant of God; the idea of the rebuilding of the Temple, which was not necessarily connected with the image of the King Messiah, as we learned here clearly; and various other elements, which combined into the shaping of what is known as the messianic idea, as it was embodied in the various forms of historical Judaism.

This paradox accompanied all forms of messianism: not only in its strikingly scandalous forms, so to speak, but in its very essence. It began in biblical exegesis in the later biblical books themselves, in the Apocrypha and Pseudepigrapha, through the Midrash, to medieval literature, and down to our own days. Within the general framework of what we have heard today concerning peace, which is the unifying force among all the various forms of messianic vision, there lurks a certain dialectical serpent filled with contradictions that seeks its own expression.

The third point that occurred to me was the unique phenomenon of Jewish apocalyptic literature, which is seen by some scholars as continuing Israelite prophecy, and perceived by others as its antithesis. Concerning this area, we are indebted to the scholars of the previous generation, who engaged in a profound examination of the messianic idea and analysis of its sources. I would like to mention here with particular feelings of admiration the work of our late colleague Joseph Klausner, *The Messianic Idea in Israel.* I think that this book will remain one of the most serious and important works attempting to define the messianic idea as it was crystallized in the history of rabbinic Judaism through the close of the talmudic period, even for future generations. Although I do not share most of the opinions of the late Professor Klausner, I believe that this is a most distinguished work. We also owe a debt of gratitude to several other books, such as *Midrashei Ge'ulah* of Yehudah Even-Shmu'el, as well as to the works of several great non-Jewish scholars (such as H. Gressman, H. Starck, and L. Mowinckel), which have illuminated our path.

It is worth mentioning here a peculiar phenomenon connected with Jewish apocalypse. There were entire generations who attempted to deny the existence of apocalypse, and directed all of their efforts toward removing it from the living body of the nation. When I began to write about this messianism as I understood it, my words were directed particularly against one very specific and clear address; namely, the late Louis Ginzberg, one of the great Jewish scholars of the last generation. I wrote against him, and against those who followed in his footsteps. In my opinion, Ginzberg set the tone for the famous book by George Foot Moore, *Judaism in the First Centuries of the Christian Era,* which was at one time considered the outstanding introduction to Tannaitic Judaism. These books were written with one explicit purpose: to negate the presence of the apocalyptic element within classical Judaism, as understood by the great figures of this school.

I do not know who, in the final analysis, will emerge victorious in this weighty polemic, or whether perhaps both sides will be found correct. In any event, it is difficult today to imagine that anyone could deny the presence of apocalyptic thought as a living and constant factor in our history. Attempts to expunge it from Judaism and to construct in its place a refined Judaism, without any apocalyptic elements, are simply not viable. The various attempts to do so took shape because recent generations were not receptive to apocalyptic ideas; they thought that such things were vain and foolish, dreamlike matters. Our colleague Itamar Gruenwald has described them as "surrealistic dreams."[2] I have my doubts as to whether the prefix *sur-* is needed, and whether such dreams are indeed outdated. In any event, messianism is distant, and is in fact diametrically opposed to the catastrophic perception of history, which concludes with the End of Days and the beginning of a new heaven and a new earth. Apocalyptic thinking established a good deal of the historical continuity of Jewish messianism, in its various and peculiar branches, about which we have heard so much today. Among those things that we have learned from the scholarly study of Jewish history is that the perception of these great scholars is hidden to us, and we have begun to better understand the hearts of those pessimistic visionaries whose optimism was intended for some other world, in which the rays of the transcendent were revealed or will be revealed with greater clarity. Apocalypse is a great but problematic principle. As a disquieting factor throughout the generations, it has also had great opponents. Those who study this phenomenon need to examine this factor, and to acknowledge its problematic nature.

Our colleague Moshe David Herr has noted this duality, and the need to distinguish between realistic messianism, which is seemingly the continuation of history, and cosmic messianism, which is built *ab initio* upon the negation of history. It seems to me that the things we have heard are correct.

Against all this is the view of Maimonides, of which we have heard quite a bit today. I do not know whether in previous generations there were those who were impressed by the tremendous daring of this genius. In any event, Maimonides' daring in *Mishneh Torah* arouses astonishment from every possible angle. We all know that there is none as great as Maimonides, yet no one has yet explained in a satisfactory manner how Maimonides dared to establish as halakhic norms, in the name of the Halakhah, things which have no basis whatsoever in any tradition of the fathers of the nation—neither in the Bible, nor in the Mishnah, nor in the two Talmuds, nor in the Midrashim! Maimonides summarized the laws of the Fundaments of the Torah, regarding much of which one is astonished. The man had the gumption to write down certain things which seemed to him to be correct, on the basis of his study of Gentile sages—Aristotle, Alfarabi, and there is no need to enumerate here all of his other sources— and converted them into halakhot. From whence did he draw this great courage, this tremendous daring, the like of which was unknown in the history of the Halakhah prior to himself? It was only in his generation that others began to follow in his footsteps and to say: if Maimonides was able to establish as law for future generations things for which there is no source in the Jewish tradition, so can we! And they began to preface their books with chapters of halakhot, which likewise aroused infinite astonishment.

Just as Maimonides had the daring to establish halakhot which had no basis in the tradition, he was no less daring when he came to reject those things with which he did not agree. Maimonides censored many things; moreover, he was successful in doing so, as many generations, including our own, have been raised upon the Maimonidean doctrine, according to which the messianic idea is very daringly explicated at the end of *Hilkhot Melakhim, The Laws of Kings.*

At one time I had the idea of interpreting these halakhot as a polemic against Jewish apocalypse, and I was attacked soundly because of it. Nevertheless, I continue to maintain my ideas on this point, in all innocence. I believe that Maimonides' remarks represent an extreme pole in the tradition of the generations, teaching a way to that public which did not wish apocalypses. Apocalyptics, even though it is a living force, could not dominate the entire nation, and Maimonides became the spokesman for all those who could not accept it. It is therefore hardly surprising that during the nineteenth century, during the age of the civil emancipation of the Jews in Europe and in other countries, it was convenient for them to use Maimonidean language and to present the messianic idea as a restorative one, ignoring all of the *aggadic* elements and reducing them to the realm of imagination and metaphor—elements which every person is free to reject entirely, because the gates of exegesis were never closed and every person is free to expound these matters as he wishes.

Maimonides established a certain tendency in Jewish thought, whose paradoxality is clearly visible to whoever reads the literature of the generations which preceded him (such as that of Rabbi Saadiah Ga'on), and even more so that of subsequent generations. He read as authoritative an *aggadic* statement by one of the great talmudic sages, cited in several places in the Talmud as an individual opinion, but nowhere cited as halakhah: "There is no difference between this world and the days of Messiah except for the [absence of] suppression by the nations." This is a tremendously daring and controversial statement. We find here the leading spokesman for one of the major tendencies, cited in the codification (which is not at all possible!) of the messianic idea for future generations.

As against Maimonides, one finds among those thinkers writing in Hebrew an opposite tendency—one whose purpose is to restore the apocalypse, so firmly rejected by Maimonides, to what they considered its proper place in the nation's tradition or, in truth, to the sense of historical reality experienced by those generations.

These ideas did not take shape in a vacuum. They are all affected by both the general historical and social background; it is quite clear that each of their advocates lived in a specific atmosphere. The tension and striking oppositions between the two tendencies—the apocalyptic, with the vision which flows from its various forms, on the one hand, and its rationalistic suppression by Maimonides, on the other—were known phenomena in every generation.

I have emphasized in the past, and I state again now, that it is extremely instructive to pose Maimonides' *Hilkhot Melakhim,* which is formulated as Halakhah, against the two great codifications of messianism, widely accepted during the Middle Ages, of Rabbi Isaac Abrabanel and of the Maharal of Prague. Maimonides would have turned over in his grave had he read their words. The contemporary reader of Maharal's *Netzaḥ Yisra'el,* which has again enjoyed much popularity in our generation and has been studied by scholars in both Israel and the Diaspora, will find there a full codification of rabbinic apocalyptics, uniting rationalistic and apocalyptic elements in one great vision. How astonished the reader will be when he compares it to Maimonides' *Hilkhot Melakhim.* True, Maimonides himself paid lip service to apocalyptism when the situation warranted it, as may be seen from his *Iggeret Teman* (Epistle to Yemen), as several of our colleagues have already noted and written. In this epistle, Maimonides is prepared to compromise with the generation, as in this concrete case he needed to communicate with the Jews of Yemen, and in the twelfth century it would have been impossible for him to address them in the language of Alfarabi or the philosophers. In this case, he too agreed to a certain compromise between apocalyptic *aggadah* and his own tendencies. However, Maimonides is unwilling to compromise with the truth when it comes to those matters which he dares to designate as Halakhah.

Maimonides' words and my comments about them bring us to another important area in the understanding of messianism: namely, the contradiction and union between restoration and utopia within messianism. Since that time in the biblical period when the messianic idea began to leave its mark, it has been accompanied by a basic question: does messianism emphasize that which has been quite appropriately referred to today as restorative messianism, taking as its motto the verse, "renew our days as of old," or does it stress the utopian side, of that which no human eye has yet seen?

In fact, generally speaking all of the principles of messianism, both in our history and in our literature, are no more than an inconvenient—at times extremely inconvenient—mixture of these two tendencies. There is no serious book in which you will not find some allusion to the utopian element. Even Maimonides, who went very far to the other extreme, left a small, albeit not an unimportant corner, for the utopian element when he spoke of the messianic age as one in which man will have the leisure to contemplate the glory of the Creator and to engage in Torah study, in contemplation and in profound reflection. The contemplative element in *Hilkhot Melakhim* is the utopian spark which remained with Maimonides after rejecting as naught all the other elements and all the other utopias. And indeed, many of the utopians of recent generations, including those who followed in Maimonides' wake, attempted in their modernistic interpretations to remove from the messianic idea specifically the restorative element (diametrically opposed to Maimonides!), which had been an important and firm element of messianism since its earliest development.

Indeed, this mixture—the controversy, the living contradiction, the back and forth, I would almost say the living debate between utopia and restoration in messianism—was that which established the living history, the heart of Jewish messianism. There were pure utopians, who completely rejected the restorative aspect of the messianic idea, while there were others, such as Maimonides, in whose teaching the restorative element predominated. Among the former group is included, for example, Hermann Cohen. Notwithstanding the love and closeness which Cohen felt for Maimonides, in whom he saw his great master and teacher in Jewish thought, this side of Maimonides' outlook did not appeal to him at all. In Maimonides' opinion, messianism is essentially political restoration—and political is almost, Heaven forbid, Zionism; and what have we to do with Zionism and such messianism, Hermann Cohen would say.

In addition to the issue of utopia and restoration, Shalom Rosenberg has taught us something new in his remarks concerning the four circles of the messianic plane: the individual, the nation, the human, and the cosmic.[3] I think that this idea is worthy of considerable further examination.

We have heard many extremely interesting things concerning messianism in the Kabbalah from our colleague Yehudah Leibis—a complex matter, which is yet to be fully exhausted. His paper is an interesting attempt to interpret a major part of *Sefer ha-Zohar* as a messianic document. I have generally read the *Zohar* as an historical document which, insofar as the messianic idea is fully expressed therein, is entirely on the apocalyptic side of the tradition, as embodied, for example, in Even-Shmu'el's *Midrashei Ge'ulah*, which I mentioned above. I do not speak here of the messianism of the *Idra*, but of a kind of typological prefiguration of a messianic possibility, at which Leibis hinted. In its beginnings, Kabbalistic messianism contains certain exceptions of acute, concrete, actual messianism—that is, a perception of it as something imminent and immediate, which we need only to take certain steps in order to realize. Such is the case, for example, in Abraham Abulafia and others. In *Sefer ha-Zohar* per se this matter does not stand out in so blatant a manner, but we would be happy to acknowledge it if Leibis's new interpretation, which is to appear in full in the future in written form,[4] is found to be correct.

Over the course of several generations, the main novellas of the Kabbalists were not primarily focused upon this issue of messianism. Being traditionalists, they repeated the words of their predecessors, united them, and drew upon them in accordance with their various tendencies. But their main yearning and desire was not to break through to the End of Days or the Apocalypse but, on the contrary, to break backwards to the original sources of Being as a whole. The Kabbalists longed to understand the act of creation. It is no matter of mere chance that the earliest Hebrew mysticism of the Middle Ages—i.e., the Kabbalah prior to the generation of the expulsion from Spain—was a quest for the way back toward the roots of being, and not a path toward the distant future—for one who is able to return to the roots of being, even if only as a means of seeking attachment to the Godhead, has found the path to God. This tendency is very remote from messianism. In a certain sense, one may even say that it is the opposite of messianism—it is a quest for a way back to the Creation, rather than a quest for the End of Days. The Kabbalists were authentically creative in their novellas concerning the quest for the path to the Creation, while it is difficult to find much original thought in their remarks about the End of Days. But with the expulsion from Spain things changed completely. More than a little has been said about this since I wrote the chapter on the period following the expulsion from Spain in my book, *Major Trends in Jewish Mysticism,*[5] and many of our colleagues here today participated in that research and enlightened us with their insights. One of the great moments, of which I took note only later, and not at the beginning of my studies or my research, was the encounter between mysticism, which seeks the path back to God, and messianism. Here we find a striking example of the problem mentioned in today's lectures, particularly in the later ones: the issue of the redemption of the individual as against the redemption of the collective, the redemption of the nation, as messianic elements. In fact, it never occurred to anyone before these questions possibly arose in Ḥasidism—or in the discussions of the colleagues today concerning Ḥasidism—and certainly not earlier—to seriously consider the redemption of the individual as messianism, and not only in a metaphorical, non-committal manner. It never occurred to any philosopher, or ethical teacher, or halakhist, to say that a person who finds wholeness within himself, who succeeds in restoring the Divine image within himself in a whole manner, to restore the image of God in his very being, to call these or their like or parts of these processes in religious life, or in the emotional life of the religious believer, by the term messianism.

Only now, in the last few generations, have things become confused, so that we are told that such an approach is possible. I must confess that the problem seems to me quite a serious one, deserving of study and clarification. But one thing is clear: in Kabbalistic literature, no one ever dreamed of calling by the term actual messianism or realization of messianism those acts by which a person prepares himself, through various stages of personal activity, for what will come about afterwards on a general human level. Lurianic Kabbalah, which is filled with general messianic tension, may serve as an example as to how this combination of the two subjects took place. We find here a marriage, not always so happy or so balanced, between messianic redemption and that which is demanded of the individual Kabbalist, who ought to perhaps become a guide for the public surrounding him.

The problem of private redemption, of redemption of the individual, is an entirely modern problem, which does not exist in the Jewish tradition prior to 1750. Whether it exists later is a debatable question, and Isaiah Tishby has already articulated his view, which differs from my own.[6]

Another issue is that of Lurianic Kabbalah, upon which I shall not enlarge here. One reads a good deal today about its messianic aspect and as to how messianism was expressed through processes of cosmic mythology, connecting the innerness of the worlds with the redemptive process. This myth connects the origin of the worlds with problems and processes requiring redemption, which is real redemption, described in special symbolic garments, the like of which are not found in the *Zohar*. In my opinion, this matter deserves further consideration. It is true that in the modern interpretations of messianic redemption, primarily those written in European languages, elements of the idea of the possible existence of utopian messianism crept in even within the activities of the individual. I will not elaborate upon the discussion of this point here, as I now wish to turn to the discussion of several subjects within the Jewish tradition.

I would now wish to turn to another subject that is deserving of attention, one that was not specifically discussed today, even though it is implicit in all of the things which were said. I refer to the two characteristic tendencies of messianic literature in all generations: the tendency toward restrictive interpretation and the tendency to expand it insofar as possible. The advocates of the former tendency wished to limit as much as possible the number of biblical verses which could be interpreted as referring to the End of Days, while the advocates of the second, world-embracing tendency see as their ideal the interpretation of every verse—if at all feasible—as referring to matters of redemption and Messiah—and this by means of all kinds of exegetical tricks in which we, as is known, are geniuses. Anyone who reads the literature will readily discern these tendencies: there are those which are restrictive and those which are expansive. The expansive tendency is reflected, for example, in the writing of the preachers from Italy and Salonica and in such codificatory works as those of Abrabanel or the Maharal of Prague.

What characterizes both of these tendencies is that anyone who ignores most of the verses and prohibits their messianic interpretation *ipso facto* assumes a certain posture regarding apocalyptic or general messianic traditions, which were interpreted and found to have sources or allusions in these verses. On the other hand, whoever expands it literally gives the entire world to messianism. The daring of the expansive exegetes finds its expression in a saying uttered, not by chance, by the well-known Sabbatian Rabbi Abraham Yakhini, who wrote that if the Torah has seventy faces, one of these is that there is no verse in the Torah which will not be interpreted in the future as alluding to Sabbatai Ṣevi. This is without doubt the most extreme formulation which may be given to this tendency: that there is no verse which will not in the future be read as speaking of the King Messiah.

The final point, upon which I shall not elaborate at length, was raised by the charming and extremely interesting lecture of our colleague Mendel Piekarcz,[7] namely, the problem of messianic interpretations found in the edificatory *(Musar)* literature of the generation of the formation of Ḥasidism. These matters reveal the expanses of the world of messianism within the totality of the various different tendencies. I will likewise not address myself to another problem—namely, secularization, and the secularization of messianism which has taken place over the course of the past two hundred years—a major and important issue, which has not yet been properly discussed in Hebrew literature, and which is certainly among the most important matters for understanding the spiritual moods, social history, and philosophy of society in the previous century and in the present one, within which secularization, including the secularization of messianism, served as a central element.

Allow me to conclude my remarks by mentioning some *desiderata.* These are matters which have not yet been discussed, to the best of my knowledge (would that I were shown to be incorrect!), and not yet studied, even though they cry out for profound explanation and clarification.

The main problem—and I call upon those scholars of Jewish studies who have not yet investigated it—is the question of the stance of halakhic figures regarding our question. I refer to halakhists in the simple sense, not to those who were interested in philosophy or some other additional area; to *poskim,* halakhic authorities, whose spiritual world is an exclusively halakhic one; for whom the world of the Halakhah is sufficient unto itself, whether its dimensions be four ells or four billion ells. I have not found any scholars who have addressed themselves to this issue, and find this rather surprising. Many people know the Halakhah; many criticize us because we do not know enough in this area. We ask them: what do you know of this subject? And they answer us hesitatingly, and to date no one has dealt with this problem. I am among those who respect the Halakhah (despite some empty and slanderous words that have been said about me), and consider it to be a central problem. I hope that during the next generation the young ones of the flock will provide a learned answer to this open question.

There are many other very complex issues involving Kabbalah and philosophical literature related to messianism requiring clarification, such as: To what extent is messianism actualized and to what extent is it hidden? To what extent is there a *sub rosa* tendency to infiltrate certain daring ideas of Sabbatianism so as to make them acceptable on the part of traditionally pious Jews?

In conclusion, allow me to quote my own personal credo regarding a topic which has not yet been mentioned today, but which is very close to my heart. I have the honor of reading to you the final page of my essay on "The Messianic Idea in Judaism," in which I discuss the price of messianism:

> One word more, by way of conclusion, should be said about a point which, to my mind, has generally received too little attention in discussions of the Messianic idea. What I have in mind is the price demanded by Messianism, the price which the Jewish people has had to pay out of its substance for this idea which it handed over to the world. The magnitude of the Messianic idea corresponds to the endless powerlessness in Jewish history during all the centuries of exile, when it was unprepared to come forward onto the plane of world history. There's something preliminary, something provisional about Jewish history; hence its inability to give of itself entirely. For the Messianic idea is not only consolation and hope. Every attempt to realize it tears open the abysses which lead each of its manifestations *ad absurdum.* There is something grand about living in hope, but at the same time there is something profoundly unreal about it. It diminishes the singular worth of the individual, and he can never fulfill himself because the incompleteness of his endeavors eliminates precisely what constitutes its highest value. Thus, in Judaism the Messianic idea has compelled a life lived in deferment, in which nothing can be done definitively, nothing can be irrevocably accomplished.

One may say, perhaps, the Messianic idea is the real anti-existentialist idea. Precisely understood, there is nothing concrete which can be accomplished by the unredeemed. This makes for the greatness of Messianism, but also for its constitutional weakness. Jewish so-called *Existenz* possesses a tension that never finds true release; it never burns itself out. And when in our history it does discharge, then it is foolishly decried (or, one might say, unmasked) as "pseudo-Messianism." The blazing landscape of redemption (as if it were a point of focus) has concentrated in itself the historical outlook of Judaism. Little wonder that overtones of Messianism have accompanied the modern Jewish readiness for irrevocable action in the concrete realm, when it set out on the utopian return to Zion. It is a readiness which no longer allows itself to be fed on hopes. Born out of the horror and destruction that was Jewish history in our generation, it is bound to history itself and not to meta-history; it has not given itself up totally to Messianism. Whether or not Jewish history will be able to endure this entry into the concrete realm without perishing in the crisis of the Messianic claim which has virtually been conjured up—that is the question which out of his great and dangerous past the Jew of this age poses to his present and to his future.[8]

Chapter Sixteen

What Is Judaism? (1974)*

Judaism cannot be defined according to its essence, since it has no essence. Judaism cannot therefore be regarded as a closed historical phenomenon whose development and essence came into focus by a finite sequence of historical, philosophical, doctrinal, or dogmatic judgments and statements. Judaism is rather a living entity which for some reason has survived as the religion of a chosen people. Indeed, for such a people to have endured for three thousand years as a recognizable entity, a phenomenal fact for which nobody has any truly sufficient explanation, is itself an enigma. The continued survival of the Jewish people seems to suggest that the Jews have in fact been chosen by someone for something.

The enigma of Jewish survival has intrigued generations. Why are the Jews there? What are they up to? Are they simply a "fossil," as Arnold Toynbee opined? If not, what are they?

Judaism, however, cannot be defined by or with any authority, or in any clear way, simply because it is a living entity, having transformed itself at various stages in its history and having made real choices, discarding many phenomena that at one time were very much alive in the Jewish

* The following text is based upon a discussion of Judaism, culled from a transcript of remarks made at the Center for the Study of Democratic Institutions, Santa Barbara, California, in 1974, and edited by Paul Mendes-Flohr. First published in *Contemporary Jewish Religious Thought; Original Essays on Critical Concepts, Movements, and Beliefs*, Arthur A. Cohen and Paul Mendes-Flohr, eds. (New York: Charles Scribner's Sons, 1984), 505–08. Published in Hebrew in *'Od Davar*, 119–22.

world. And having discarded these phenomena, Judaism bequeaths to us the question of whether that which was historically discarded is also to be discarded by present-day Jews or by the future Jew who wishes to identify himself with the past, present, and future of his people.

If Judaism cannot be defined in any dogmatic way, then we may not assume that it possesses any *a priori* qualities that are intrinsic to it or might emerge in it; indeed, as an enduring and evolving historic force, Judaism undergoes continuous transformation. Nevertheless, although Judaism is manifestly a dynamic, historical phenomenon, it has evolved under the shadow, so to speak, of a great idea, namely, monotheism—the idea of one unique God, the creator of the universe. Yet it is clearly impermissible to understand this idea in such a manner that whatever follows or does not follow from it must necessarily be referred to the Halakhah. To be sure, the Halakhah is certainly an overwhelmingly important aspect of Judaism as an historical phenomenon, but it is not at all identical with the phenomenon of Judaism per se. Judaism has taken on many varied forms, and to think of it as only a legislative body of precepts seems to me as an historian and as an historian of ideas to be utter nonsense.

If I say that Judaism has no essence, this means two things. First, I do not accept as valid the all-embracing, Orthodox, or what I prefer to call fundamentalist definition of Judaism as a given law in which there are no differences between essential and quintessential points—which, of course, is the point of view of strictly Orthodox halakhic Jews. Neither am I a partisan of the school that defines the essence of Judaism by reducing it to some essential spiritual statements such as those made by Moritz Lazarus, Hermann Cohen, Leo Baeck, Martin Buber, and many others during the last hundred and fifty years. Under a dominant Protestant influence, this tendency of modern Jewish thought has regarded Judaism as a purely spiritual phenomenon. But it is incorrect to consider Judaism in spiritual terms alone. Judaism certainly is a spiritual phenomenon, but it is a spiritual phenomenon that has been bound to an historical phenomenon, namely, to the Jewish people and the Jewish nation. To try to disassociate one from the other has proved impossible, as evidenced by the unsuccessful attempt made by Reform or Liberal Judaism to denationalize Judaism.

Similarly, Zionism's reaffirmation of Jewish nationality would be ill-advised to attempt severing its link with the spiritual dimension of Judaism. In fact, Zionism does not attempt to do this; it merely seeks to sponsor the return of the Jewish people and its spiritual life to history. When the Halakhah governed their life, the Jews were not masters of their own destiny. This is one of the most problematic aspects of the Halakhah, paradoxically, since the Halakhah did play a very positive role in preserving the Jewish people. Yet it is nonetheless true that the Halakhah as a body of laws and way of life ultimately relinquished responsibility for the historic destiny of the Jewish people.

One cannot, of course, anticipate what will become of Judaism as it reenters history, as the Jews become newly responsible for their own history. It has been said that the very success of Zionism—meaning the dialectical success it manifests in its historical founding of a state— constitutes a betrayal of the mission of Judaism. But this theory of mission, to be a light unto the nations, which over the last hundred and fifty years was accepted by a large part of Jewry, was invented ad hoc by a people who were aware of their historical importance, that is, their lack of vital resolve to live as a people. It was invented as a kind of spiritual recompense, a lame justification for the existence of Judaism in the Diaspora. The mission theory is one of the most dialectical (in some ways praiseworthy, in some ways shameful) aspects of Jewish experience since the emanicipation. Thus, Zionism may indeed be a betrayal of the mission of the Jews invented by German, French, and Italian Jewry a hundred and fifty years ago. That it is a betrayal of the real mission of the Jews, namely, to face history in a social way as a people seeking to order their affairs, I disagree. To be sure, the return to Zion could be construed as the Jews' betrayal of their vocation to be a transcendent people—to be a people that is not a people, to quote Heine, a *Volksgespent* (literally, phantom people), a people whose essence it is to disappear. That the essence of the Jewish people is to cease to be a people is, in my opinion, a highly perverse proposition.

Zionism, whimsically defined as a movement against the excessive inclination of the Jews to travel, is the utopian return of the Jews to their own history. The fathers of Zionism simply dreamt of bringing order into their own world as Jews, and of doing so under the shadow of some great ethical ideas such as socialism or other humanistic and religious ideas of elevated character. This is all that Zionism sought. Parenthetically, Zionism is not to be regarded as a species of messianism: I consider it the pride of Zionism that it is not a messianic movement. It is a great error, therefore— for which Zionism may have to pay dearly—if the movement attributes to itself messianic significance. Messianic movements are apt to fail. Zionism is rather a movement within the mundane, immanent process of history; Zionism does not seek the end of history, but takes responsibility within the history of an unredeemed and unmessianic world. To be sure, as an attempt to build a new life for the Jewish people in an unredeemed world, Zionism may have to confront certain messianic overtones that are manifestly inherent in the idea of the return of the Jewish people to Zion.

As regards Judaism in the State of Israel, it is the living force of the people of Israel. As such it does not recognize an essence. There will be forms of Judaism devolving from the whole whirlpool, as it were, of Jewish history, from the struggle to create a just society and all that is implied by this struggle. Jewish theology may hence undergo radical changes in the State of Israel because secularism is a powerful reality, the meaning of which has to be lived and confronted squarely. This confrontation will be between transcendental values and secular, that is, relative, values—essentially and principally relative values. It will be a fruitful confrontation because it will not be confined to a spiritual, abstract realm, but will occur within a living society of a people struggling for its liberation. Halakhah may emerge as one of the presuppositions of a future theology of Judaism to evolve in Israel, but it will only be one of many; *aggadah* will not remain any less creative and enduring. Furthermore, as noted earlier, those phenomena of Jewish history that were discarded by Diaspora Judaism from the talmudic period cannot be assumed to have been lost forever to Judaism.

It will be necessary to rethink Judaism in broader terms, and in much broader terms than those of halakhic Judaism. We have to face the question: How will a Judaism that evolves in a society of Jews work without taking refuge in traditional forms of ritual or of theology? I am not a prophet, but I welcome the struggle. I am not sure of its outcome. It might be deadly for the Jews. There is no guarantee that the State of Israel is or will be a full success in any sense, but I welcome the struggle because it will call forth the productive powers—whatever they are—of Jews. These productive powers will be dedicated to their own progenitors and will, if there is anything to radiate, radiate beyond them. We are not obliged to justify our existence by working for the world. Nobody, no other nation, has ever been put under such an obligation, and some of us see it as scandalous that unlike everyone else, we have to justify being Jews by serving some further purpose. No one asks a Frenchman why he is there. Everyone asks a Jew why he is there; no one would be content with the statement, I am just a Jew. Yet the Jew has every right to be just a Jew and to contribute to what he is by being just what he is. We are always asked to be something exceptional, something supreme, something ultimate. Maybe that very expectation will come to fruition one day, and perhaps then even the enigma of being the chosen people, which is not easily discarded, will be resolved.

Part Four

Judaism Through the Ages

Chapter Seventeen

The Historical Development of Jewish Mysticism*

By the term Hebrew mysticism or *Kabbalah,* in the broad sense, we refer to the totality of those religious streams within Judaism which strive to arrive at a religious consciousness beyond intellectual apprehension, and which may be attained by man's delving into himself by means of contemplation, and the inner illumination which results from this contemplation. Simultaneously, these streams tried to maintain their position within the existing Jewish framework of their time and to refrain from controversy with it, insofar as this was possible. One can discern certain broad lines of organic development within Jewish mysticism, which reveal in a striking way certain aspects of the history of Jewish religion, specifically that of folk religion. All told, if we do not confine ourselves to the Kabbalah in the narrow sense of the word, the history of Jewish mysticism embraces the past two millennia. Its particular development may be divided into six periods:

First Period: Merkabah mysticism, centered in the Levant during the first millennium C.E.

Second Period: Ashkenazic Hasidism, whose center was in Germany, initially during the period ca.1150–1300, but which had an ongoing vital impact thereafter, as late as the fifteenth century.

* Originally published as a pamphlet-essay under the title *Jewish Mysticism and Kabbalah* (*Ha-mistorin ha-yehudi veha-kabbalah;* Tel Aviv: Sifriyat ha-Sha'ot, 1944); reprinted in *Devarim be-go,* 230–61, in a version revised and edited by Avraham Shapira.

Third Period: The development and rise of Kabbalah proper, centered in Spain, from the year 1200 until the expulsion in 1492.

Fourth Period: The later Kabbalah, centered around the Land of Israel, during the period 1500–1650.

Fifth Period: The Sabbatian movement and its offshoots, ca. 1665–1800, in the Near East and in Europe.

Sixth Period: Ḥasidism, in the lands of Eastern Europe, beginning approximately 1750.

Notwithstanding the fact that a common line of development unites the last four groups in particular, we shall not speak here extensively of either the Sabbatian movement or Ḥasidism. However, these may not be entirely excluded from any discussion of the characteristics of Jewish mysticism in general.[1]

GENERAL FEATURES

If one were to summarize the development of Jewish mysticism from an historical viewpoint, one would need to say that its unique nature and the specific character of its development derive from the fact that these were mystical movements which strove increasingly for influence in the social and national realms. This tendency is not yet discernible during the first period. It began to be felt with varying degrees of clarity during the second and third periods, while in the last three periods it became manifested with a sharp dialectic. Hence, there took place here a peculiar development, unique to the inner laws determining the history of Jewish religion. On the other hand, throughout all of these periods one may also clearly see the influence of the general environment and tendencies of these periods in the non-Jewish world, albeit not always in equal measure. Nevertheless, Jewish historiography generally, and that of the nineteenth century in particular, erred in placing excessive emphasis upon external influences. In point of fact, during each period Jewish mysticism revealed original Jewish aspects, notwithstanding outside influences. Moreover: among the religious streams in Judaism following the destruction of the Second Temple, the Kabbalah was that which, on the basis of religious impulses, succeeded both in moving great masses of people to the depths of their souls, and also in controlling them.

This phenomenon may be explained in light of the unique nature of Jewish mysticism during the Middle Ages. Mysticism competed here with the rationalistic trends, particularly those manifested in Jewish philosophy of the twelfth and thirteenth centuries. Both movements, that of philosophical rationalism and that of Kabbalistic mysticism and esotericism, bore an aristocratic character. They emerged with the explicit intention of disseminating their teaching to a small elite who had a special claim to it. However, in terms of the sources upon which it drew, Kabbalah had deep roots within popular religion. So long as it was in fact a vital religious force, we find it maintaining vital contact with the national myth, and with the religion of the ordinary, simple Jew. From this there follows an additional paradox: that the Kabbalists appear as the representatives of the religious forces and beliefs which were active among the masses of the people, despite these being expressed in the language of religious ideology, and in many cases even through means of the thought and speech of philosophers. However, as against the rationalistic thought of the philosophers, the main stream of Kabbalistic thought was determined more by the colorful imagery of myth, giving it a greater connection with the masses than would seem to be the case from the images of its external appearance and from the course of its thoughts, which frequently seem quite bizarre and convoluted. There is a mutual relationship and interdependence within this movement between myth and mysticism. Myth, against which the classical forms and expressions of Jewish religion waged war and was thus suppressed, or at least marginalized, frequently burst forth with tremendous power from the different forms of mystical thinking and revealed itself as a force which now, as in the past, enjoys a firm and strong position within Judaism. Indeed, from this point of view many Kabbalists are extremely interesting, in their attempt to combine mythic and at times even primitive thought processes together with the strict monotheism of Judaism. During certain periods of Jewish mysticism, particularly following the expulsion from Spain, these attempts led to an extremely important result: Kabbalah became manifested as a force which, in its own way, wrought a revolution in Jewish consciousness. True, in the thought of the Kabbalists themselves, old and new were quite neatly united. They frequently felt themselves to be traditionalist, conservative spokesmen for the old religious authority when, in point of fact, the impact of their activity tended to be the exact opposite. So long as the Kabbalists knew that their ideas were revolutionary in terms of rabbinic Judaism, they approached the brink of mystical heresy and nearly came into conflict with the official Judaism of their time—a conflict which was at times covert and at times completely open.

Mysticism rapidly disseminated its ideas of unceasing ascent to God and of unmediated religious illumination and contemplation—but nevertheless did not wish to lose its connection with the classical forms of Jewish religion, nor with popular religion. This provides the explanation for two other characteristic phenomena:

First: that, notwithstanding the mystical and intuitive nature of this system, it claims to be no more than Kabbalah (literally, that which has been received)—that is, the authentic tradition, passed on secretly from generation to generation since the existence of man upon the earth. This is expressed in various mythological forms: Kabbalah is, so to speak, the authentic wisdom and knowledge given to Adam by the angel Raziel; or it is, as it were, the essence and inner core of the Oral Torah given to Moses at Sinai; or it attempts to demonstrate, by means of a long chain of tradition from one generation to another, the authenticity of the teaching which it would promulgate. Strangely enough, notwithstanding the claim that they are no more than conveying the hidden wisdom which they had received as tradition (Kabbalah) from previous generations, never in the history of Judaism—not even among the philosophers—have there appeared so many new ideas as there did among these Kabbalists. On this point, they were also influenced by certain messianic ideas. We constantly find among the mystics the idea that the true and perfect wisdom will spread over the entire world, albeit only in the days of the Messiah. However, on the eve of the redemption it will already be possible to record them in writing or to convey them to those select disciples who have been initiated in the divine mysteries. Since many of the greatest Kabbalists were certain that the Redemption would come in their own days, they found here adequate justification for all of those novel ideas which did not correspond to what had been given over and received from generation to generation. In most cases, this new element took the form of an interpretation of the old, albeit the new ideas were not always really the result of such interpretation. The more daring the new idea, the more firmly they argued that this was merely a revealing of the true and original contents of the religious tradition from the Six Days of Creation—contents which now, with the onset of the Eschaton, were fully understood and restored in all their brilliance. Such an approach was customary among the Sephardic Kabbalists, no less than among those of Safed or among the ideologists of Sabbatianism.

Second: the relationship between mysticism and magic, which is a feature of all six periods of Jewish mysticism, may be explained in terms of the strong connection to folk religion. In general, only rarely were certain very specific forms of mysticism entirely separated from the magical element, as in certain Indian systems and in fourteenth century Christian mysticism. Such a complete separation, however, hardly ever occurred in the history of Jewish mysticism. In all periods, Kabbalah is associated to a greater or lesser extent with both popular and learned magic. What has been known since the fourteenth century under the title "Practical Kabbalah" is simply magic, incorporating various earlier and later elements. On occasion, it also has some slight connection with the religious speculations and quest of the mystics. Even in those cases in which the Kabbalists developed a theoretical doctrine of such magic (as, for example, in the fourteenth century work *Berit Menuḥah),* its actual, concrete contents—the raw material of magic—is generally not at all related to the specific views of the Kabbalists. In any event, "Practical Kabbalah" is much earlier than theoretical Kabbalah which, even when directed toward practical concerns—namely: to show man the way toward God—has hardly any relation to "Practical Kabbalah."

Each one of the six periods of the development of Jewish mysticism created for itself a unique religious language and conceptual world, by means of which one may clearly distinguish one period from another. Of course, each new period is also accompanied by the heritage of the earlier periods; there are cases in which a transformation takes place in the earlier heritage, new vitality being discovered therein as a result of a new attitude and new perspectives. The religious terminology of the Kabbalists, its abundant and complex language of symbols, epithets and allusions, is one of the explicit factors making it so difficult for the contemporary reader to penetrate the infinitely rich literature of the Kabbalah, especially that of the last four periods.

THE BEGINNINGS OF JEWISH MYSTICISM

One may conjecture that Jewish mysticism developed as an independent entity shortly before the appearance of Christianity and shortly thereafter, that is, during the century prior to the destruction of the Second Temple. The details of these beginnings have not on the whole been sufficiently clarified, for which reason there has been much speculation concerning this matter, including certain extremely dubious theories for which there is no basis. For example, the role of the sect or order of the Essenes in this development has often been emphasized, although in point of fact this matter is not at all clear. One can say with some confidence that the origin of Jewish mysticism is associated with two factors: first, the fashioning of the classical forms of rabbinic Judaism by the Pharisees. The fixed and crystallized lines of this religious form led to the fact that new religious impulses, seeking expression within the fixed framework of this Judaism, were easily channeled into a mystical direction—that is, toward the reinterpretation of the traditional contents of the religion in a mystical spirit.

Second, a great deal of importance must be attributed here to the all-embracing and deep religious ferment in the non-Jewish world, expressed in the breakdown and mixing of the earlier pagan religions. This mixing (known as syncretism) frequently took place by means of mystical slogans. There is doubtless also a certain connection between the origins of Jewish mysticism and the religious world of syncretism. Such a connection may be seen, for example, in beliefs concerning primordial Adam as a unique sort of spiritual power, in beliefs concerning the ascent of the soul to heaven and its various stations, and in ideas relating to the divine qualities and attributes, understood in a more or less personal and autonomous manner (e.g., the attribute of Justice, the attribute of Mercy, etc.).

The earliest mystical development in Judaism itself is rooted in two factors: (a) the longing for greater and more objective immersion in the study of Holy Writ; and (b) the longing for subjective, personal experience of divine matters.

The former led to an extension of the boundaries of Torah and its significance: from now on, it was no longer seen as the law of the Jewish nation alone, but as the hidden law of the entire cosmos. Such an inner interpretation of the Bible was primarily based upon: the first chapter of the Book of Genesis; the subject of the rationale for the commandments; those verses which speak of Divine Wisdom (especially in the Book of Proverbs), which were interpreted as referring to the Torah; and finally, the vision of the prophet Ezekiel, who saw the Divine Chariot carrying the throne of Glory, "and seated upon the likeness of a throne was a likeness as it were of human form." (1:26)

The second type of longing led to the creation of new forms in place of the earlier prophetic one. Especially pertinent here is the practice of gazing upon the Chariot and the vision of the End among the apocalyptics, who revealed the secrets of the approaching redemption. Regarding several points, the dogmatic contents of Jewish religion had not yet been unequivocally formulated during this period. Hence, one cannot attribute the same importance to the question of the orthodoxy of these early mystical ideas as it would assume among Christian scholars. For a long time thereafter, other religious streams continued to exist within Judaism alongside the rabbinic mainstream, whose image became progressively fixed, and the boundaries between them cannot always be ascertained in a clear way.

MERKABAH MYSTICISM

This form of Jewish mysticism exists in recognizable form, to a certain extent, as early as the first century. It underwent two main stages during the course of a very long development. In the earlier stage, its main spokesmen were certain circles in Palestinian Judaism, including the *tannaim,* the sages of the Mishnah. We know of mystical activity within the circle of Rabban Yoḥanan ben Zakkai and his disciples, of Rabbi Akiva, and of other sages from the Mishnaic period. Even before their time and contemporaneous with them, we may identify the activity of anonymous circles, whose identity it is impossible to determine exactly, from whom there have come down several esoteric books composed in the name of pious and holy men of hoary antiquity (pseudepigraphic), such as the *Books of Enoch* and the *Apocalypse of Abraham.* In the amoraic period as well, particularly during the third and fourth centuries, we may identify several notable talmudic sages who represent mystical ways of thinking (such as Rabbi Yehoshu'a ben Levi, Resh Lakish, and especially Abba Arikha, known as Rav). With Rav, mystical thought spread to Babylonia, where it continues over a long period of time and develops in an extremely vital way. On the other hand, during the subsequent period, from the fifth century on, the leaders of the movement again disappear. One can no longer speak of an historical figure who stands at its head; instead, they are all mixed together in an anonymous mass, or else hidden behind the distinguished names of the great talmudic rabbis. No complete written documents are extant from the earlier period (unless we assume that *Sefer Yetzirah* belongs to this period, a rather dubious conjecture). However, here and there in the Talmud and Midrashim we do find remnants of the ancient mystical tradition. By contrast, from the later stage of development—which is admittedly connected with the earlier stage by a continuous chain of development and which preserved many early traditions—there is an entire extant literature, consisting of those works known as the Hekhalot books *(Hekhalot Rabbati, Hekhalot Zutarti, Masekhet Hekhalot, Merkabah Rabbah,* etc.), as well as a number of later related Midrashim (especially *The Alphabet of Rabbi Akiva, Pirkei de-Rabbi Eli'ezer,* and *Midrash Konen).*

The greater part of these writings seem to have been edited in Babylonia, but they also include extensive Palestinian material. In any event, the religious movement reflected therein was centered in the East, in the Persian and Byzantine Empires.

This movement has a very striking character. Its practitioners, rather than build a theology, a theoretical mystical doctrine, sought to guide man toward certain mystical experiences, which they are intent upon describing. They also engage in speculations concerning the creation of the world (Acts of Creation). The focus of mystery here is doubtless the mystery of the Throne of Glory. Their intention is to instruct those select few who are capable of doing so to climb the ladder of ascent of the soul, via all the heavens and palaces, until reaching the Throne of Glory. The moment it reaches the Throne of Glory, in the world of the Merkabah (the Divine Chariot), the soul receives revelations of those things which most engaged the hearts of these mystics, such as: the curtain of the Throne of Glory, which is understood as the place where the Godhead stands and from whence He creates and rules the world; the order of Creation (cosmology); the ministering angels and destroying angels; and the final redemption and End of Days. In one line of development of the secret of the Chariot, there was added to these an extremely holy doctrine, known here as *Shi'ur Komah* (The Measure of the Shape)—that is, the revelation of the dimensions of the divine body in which is revealed His Glory as the Creator and as He who sits upon the throne. All of these things are very close to myth, even in those cases in which the ideas invoked are based upon verses from the Bible and the like. At a later date, the traditions of *Shi'ur Komah* aroused particularly intense opposition among the theologians of a purified Judaism (e.g., Saadiah Ga'on, Maimonides), who saw in it a stumbling block to faith. Meanwhile, it would appear that the advocates of these opinions held a certain negative attitude toward historical reality: their apathy toward this stands out even more strongly than it does among contemporary *aggadic* authors. The disasters and sufferings of the period, the persecutions on the part of the Christian church, beginning from the fourth century C.E., directed the religious interest of these mystics ever more strongly toward the supernal world—that is, toward the world of the Chariot, to the pre-history of Creation—or to the end of history, to the day when the son of David would come. These thinkers completely ignored the historical world in the real sense of the word, something which is quite characteristic. Unfortunately, it is impossible on the basis of the sources available to us to arrive at a clear picture of the social background of the Merkabah mystics during this latter period. Man as such is of almost no interest to them. Their yearnings and concentration are directed exclusively toward God and the worlds of light and brilliance surrounding Him, which constitute the Chariot.

The Merkabah mystics longed for elevation of the soul, for ecstasy. The perfect man, according to their deepest wish, is the ascetic who separates himself from the world, who prepares his soul for the ecstatic ascent to the supernal world of the Divine Throne by fasting and descending to his own deepest essence. This ascent of the soul—which is referred to in the books belonging to this second stage by the surprising name, "The Descent to the Merkabah"—is here the center. All of the ideas of the Merkabah mystics concerning the ascent of the soul, its stations and levels and the dangers involved therein—strongly connect these circles with the gnostic tendencies in the religions of late antiquity.

This mysticism restricts its wisdom to a limited circle of those who have been initiated into the divine secrets, who fulfill certain conditions: it appears initially as a secret doctrine to be revealed only to the modest ones, a kind of Jewish mystery religion cognate to the other mystery religions known from that period. All this lends the Merkabah mystics a certain place within the framework of religious life of that period, which embraces extensive circles. Graetz, Zunz, and others thought that the mysticism of the Hekhalot literature originated in a later period, and that one can find therein signs of Muslim influence; however, this view is no longer credible. All of the major elements of this Jewish gnosticism had already been shaped prior to the seventh century, when Islam began.

The image of God is clearer here than that of the human seeker of the divine secret. On this point, the Jewish form of gnosticism is strikingly different from its Christian and pagan counterparts. These other forms posit a deep chasm between the true, hidden God, who is the good God of the soul, and that God who is the Righteous, who is the Creator and ruler of the world. Gnosticism is fond of bringing this Creator God down from His sublime heights to a lower place, seeing in Him the God of the Jews. By contrast, such dualistic belief is unknown to the Hekhalot literature. They wish to develop a strictly monotheistic form of gnosticism, according to which the God of Israel is the true God of the mystics.

Regarding their conceptions of the Divine word, one should note the following characteristic features: first, that this God is first and foremost the holy king. The hearts of the mystics are aroused to boundless ecstasy when they contemplate those attributes of God expressing the sublimity and loftiness of His kingdom, the unending influx of His holiness, and the pleasing solemnity of His otherness. Their hearts are not particularly attuned toward God's compassionate aspects; this aspect of Divine Revelation fails to attain living expression among them. The descriptions of their visions, as well as their songs and praises—which the Merkabah mystics heard when they stood before the Throne of Glory, and which are repeated in their writings, especially in *Hekhalot Rabbati*—stress the above-mentioned aspects in extremely exaggerated fashion. God's sanctity is not subjected here to an ethical interpretation; His sanctity is synonymous with the sensations of awe, fear, and trembling that surround Him. This sanctity imposes irrational fear upon one who gazes at the sight of the Merkabah, and in this sense only a holy king emerges in the living religious experience of this mystic. Even at the heights of ecstasy, the Merkabah mystic maintains the integrity of his personality—he stands in the presence of the Divine throne as a creature, as one who acknowledges and declares the mighty majesty of his king. There is no room here for confusion of God and man, nor does this mysticism know of the negation of the human personality in the depths of godliness. The strictly monotheistic interpretation which they give to the acts of enthrallment and of descent before the throne leave no room for pantheistic elements that obscure the depth separating Creator and creature. What is predominant here over the religious sentiment is the mysticism of God as emperor, as the cosmocreator or absolute ruler—i.e., what is known to us from the end of antiquity and the early Middle Ages in Western countries as emperor mysticism.

The influence of the Merkabah mystics is still felt in certain sections of the *Siddur* as well as in liturgical poetry *(piyyut)*. From these circles there originates in particular the formulation of the *Kedushah* (doxology) in the morning prayer for weekdays and Sabbaths. One of the most characteristic Hekhalot poems, *Ha-Aderet veha-Emunah le-Ḥay ha-'Olamim* (Glory and Faith to the Life of the Universe!) even entered into the Yom Kippur *Maḥzor,* while several works of the earliest *paytanim* were composed in the style of these songs and hymns.

Mystical tendencies of the opposite kind, which did not find clear and systematic expression such as those in the movement of Merkabah mystics, may be found in both the earlier and later *aggadah*. To these belong the fashioning of the concept of the *Shekhinah,* so characteristic of the *aggadic* Midrashim. The *Shekhinah* is that aspect of God which dwells within the creation and is revealed to man. In the later Midrash, we find signs of a tendency toward its personification, of the shaping of its image as a divine quality, analogous to that process which had occurred earlier in the shaping of the figures of the Attribute of Judgment and the Attribute of Mercy. But there is still no connection between the idea of the *Shekhinah* and the understanding of God by the Merkabah mystics, who found God, not within the world, but outside of it and separate from it in an absolute way, in the image of the holy king who dwells in the chambers of the palace of pride.

But there were also circles which engaged in gnostic speculations and gnostic mythology to a far more striking degree than that to be seen in the Orthodox Jewish gnosticism of the Hekhalot literature. We do not have any exact information concerning these circles, but certain echoes of such ideas and traditions came down to the earliest medieval Kabbalists, such as the editors of *Sefer ha-Bahir.*

We also find a unique form of mystical meditation in *Sefer Yetzirah,* which at least in terms of its language is strongly connected with the Merkabah literature. It is difficult to establish its date, which is evidently somewhere between the third and seventh centuries. This book represents the first known attempt at theoretical thought in the Hebrew language. The words of this short book are formulated with great solemnity, but also in very confused fashion with regard to the major elements of its teaching, but it seems at times as if the things flowed from mystical contemplation. The book is multi-faceted, for which reason it was used by both philosophers and Kabbalists during the Middle Ages. The book deals with the basic elements of the world which are, in its author's opinion, the ten primal numbers, which he calls the ten *Sefirot* of *belimah* (possibly nothingness), and the twenty-two letters of the Hebrew alphabet. The letters and numbers of the Torah conceal secret powers, and every thing in the world, in the year, and in the soul is created from their combination. The *sefirot* and the letters are the thirty-two wondrous paths of wisdom, by whose means God created everything and will create everything which is to exist in the future. By means of brief aphorisms, the author explains the secret significance of each letter in terms of its function in the three circles of creation of which he knows, namely: man, the world, and the rhythmic progression of time in the year. *Sefer Yetzirah* seems to combine together ideas from the late Greek philosophers concerning the secret of numbers with original Jewish thought concerning the secrets of letters and language. This thought is based upon the assumption that, if by the word of God the heavens were created, the letters are the basis of this divine word and those selfsame ten sayings by which the world was created (according to the statement of the Mishnah).

ASHKENAZIC ḤASIDIM

From the Eastern lands, where it had already reached its peak, Merkabah mysticism moved into southern Italy (ca. eighth century), and from there to France and Germany. There were several circles there which engaged in it and cultivated it as an esoteric doctrine. Thereafter it became associated, particularly in Germany, with later elements: one finds influences from the teachings of R. Saadiah Ga'on, as well as various ideas associated with the neo-Platonists (especially in the writings of Rabbi Abraham Ibn Ezra and Rabbi Abraham bar Ḥiyya), as well as esoteric doctrines related to prayer, which sought to uncover secrets and allusions in the fixed text of the prayers, in the numerical values *(gematria)* of individual words and of entire sentences, etc. However, these elements only acquired true significance and influence once they had been absorbed by a new religious movement which reworked them according to its own spirit. The bearers of this movement were the circles known as Ashkenazic Ḥasidim *(Ḥasidei Ashkenaz)*, first known in the twelfth and particularly in the thirteenth century, but who continued to exercise profound influence upon the spiritual life of German Jewry long thereafter. From the religious viewpoint, the central personality of this movement was Rabbi Judah ben Shmuel he-Ḥasid, who died in 1217 in the city of Regensburg. However, its most important literary spokesman was his main disciple (who was not much younger than him), Rabbi Eleazar of Worms (Wormiza), who died ten or fifteen years later. The most important document of this movement was *Sefer Ḥasidim,* which is extant in a variety of versions. This wonderful book gives us a glimpse of the concrete life of the Jewish community and society in all of its manifestations and phenomena. The life of the Jews in Germany during this period is portrayed here in extremely realistic terms, albeit in light of a tremendous religious idea. The book did not undergo the same dogmatic or halakhic self-censorship such as that found in most other works of rabbinic literature; neither did there operate here those modern distortions which present the past life of the Jews as an idyll.

Mysticism appeared in an entirely new form among the circles of Ashkenazic Ḥasidim, even though they attempted to preserve the earlier heritage. There is hardly any doubt that the movement arose in response to the tremendous shocks brought about during the period of the Crusades and the related persecutions of Jewish society. Completely new ideas concerning God and man appear here upon the horizon of the masters of Jewish mysticism.

Ashkenazic Ḥasidism promulgates three main teachings pertaining to man's religious life: the new ethical ideal of the Ḥasid (the pious man) and pietism; its view of repentance and the act of repentance; and the esoteric meaning of prayer. A very striking human type is portrayed here as the ideal: essentially, the Ḥasid is the ascetic monk of the Middle Ages in Jewish dress. The true hero and possessor of mystical consciousness is not the master of ecstatic experience, but rather the Ḥasid, who is marked first and foremost by three characteristics: asceticism and abstinence from things of this world; complete equanimity, to the point where he is affected neither by words of praise nor by words of condemnation; and finally, love of others, carried here to an extreme. Underlying all this is a decidedly pessimistic world-view. The true Ḥasid is no longer the keeper of the keys of the secrets of the world of the Merkabah, but the humble, devoted ascetic who forgoes his own self. The social and ideological background of this entire movement, concerning the order of the world and its correction, and the perfection of man and society, are all elucidated by Yitzhak Baer in his study, "The Social-Religious Orientation of *Sefer Ḥasidim,*"[2] which likewise sheds light upon the connection between this Ḥasidism and the religious and ethical-social ideas of Christian movements during the same period.

At the beginning of his great work, *Sefer ha-Rokeaḥ,* Rabbi Eleazar of Worms formulated the extreme demands of Ḥasidic ethics in the form of laws of Ḥasidism, just as the understanding of repentance and its laws were formulated in the laws of *teshuvah* which follow them. There is a striking and very characteristic contrast here to Maimonides' *Mishneh Torah*, which was composed only a short time before *Sefer ha-Rokeaḥ*. In the former, there appears as the very keystone to this new structure of ha-lakhic rulings a chapter on metaphysics, which is completely alien to the spirit of the old Halakhah; whereas here we find chapters (likewise new in spirit, notwithstanding their reliance upon talmudic material) dealing with the ethics of asceticism and questions of social ethics. In *Sefer Ḥasidim* there is, so to speak, a formulation of that selfsame Ḥasidic teaching which had emerged previously here and there in the religious tradition. True, there is a possible conflict between the laws of Torah of the existing Halakhah practiced by the public, and the Ḥasidic laws of heaven, based upon natural honesty and trust. But the Ashkenazic Ḥasidim did not in fact seek conflicts with the Halakhah, and refrained from them in practice, because their extreme ethical demands were directed towards themselves and not toward the surrounding society. A person who trains himself to practice this central aspect of Ḥasidism attains the love of God, which the authors of this circle describe in the strongest sexual imagery.

Repentance, which did not occupy an important role in the thought of the mystics prior to this period, now received the most intensive treatment. The treatment of this issue by the Ashkenazic Ḥasidim and the principles expressed in its Laws of Repentance betray the powerful influence of customs and views found in their Christian surroundings. Thus, we find here certain tariffs fixing the precise act of repentance and its degree, according to each particular sin. The Ashkenazic Ḥasidim earned a reputation throughout the Jewish world for their mighty acts of atonement and their unusual and exaggerated penitential practices, such as rolling in snow or sitting on anthills. The concept of repentance by balance is characteristic of the new arrangements: the weighting and evaluation of repentance to correspond to the degree of pleasure which the person enjoyed from the sin.

Prayer likewise assumes here the nature of an esoteric enterprise filled with secrets, creating a connection between man and hidden forces. Instead of the enthusiastic and ecstatic prayer of the early Merkabah mystics, here prayer tends more toward the realm of magic. These magical practices (which afterwards became known by the term "Practical Kabbalah") altogether assume a very significant place in the words of many of the Ḥasidim. The true Ḥasid, who seeks nothing for himself, appears in folk legend as a master of the hidden powers, ruling over the secret names, the spirits, and angels. Everything belonging to this realm of false beliefs had a very decisive influence far beyond the ken of Askenazic Ḥasidism, even in the Judaism of subsequent generations.

In their rich literature, there likewise stands out their interest in questions concerning the World to Come. The life of the soul after death, the nature of the supernal pleasure and delights awaiting the righteous in the Garden of Eden and in the days of the Messiah (anticipated particularly for those killed for the Sanctification of the Name—*kiddush ha-Shem*), recompense and punishment in the World to Come—all these questions profoundly interested folk religion and the Ḥasidism which stemmed from it. By contrast, the majority of the theologians, who engaged in profound abstract speculations, did not at all crystallize their thoughts on these issues and did not formulate clear dogmatic definitions which obligated the believers. The uniquely trying circumstances of the period of the great persecutions added a strong stimulus to the imaginative power of these mystics.

Even the God of the Ḥasidim had completely new features. Alongside the old mysticism of the king of the Merkabah, "who sits in the chambers of his palace of pride," there appears the rationalism of R. Saadiah Ga'on as well as the original mystical thought of the Ḥasidim. Alongside the holy monarchy of the Holy One blessed be He, considerable place is taken by His absolute spirituality and infinity (which were so much stressed by R. Saadiah Ga'on), and particularly God's existence in every place. There are cases in which this great emphasis upon God's presence in everything and in every place is tantamount to a doctrine of immanence, the existence of God within the creation and not outside of it. God is at once the revealed and the hidden, the near and the far; in the words of the poet, "Further away than the highest heavens, closer to me than my flesh and blood" (from a poem by Abraham Ibn Ezra, *"Eshtaḥaveh apayim artzah"*). A completely different feeling emerges from the words of the Ḥasidim than from those of the early mystics. R. Eleazar of Worms says:

> For He is in every place, and sees the wicked and the good . . . And when [a person] blesses, he should turn his heart toward the Omnipresent. Therefore they established [that one should recite,] "Blessed art Thou," like one who speaks to his friend.

This feeling of intimacy with God is completely new in rabbinic Judaism. The presence of God within the world is stressed in a manner that is at times close to pantheism. The Song of Unity, adapting the doctrine of R. Saadiah Ga'on to the religious needs of the Ḥasidim, was composed in these circles. Here it says concerning the created beings and God: "All are within You, and You are in all of them; surrounding all and filling all;

being all, You are in all; before all, You were all; and when all was, You filled all." Another Ashkenazic Ḥasid said: "Everything is in Him, and He sees everything, for He is all-seeing, and He has not eyes to see with them, for He has the power to see within Himself."

In addition to this, the Ḥasidim had a unique esoteric doctrine. The secrets of the Godhead and of the divine Glory; the secret of the special cherub which sits upon the Throne, the matters of the throne itself, and the doctrine of the pre-creation images inscribed upon the curtain that is set before the Throne—these are the major elements of the doctrine of Ashkenazic Kabbalah in the Ḥasidic circles. A rather naive mythology is connected here to mystical experience and contemplation, without this connection bringing about a unity. In this doctrine, the *Shekhinah* is identified with the appearance of God above the Throne of Glory, but also with that of the immanent God who dwells in the world and in the inwardness of the soul.

SPANISH KABBALAH

From the end of the twelfth century on, a mystical movement of even greater importance emerges into the light of history for the first time. Its leaders and devotees call themselves *ba'alei kabbalah* (that is, masters of the [true mystical] tradition), *ba'alei ḥokhmah* (masters of wisdom), *ba'alei emunah* (masters of faith), or *ba'alei ha-'avodah* (masters of [divine] service). The earliest origins of this movement predate its historical appearance, which took place in the Provençal district of southern France and in Catalonia. Analysis of the earliest sources of this Kabbalistic literature (particularly *Sefer ha-Bahir)* indicates that its historical manifestation was preceded by a certain development which took place in France, evidently among circles which were not necessarily learned in Torah. There arrived in these circles, at first directly from the countries of the Levant and thereafter via the circles of Ashkenazic Ḥasidism, a variety of ancient traditions and teachings. These were the remnants of early writings of a Gnostic-Jewish character, expressing extraordinary ideas of a mythological nature concerning God and His powers. In any event, it is impossible to determine on the basis of these surviving remnants whether this early Kabbalah was particular orthodox in outlook. In fact, *Sefer ha-Bahir* was initially considered among the pious as an heretical book; we have extant complaints concerning it from the rabbis of southern France.

But these ideas only achieved importance once they were combined, beginning in the second half of the twelfth century, with the intellectual heritage of the schools of neo-Platonic philosophy of that period. These

combinations of ideas developed in the Spanish Kabbalah of the thirteenth and fourteenth centuries with tremendous power and in a variety
of different directions. One should emphasize that this development took
place within the geographic and spiritual sphere of the Western-Christian
world, and had a strong connection to the religious life of that world, so
that the possible importance of the Muslim mystical influence ought not
to be exaggerated. Large areas of the Provençal district, where this new
mysticism initially struck roots, were at the time decisively influenced by
the Christian movement of the Catharists or New Manicheans, who held
a dualistic world-view (the good God—creator of the soul; the bad God—
creator of nature and of the body). This strong folk movement was only
suppressed during the course of the thirteenth century, by fire and sword,
by the Christian church. Thus, the first stages of the development of Kabbalah, during the twelfth century, occurred in a religious atmosphere filled
with tension and great excitement. It succeeded in attracting a number of
outstanding Orthodox talmudic scholars; from then on, Kabbalists always
appear in the guise of faithful, pious Jews, and it was in this image alone
that Kabbalah fulfilled its historic task.

Around 1200 the Kabbalah moved to Spain. Centers of the new movement were established in the small town of Gerona (in Catalonia), in Burgos, in Toledo, and in other places. The most important center was that of
the Kabbalists of Gerona. Here the new teachings and impulses which had
found their way to the members of this circle via the Provençal Kabbalist
Rabbi Isaac Sagi Nahor (the Blind; son of Rabbi Abraham ben David of
Posquières, contemporary and critic of Maimonides) were formulated and
expanded, and a rich Kabbalistic literature was created. Rabbi Moses ben
Naḥman (known as Ramban or Naḥmanides), the most important religious personality in Spain between 1230 and 1270 and a recognized halakhic authority, stood at the head of this camp. The number of Kabbalists
in Spain became progressively greater during his generation and the following one, and the religious ferment among them impresses us by its
great power. We find here profound attempts to develop the theory of Kabbalah (Rabbi Azriel of Gerona), and to create a synthesis with the contemporary philosophy which followed in the footsteps of Maimonides (Isaac
Ibn Latif). Alongside these, there developed streams of a totally different
direction, among whom the world of myth and of mythological thought
were strengthened, assuming an old-new guise. To this group belong the
brothers Jacob and Isaac Ha-Cohen, Rabbi Todros Abulafia, and Rabbi
Moses of Burgos. The greatest Kabbalists (such as Rabbi Isaac the Blind)
were considered to have been graced with the Holy Spirit and to have received their doctrines from Elijah the prophet, while others (such as Rabbi

Jacob Ha-Cohen of Segovia) relied explicitly upon heavenly revelations and drew their thought from visionary sources. Abraham Abulafia was the most extreme spokesman for a school of theoretical and practical mysticism which unabashedly yearned for the renewal of prophecy and a new revelation. He was born in Saragossa in 1240 and received his prophetic revelation in Barcelona in 1270, but most of his subsequent life was spent in Italy and Sicily. He systematically developed the doctrine of prophetic Kabbalah, which instructs how, by means of certain guided contemplative exercises, man may prepare himself to receive prophetic states of departure from one's bodily vessels and revelation of the *Shekhinah*. According to his own testimony, he also had connections with non-Jewish mystics. Among his disciples and later, during the fourteenth century, his doctrine of contemplation, based upon combination of the letters of the Hebrew alphabet (the wisdom of combination), became mixed with other branches of Kabbalah, and was highly influential. Ignorant people were also involved in this new movement, as shown by the awakening of the prophet in Avila in 1295: the prophet was a simple artisan who wrote a book of secrets which he received from one of the angels.

During the second half of the thirteenth century, we find an impressive mixture of all of the streams of Spanish Kabbalah in the kingdom of Castile, particularly in the numerous works of Rabbi Joseph Gikatilla (author of *Sha'arei Orah*, the best introduction to the teachings of Spanish Kabbalah) and of Rabbi Moses de Leon (from the city of Guadalajara), who evidently died in 1305. Moses de Leon is to be considered the principal author of *Sefer ha-Zohar*, the major literary document of Spanish Kabbalah. This book appeared under the guise of an Aramaic Midrash which reputedly originated in the circle of R. Simeon bar Yoḥai during the second century C.E. Its author does not attempt a systematic, theoretical exposition of the teaching of Spanish Kabbalah—such as is found in that generation, for example, in the work *Ma'arekhet ha-Elohut*, whose author is not known with certainty. The author of the *Zohar* made these doctrines the basis for his homiletics, utilizing them rather than expounding them. A homileticist of great sweep, his book is the most convincing testimony to the revival of myth and mythic thought in the heart of medieval Jewry. The main bulk of the book was composed between the years 1275–1285, while in the last years of the thirteenth century two additional books (possibly by a different author) were added, which claim to be a kind of continuation of the main work: *Sefer Ra'aya Mehemna* (The Faithful Shepherd), concerning the rationales for the commandments; and *Sefer ha-Tikkunim* or *Tikkunei ha-Zohar*, expounding the first word of the Torah, *Bereshit* (in the beginning).

Prior to the acceptance among wider circles of the *Zohar* as a holy and authoritative book (a process only completed after the expulsion from Spain), several other developments occurred within Kabbalah during the course of the fourteenth century. A particularly central role was played here by the polemic within Jewish philosophy. Among the Kabbalists themselves, one finds an opposition between theistic and pantheistic tendencies regarding the understanding of the doctrine of the Godhead. Several Spanish Kabbalists continued the line of the *Zohar* and composed various other books under the guise of the ancient sages, and here too Kabbalah reached its most extreme stage: during the second half of the fourteenth century, were composed *Sefer ha-Peli'ah* (on *Parashat Bereshit)* and *Sefer ha-Kanah* (on the commandments). In the course of a severe critique of Halakhah and of a simplistic halakhic Judaism, the anonymous author of these works arrives at the conclusion that there is no *peshat* (literal meaning) at all, either of the Oral Torah or the Written Torah, and that the secret, esoteric teaching is in fact the only authentic content of Judaism. Thus, the traditional halakhic way of life only receives its confirmation and justification from the Kabbalistic interpretation given to it. After the edicts of the year 1391, Spanish Kabbalah did not create anything original.

What historical and social function was fulfilled by Kabbalah among Spanish Jewry from the year 1250, in light of the special conditions of this Jewry? How is one to explain the fact that the Kabbalah, which was created within a narrow esoteric elite, a spiritual aristocracy, became transformed over the course of time into an historical and social force in Judaism? The answer is that the Kabbalists appeared not only as mystics and esoteric devotees, but also as ideologists defending the folk religion. Kabbalah fought the tendency toward excessive abstraction of the contents of Judaism, strongly manifested in the rationalistic philosophy of the enlightened ones of that generation, in which it saw a danger to Jewish life. In other words: if philosophy was interested in purifying faith in correct conceptual formulation so as not, Heaven forbid, to harm the unity and transcendence of God, the Kabbalah was interested in the vitalization of this belief. It came to save holistic and non-emptied Judaism, the Judaism of the simple believer who was confused by new historical conditions, through simplified formulations. In such works as *Sefer ha-Zohar, Sefer ha-Peli'ah* and *Sefer ha-Kanah,* the function of Kabbalah as "a project of national-religious romanticism and of mystical-ascetic reform" stands out (Yitzhak Baer). The Kabbalah is initially concerned with only a small number of problems (the secret of the Godhead, the secret of prayer, and the reason for the mitzvot and for the non-rational laws of the Torah).

However, it gradually expands its ken to encompass most realms of religious life in its mystical interpretation of Judaism. It felt itself to be a conservative force, the spokesman of the tradition against innovators, in its war against philosophical enlightenment. However, during the course of this struggle Kabbalah developed a completely new understanding of Judaism and of its values. Among the decisive reasons for the success of Kabbalah, one must take into consideration the fact that, by means of its own axioms, it was capable of shedding much light specifically upon those realms concerning which the Jewish enlightenment of the Middle Ages had nothing vital or original of its own to say, such as the reality of exile or the entire realm of the way of life created by the Halakhah.

On this basis, it seems reasonable to assume that the small class of wealthy court Jews who were involved with the interests and intrigues of politics or tax and tariff farming did not see the Kabbalists as representing them. On the other hand, the Kabbalah became the spokesman for poor talmudic scholars and pious householders. The ideas of the Kabbalah helped to free them of the entanglements of history from which they suffered, on the basis of its own unique approach: rather than leap forward toward the miraculous messianic End, the Kabbalist sought to return to the pristine beginnings of the Creation. This flight from history is characteristic of Spanish Kabbalah, which was wholeheartedly devoted to questions of the Creation—and there were even those Kabbalists who were interested themselves particularly in those acts of creation which preceded Genesis, in the "worlds which were destroyed."

In order to describe the world-view of Spanish Kabbalah, we shall need to focus upon a number of main points. In terms of the detailed solutions, these basic problems are discussed in several different approaches and tendencies. There is no complete uniformity in the answers (albeit they do have a great deal in common), but there is coordination and unity in the posing of the questions.

1. Mystical Symbolism

The philosophers fashioned concepts, while the mystic created symbols. What is the meaning of the mystical "symbol"? The allusion, the metaphor, the allegory—all these are regular forms of thought even outside of the realm of Kabbalah. The rationalistic philosophers, no less than the Kabbalists, took trouble to discover the inwardness, the hidden things of Jewish teaching and of the world as a whole. But the symbol, the *sod* (secret) of the Kabbalist, has a special character. The allusions of the philosophers and the homilies of the *aggadah* both begin and end within

the world of human speech and expression, in which the metaphor belongs to the same universe of discourse as the object to which it refers.
Thus, in principle it should be possible (should one wish to do so) to express them directly, in their own right, without resorting to metaphor at
all. If the stories of the Torah allude to the philosophical truths of Aristotle, if Ezekiel's tale of the chariot alludes to the celestial spheres and as-
tronomy, then that which is alluded to is not beyond the boundaries of
expression and does not necessarily require the metaphor in order to be
expressed.

Not so the Kabbalistic symbol. It is true that here too there are many allusions of the former type. But it is not they which determine its true face.
In Kabbalah, one is speaking of a reality which cannot be revealed or expressed at all save through the symbolic allusion. A hidden authentic reality, which cannot be expressed in itself and according to its own laws,
finds expression in the symbol. It follows from this that every authentic
symbol involves an aspect of mystery. It expresses in brief that which the
mouth cannot utter and the ear cannot hear. The Kabbalist discovers the
duality within everything: he finds in it an entire revealed world: everything is reflected in everything, but in addition to this he finds there
something else mysterious, which is not taken into consideration by its
meaning and expression. Anything that becomes a symbol can take us
into the great depths that lie beneath, to the great inexpressible, to the aspect of the Nothing. Through means of the symbol, there is revealed hidden light from the concealed life of the Infinite that illuminates from
within. This light, which comes as it were from afar, and which is nevertheless intermingled within the essence of everything, is that which designates the level of reality upon which the Kabbalist draws. One could say
that all of creation is only a language, a symbolic expression of that level
which cannot be apprehended by thought, and that this level serves as a
basis for every structure which is subject to apprehension through
thought. The entire world is thus a symbolic body, within whose concrete
reality there is reflected a divine secret.

2. The Torah

If the entire world is one great symbol and it is entirely filled with symbols
in each and every detail, how much more so the Torah![3] This symbolic
understanding of the nature of the Torah is primarily expressed in three
things. First: the Torah is a living organism, a tapestry woven from the In-
effable Name of God. The Divine Name is itself a mysterious organism,
containing the hidden life of the Godhead and of all the worlds. In the

weave of the combinations of the Divine Name there appears the primeval
subject of all revelation. The Torah is therefore not a dead or calcified
thing. Rather, in each of its "limbs," in each and every word, there shine
forth an infinite number of lights and secrets, the literal meaning of the
verse being no more than the outermost one of these lights. "The Torah
has seventy faces," and any contemplation of it exposes new faces. One
must add to this, secondly, the understanding of the Torah as a complex of
laws determining every hidden event within the world. Any historical element within the Torah alludes to the hidden history of the world, to the
hidden process of the life of the cosmos which is none other than the concealed life of the Creator contained in the Torah and revealed from within.
Finally, one must mention here the concept of the four methods of interpreting the Torah. This idea first appears in the *Sefer ha-Zohar*, but there is
no doubt that it was borrowed from medieval Christian exegesis. The
Torah may be interpreted in four different ways: *peshat*—the literal meaning of Scripture; *derash*—*aggadic* elaboration; *remez* (or *muskal*)—the allegorical interpretation, based upon philosophical premises; *sod*—the
revelation within the verse of a hidden symbol of the secret of the Godhead. These four methods are alluded to, through their initial letters, in
the word *pardes*—the hidden garden which the Kabbalist enters through
his studies. These ideas also imply a certain critique of the Torah, concealed in Kabbalistic garb: if the narratives of the Torah really only contain
that which the literalist exegetes claim to find therein—says the author of
the *Zohar*—then on the basis of its surface contents we could write a better
Torah today! Some particularly extreme Kabbalists, such as the author of
the Zoharic *Ra'aya Mehemna* and others who followed his approach in the
fourteenth century, did not hold back curses and vigorous attacks upon
the devotees of literal interpretation and philosophical allegory, and attempted to prove that there is no place for these approaches at all in the
understanding of Torah.

3. The New Theosophic Concept of God

The central importance of the new theosophic concept of God developed
by the Kabbalists. By its means, they attempted to save the living God of
popular faith from the emptying which came about through the philosophers' rationalistic understanding of God. The two poles around which
the theoretical interest of the Kabbalist revolve are the new God (who is
essentially, according to Kabbalistic belief, none other than the old God,
the Creator of Genesis and the giver of the Torah) and man who confronts
Him. The Kabbalists distinguish two aspects within the Godhead. The one

is God as He is in His own essence, God who hides within the depths of Himself, whom they called the "Infinite"; the second is the God who reveals Himself as Creator and guide of the worlds. There are cases where this Infinite is understood in a personal way (He who has no End!) and others where it is understood in a non-personal way (that which has no end!). Insofar as the Infinite was understood as the non-personal, concealed element within the Godhead, it becomes a personal image when it awakens and is revealed as emanating and creating.

Only God in His aspect of Creator is the living God of religious faith, the God of Israel. He is portrayed and revealed in ten images or qualities or descriptive terms, which the Kabbalists referred to by the set term, *sefirot*— a term borrowed from *Sefer Yetzirah,* albeit here it acquires an entirely different meaning. The Kabbalist, who yearns for the hidden flow of life in everything, finds it even in the Godhead itself. God's unity is the unity of His hidden life, present in the life of man and in the life of the entire universe. This flow of life and its fixed pace is revealed in the *sefirot,* with which all Kabbalistic books deal at length, using every possible kind of symbolic and allusive language. The *sefirot* are the waves of hidden life within the Godhead, which flow from the depths of the Infinite into the created world, the emanation of this fullness being the hidden and mysterious innerness of Creation itself. When we speak of the secret of the act of creation, we are speaking of this innerness and emanation of the realm of the *sefirot.* The existence of this hidden life, around which revolve all the secrets of the Kabbalists, is only attained by means of symbols. Each *sefirah* has any number of names or terms—that is, symbols which allude to them.

The Kabbalists love to describe the *sefirot* as different levels of revelation of the Godhead in His emanation and creation, from the very highest level in the aspect of divine "Nothingness" *(ayi"n)* down to the *Shekhinah,* which is the aspect of the "I" *(an"i)* embodying the personal image of the Godhead. The following is the order of the ten *sefirot,* using those names by which they were most usually designated by the Kabbalists of Gerona:

  a. Keter 'Elyon (Supreme Crown), also known as Primeval Will or Nothing.

  b. Hokhmah (Wisdom) or Thought, or Primal Point, or The Source of Life.

  c. Binah (Understanding, Intuition) or Divine Intellect or The River That Goes out of Eden from the Source of Wisdom.

  d. Hesed (Kindness / Grace) or Greatness or The Right Hand of God.

  e. Din or *Gevurah* (Judgment or Strength) or The Left Hand of God.

  f. Rahamim or *Tiferet* (Mercy / Compassion or Grandeur), the power that mediates between *Hesed* and *Din.*

  g. Netzah (Eternity or Victory).

h. Hod (Splendor).

i. Yesod (Foundation) or *Tzaddik Ḥay 'Olamim* (The Righteous One, Life of the Worlds). In this last *sefirah* all the flowing and fructifying forces of the divine life are concentrated, and it is therefore considered to be the male element. From there they flow into the tenth *sefirah.*

j. The final *sefirah,* identified by the Kabbalists with the *Shekhinah* of the Midrash, is called *Malkhut* (kingship) or *'Atarah* (crown). This last *sefirah* is the vessel which receives all of the active attributes, and is considered the female component within the Godhead, the Queen or Matron *(Matronita).* This power of the *Shekhinah,* resident in every place, is none other than the hidden radiance of the totality of the hidden divine life which dwells in every created and existing being.

These, then, are the ten "powers of the Holy One blessed be He." When they develop from one another in an organic way, they constitute the tree of the *sefirot,* in which the divine organism grows, like a tree which grows from its hidden root until its full manifestation.

The Kabbalists used an endless number of symbols to describe the inner world of the *sefirot,* using all sorts of metaphors to describe the divine reality which is beyond description. Thus, the God revealed in the *sefirot* is thought of as the "Primal Man," the spiritual model in whose image Adam was created. One may also understand from this why the Kabbalists to a certain extent defended the principle of corporeality—that is, the material expression used by the language of faith in relation to God. Nowhere do the books of the Bible or the other sources of faith speak about the Infinite, or the hidden God, but only of the living, revealed God. Yet it is to Him, the Hidden Face of God—that is, to the Primal Man that sits upon the throne of the Chariot—and only to Him, that these symbols allude which, being of necessity borrowed from our world, must be corporeal and human. On this significant point as well—and the relentless struggle of the philosophers against the corporealizers is well known—the Kabbalists appear explicitly as the theoretical defenders of the concept of God as imagined by the simple and naive pious Jew. Nor do the Kabbalists hesitate to use language of great daring and extreme corporeality in their books as well (as in the *Zohar)* when they wish to refer to the most delicate and subtle matters. The many logical difficulties and contradictions, which could easily be discovered in the concept of the *sefirot,* served subsequent generations as stimuli to the further development and shaping of the theoretical teachings of the Kabbalists regarding the secret of the Godhead. Rabbi Moses Cordovero in Safed and Rabbi Joseph Ergas in Italy were outstanding for the theoretical depth of their attempts to introduce conceptual clarity into the theosophic doctrine of the *sefirot.* But one can-

not ignore the truth imminent in the descriptions of the world of emanation and of the *sefirot*. In the works of the Spanish Kabbalists, we frequently find the strengthening of an ancient mythology which they
attempted to connect with monotheistic faith, if not always with great
success. But then neither did the living God of folk religion ever correspond to the God of theological orthodoxy, to the refined faith of the
philosophers in a God who was confined to the realm of abstract concepts.

4. Creation and the Cosmic Processes

Creation of the cosmic processes were understood by many Kabbalists as
the emergence of the hidden divine life. Hence, the *sefirot* act here too in
the external realm which reveals and reflects the inner. The divine light
descends in many stages and is emanated below to bring about the lower
creation, except that within the innermost part of the creation there remains an emanation or residue of these powers of creation, which gives
the world its symbolic radiance and glory. Within this overall world picture may be found various lines of a theistic or pantheistic direction and,
depending upon the tendency of the individual Kabbalist, one aspect or
another is emphasized within their system, the dispute between the two
tendencies never being ultimately decided. A strictly theistic formulation
of the Kabbalistic position is found, for example, in Joseph Ibn Waqar of
Toledo (ca. 1330), who was anticipated by one generation in a pantheistic
formulation of this idea by David ben Abraham Ha-Lavan, in his book *Ma-
soret ha-Berit*. The *Zohar* fluctuates between the two positions, but tends
to formulate the relationship of God to the world more in terms of a theistic approach. All of the great Spanish Kabbalists agree on one point: they
do not understand the doctrine of the creation of the world *ex nihilo* literally, using these words in the exact opposite sense: the "Nothing" from
which everything was created is not outside of the divine being (as the literal meaning of this doctrine would have it), but is itself the hiddenmost
aspect of God. This Nothing is in fact the first *sefirah,* so that even in the
transition from the world of the *sefirot* to the world of created things there
is no room for a new act of creation literally from nothing. This is an outstanding example of preserving a theological formula while emptying it
of its content.

5. Man

Man appears here in an unmediated relationship to God, which has only
been interrupted since Adam's sin. The nature of sin and of evil in general is

separation, that is, the placing of being cut off from God in its own domain. The good places man within the flow of uninterrupted divine life; evil cuts him off from it. The authentic man (who is, of course, the authentic Jew) is the master of the creation, and this in a very explicit sense: the cosmic process is carried on without disturbance by virtue of man's activity, which serves as a balance to this process, or at times, in a more mechanical approach, even as its mechanic. The entire life of creation is reflected therein and is itself a microcosm, but since it is composed of everything and connected to everything, it can also act upon everything. The observance of the Torah and the commandments returns man to a state of direct connection with God. Through the fulfillment of the Torah, man becomes subjugated, not to the laws of the Torah, but to the hidden law determining the life of the universe that is included within the Torah. The life of the Jewish person is not subject to the laws of nature, but is a continuous line of hidden miracles in which God acts, not merely as the ultimate first cause at the end of a long chain of causality, but as the unmediated cause of every situation and of every event. All of the goals of the Torah and everything which occurs in the Land of Israel are such hidden miracles.

6. The Secret of the Positive Commandment

This, then, is the secret of the positive commandments: to awaken an impulse in the right place in the inner world; while the secret of the negative commandments is to reject those impulses which are likely to disturb the secret order of the unity of creation. In the act of mitzvah, the life of the Jew is manifested as a symbol for the primeval secret itself. Since every step in the life of the Jew is of importance for the world as a whole, the Kabbalists were able to create an ideology of Halakhah which had profound influence upon the Jewish community. Such an ideology is fully developed in the later level of the *Sefer ha-Zohar*, namely, the *Ra'aya Mehemna*, and in no less extreme form in *Sefer ha-Peli'ah*, and *Sefer ha-Kanah*.

Thus the *Shekhinah* itself dwells within the Congregation of Israel, which conducts its life according to the secret rhythm of the life of the universe. The law of the world, the conduct of the world which is none other than the hidden life of the Godhead itself, is embodied in the personal image of the symbol of the *Shekhinah*.

The explicitly Jewish character of this mystical doctrine of the nature of man is also revealed in its positive evaluation of sexual life, within the limits of the Halakhah. While it is true that the Kabbalah is not without ascetic tendencies of abstinence and renunciation, it does not in principle counsel sexual celibacy (as do several movements of religious mysticism among the other nations). On the contrary, since the *Iggeret ha-Kodesh* attributed to Naḥmanides, the Kabbalists saw in the union of man and wife a holy and sacred mystery.

7. Mystical Psychology

Suitable to its understanding of man is Kabbalah's mystical psychology. The various levels of the soul likewise emanate from a supernal source in the *sefirot* world. One should in particular note the *Zohar*'s doctrine of the existence of an intuitive psychological power within man (the *nishmata kaddisha* or "holy soul," in the language of the *Zohar*), which is not part of the psycho-physical organism, but develops within man insofar as he is steadfast in acquiring and actualizing religious apprehensions and values. This holy soul contains the deepest religious consciousness. In this highest secret level of the soul, into which there shine the supernal *sefirot*, man connects with God via the *kavvanah* (intention) that penetrates to the depths of the Godhead and opens the sources of supernal plenitude which shine upon man, particularly during the time of worship. (Incidentally, this doctrine involves a substitution for and mystical reinterpretation of the medieval Aristotelian doctrine of cognition concerning the acquired intellect in man and its connection to the divine active intellect.)

8. Devekut

The ultimate religious value placed by Spanish Kabbalah in the center of its ethics is *devekut* (communion with God). This term refers to constant attachment to God, to the unmediated connection which occupies here almost all of that place which in other mystical doctrines is taken by the ecstatic experience. While *devekut* is, it is true, the closest and most intimate relation to God, it is not *unio mystica*—it is not the union of the soul with the Creator, nor does it entail negation of the independent existence of the soul or its complete intermingling within the ocean of God. Hence, *devekut* does not depend upon abnormal states of mind, notwithstanding its realization through acts of contemplation and meditation. Naḥmanides already taught that true *devekut* can be realized specifically through the life of the individual within society, and not necessarily through withdrawal from it. It is likely, therefore, to appear as a mystical social value. All of the other values in Kabbalistic ethics—fear of God, love of God, love of man, purity of heart and modesty, acts of kindness, Torah study, repentance, and prayer—are hence directed toward *devekut* as a supreme value. It is these ethical commandments in which *Sefer ha-Zohar* is most interested.

These values and their interpretation by the Kabbalists lend a certain supernal radiance to the qualities of the humble and the pious, and one also receives a very characteristic picture in terms of social ethics. This situation likewise suits the notion of poverty as a religious value, a doctrine which appears in rabbinic Judaism for the first time in *Sefer ha-Zohar* and the *Ra'aya Mehemna*.[4] The poor are the "broken vessels of the Holy One blessed be He," and in a certain sense the *Shekhinah* itself is "poor." The righteous man *(tzaddik)* of the *Zohar* is one who manifests attachment to God through means of Torah, mitzvot, and prayer, but first and foremost one who "guards the covenant"—that is, who observes the strictest sexual chastity, although he is forbidden to practice total abstinence. It is also hardly an accident that, among those values that are cherished in the Kabbalah, there is hardly any room for those of an intellectual nature (apart from Torah study). In their ethical teaching as well, which is directed more to the values associated with the will than to those of intellect, the Kabbalists appear as the mystical ideologues of a folk religion.

9. Eschatology

The Spanish Kabbalah likewise gives great weight to ideas concerning "the final things" (i.e, eschatology). Here too, as in Ashkenazic Ḥasidism, less stress is placed on the subjects of messianic redemption and the End of Days than on those pertaining to the life of the soul after death. The belief in the "metempsychosis" *(gilgul)* or reincarnation of the soul from one body to another (even to that of animals) appears here in various forms and variations. To a certain extent, the idea of reward or punishment for man's acts by means of reincarnation contradicts the rabbinic doctrine concerning punishment in *Gehinnom.* For most Kabbalists (including *Sefer ha-Zohar*) these two doctrines complement one another: the soul undergoes metempsychosis only for certain sins, or if a person dies without children. However, from the fourteenth century on, we find Kabbalists who interpret the entire doctrine of *Gehinnom* and its punishments as a metaphor for man's falling into the realm of transmigration, thereby removing the idea of *Gehinnom* from Jewish teaching entirely and interpreting metempsychosis as a general law of the cosmos. According to this view, all of man's deeds bring about reward or punishment in different forms of being, and all created things, from the angels down to the plant and mineral realms, are in a constant flow of transformation from one form to another, in accordance with this "law of transformation."[5] The pleasure of the righteous in the World to Come is no more than an additional measure of *devekut,* beyond that which they have already attained in their life in this world. The absorption of the soul within the "bundle of life," which is tantamount to the flow of hidden life, is the eschatological goal of the ascent of the soul to the world of the *sefirot*.

Thus, Spanish Kabbalah forged for itself an entire world-view of Judaism, as it appeared in the eyes of these mystics. However, except for certain isolated attempts, especially during the second half of the thirteenth century, the Kabbalists chose to forgo their wish to influence and to bring their contemplative world-view into the everyday life of the Jewish community on all its levels. The most outstanding spokesman of a Kabbalah which struggled to correct Jewish society in accordance with its principles was the author of *Ra'aya Mehemna,* the later part of the *Zohar,* and in his wake the author of *Sefer ha-Peli'ah.* It is true that most of them thought and even proclaimed that they alone had the correct key to the understanding of the Congregation of Israel and of Jewish life, but they did not seriously attempt to realize their demands in the historical life of the nation. Proof of this is found in those ethical works of that same period which were intended for the masses of people, where one finds only a small amount of propaganda on behalf of the Kabbalah, and hardly any mention at all of Kabbalistic doctrine. The major exceptions to this are the writings of Rabbi Baḥya ben Asher at the end of the thirteenth century.

KABBALAH AFTER THE EXPULSION FROM SPAIN

The status of the Kabbalah, as it has been described thus far, changed fundamentally following the expulsion from Spain. With the catastrophe of persecution and expulsion, the old intellectual world of the rationalist philosophers completely collapsed, the Kabbalah remaining the only force with religious vitality and renewed creative powers. It now undertook the project of the realization of its demands to remake Jewish society and began to penetrate into all of its levels. Only now does the *Zohar* begin to be recognized on much broader levels as a holy book, possessing religious authority alongside the Bible and the Talmud.

The entire sixteenth century was filled with intense religious ferment, and quite a few transformations began to take place in the heart of the Kabbalah itself under the influence of the expulsion from Spain. The most important factor in this process was the association of Kabbalah with messianism, which began to develop with tremendous power. Its combination with messianism gave Kabbalah its social impetus, and it was that which assured its supremacy in the nation for several hundred years.

Initially, a number of attempts were made to preserve Kabbalistic doctrines in their earlier form, alongside the messianic agitation which emerged from the Kabbalistic circles, especially in Italy and the Land of Israel. During the first forty years following the expulsion from Spain, the hope for immediate redemption was disseminated by means of this agitation. When these hopes failed to be realized, messianism assumed other forms and passed into deeper levels of religious life, penetrating the actual doctrines of the Kabbalists. This process occurred primarily in the new religious center of the Jewish people which took shape from about 1530 on in the town of Safed in the Upper Galilee. In Italy (where it underwent a great flowering), Kabbalah was influenced by the neo-Platonic philosophy which was widespread among Christians during the period of the Renaissance, whereas the new Kabbalah in Safed was almost entirely free of such influences. In the latter place, there lived together in one community an entire circle of Kabbalists who were gripped by deep religious enthusiasm. These included: Rabbi Joseph Caro, Rabbi Solomon Alkabez, Rabbi Abraham Galante, Rabbi David Ibn Zimra, Rabbi Eliezer Azikri and, especially, the three creative geniuses of the new movement: Rabbi Moses Cordovero (1522–1570), Rabbi Isaac Luria Ashkenazi (1534–1572), thereafter known by the acronym *Ar"i* ("Our Master Rabbi Yitzhak"; literally, "the Lion"), and his outstanding disciple, Rabbi Ḥayyim Vital (1543–1620).

Rabbi Moses Cordovero was the outstanding and most profound theoretician of the Kabbalah, as indicated by his books *Pardes Rimmonim, Shi'ur Komah,* and *Elimah Rabbati.* Luria himself, whose entire activity in Safed lasted for only two years, was the central religious personality and creator of the new myth in Kabbalah, while in Rabbi Ḥayyim Vital, Luria's teaching found its outstanding author, who reworked it and presented it systematically. The extensive literature known as the "writings of the *Ar"i"* was in fact written primarily by Vital, only a small part of it being written by other disciples of Luria or their disciples *('Etz Ḥayyim, Shemonah She'arim).*

In Safed were created religious societies which did not suffice with the cultivation of a Kabbalistic way of life among their own members, but which also disseminated this way of life among wider circles. Here were also composed the outstanding works of ethics *(Musar)* of the new Kabbalah, which were far more instrumental in bringing it to the popular consciousness than the careful learned presentation of Kabbalistic doctrine in the writings of Cordovero or Vital. The most important of these were Cordovero's *Tomer Devorah* (which expounds the ten *sefirot* as alluding to the scale of ascent of man's ethical perfection), *Reshit Ḥokhmah* by Rabbi Elijah de Vidas, *Sefer Ḥaredim* of Rabbi Eliezer Azikri, and *Sha'arei Kedushah* of Rabbi Ḥayyim Vital. These works paved the way for an extensive popular ethical literature which drew primarily upon the Kabbalah and which constituted the most characteristic testimony of the religious make-up of Jewish society until the end of the eighteenth century. Two great and comprehensive books enjoyed particularly profound influence: among the Ashkenazim, *Shenei luḥot ha-Berit (Shela"h)* by Rabbi Isaiah Horowitz and, in a later period among the Sephardim, the anonymously published *Ḥemdat Yamim*.

The ideas of the Safed Kabbalists became widely known due both to the impact of this literature and because of the agitation of religious associations which were organized, particularly in Italy, to disseminate the way of life of this new movement. This Kabbalah was spread and absorbed with great speed and remarkable power through all corners of the Diaspora: in Persia and Yemen, in Morocco and Turkey, no less than in Italy and Poland, Germany and Holland. From approximately 1625 on, the unique doctrines of Luria and his school began to predominate throughout the Jewish world. But not only did their religious ideas take root in the public; there were also numerous new customs promulgated by the Safed Kabbalists, rooted in esoteric teaching. Not always, but in most cases, these were habits and customs involving ascetic principles, subjugation to which became stronger in the life of both the individual and the public. Examples of these pious customs are the custom of not sleeping on the nights of Shavuot and Hoshana Rabbah, the transformation of Hoshana Rabbah from a festive day to one devoted to repentance, the transformation of the eve of the New Moon to a fast day known as "Little Yom Kippur," the introduction of numerous immersions in the ritual bath, and certain burial rites (such as processions around the dead body, etc.). Prayer, which in every period serves as a reflection of religious life, reveals the profound influence of the Kabbalists more emphatically. Many prayers written by Kabbalists, whether for the individual or the community, penetrated into the *Siddur* (such as the hymn *Lekhah Dodi* by Rabbi Solomon Alkabez, which was introduced for the Kabbalat Shabbat service) or into the most widespread collections of prayers. In general, the hidden meaning of prayer is greatly emphasized here, in accord with an original theory of intention *(kavvanah)* in prayer.

Both in its theoretical outlook and in its practical institutions, this new Kabbalah was based upon the central idea of redemption. One may speak here without hesitation of the penetration of the messianic idea into all realms and levels of Jewish existence. The central subjects which constantly occupy the Kabbalists anew are the nature of exile and redemption. In posing these questions, the Kabbalists clearly reflect the historical state of the Jewish masses from the sixteenth until the eighteenth century.

Around these ideas there revolves, first and foremost, the new myth revealed by Rabbi Isaac Luria, which his disciples and devotees made efforts to base, to rework, and to fashion in all kinds of ways. The three key terms in Lurianic Kabbalah are: *tzimtzum* (contraction), *shevirah* (breaking), and *tikkun* (correction).

The doctrine of *tzimtzum,* or God's self-limitation, states that the primeval act of creation by God was not one in which the Infinite left its mysterious depths, an act of emanation from within to without, as in early Kabbalah, but that this primal step was in fact "the contraction of the Infinite from Himself to Himself," an act of self-gathering and contraction within Himself in order to create the possibility of the processes of the world. Without contraction there is no creation, as everything is Godhead. Therefore, already in its earliest origins, the creation is a kind of exile, in that it involves God removing Himself from the center of His essence to His secret places. Only after this act of contraction does the Infinite turn outwards, sending a thread of the light of His essence into the primeval void created by *tzimtzum,* from which there emanate the *sefirot. Tzimtzum* is repeated in each new stage of creation, thereby preventing the world from returning to its origins in the Infinite. The process of the world is created and developed in all of its stages through the meeting of the lights that move in two opposite directions: the lights which retreat to their source and seek to return to the bosom of the Infinite, and the lights which burst forth and descend from there *(histalkut ve-hitpashtut).*

The symbol of *shevirah,* the primordial "breaking," signifies the coming into being of evil or its going into its own domain through the "breaking of the vessels" which were needed to receive the lights which built the creation. The vessels were unable to stand the abundance of divine light poured into them: most of them were broken, while all of them were harmed in some fashion. Thus, the universe did not develop in accordance with the ideal order which first arose in the Divine mind, but rather each thing was to some extent removed from its path so that nothing was left in the proper place originally intended for it. "Sparks" from the flow of Divine light descended into the depth and were imprisoned there by the powers of darkness or the "shells" made from the broken vessels. Therefore, the *shevirah* is the great crisis in the structure of creation, in the cosmic drama, albeit according to the Kabbalists the secret of the breaking refers to an event within the divine being. All of the worlds, from the world of emanation down to our lowly world of action, came about through a fixed law that is rooted in the breaking.

To counteract the *shevirah,* there came about the third element, *tikkun* (correction)—that is, the process of restoration of all things to their proper path and place, and correction of the fault which has existed since the *shevirah* in the heart of each created thing. *Tikkun,* which is essentially the positive content of the entire world process, and of human history in particular, comes to restore the full connection between the Creator and the creation which was originally disturbed by the breaking and thereafter, on a different level, by the sin of Adam and by the sin of each one of us. The Infinite emanated new lights that came to heal the break and to introduce a corrected order into the confusion that has fallen into things. But the act of *tikkun* is not left to God Himself: there are certain tasks of *tikkun* which have been given over to man and which constitute the primary goal of human life. All those human acts which come from the realm of holiness, in Torah and prayer, are directed toward the completion of the task of *tikkun*. It follows from this that the concept of *tikkun* belongs to the realm of mystical messianism. When the fault that attaches itself to all existing things by virtue of the breaking of the vessels will be corrected, this will bring about the redemption of the world and the Messiah will come. Redemption is dependent upon the progress and completion of the task of *tikkun,* that is, upon the deeds of man, more than it depends upon God's mercies or the miraculous acts of the Redeemer himself. Therefore, every act of religious value plays a certain role in the correction of the inwardness and outwardness of the universe. Hence, Lurianic Kabbalah is intended to define the exact place of the action of each mitzvah within the chain of *tikkunim.*

It was within this theoretical framework that, according to the understanding of Luria's disciples, Jewish teaching was developed. It would appear as though this were no more than a definitive myth of exile and redemption. The doctrine of the breaking, too, is meant to imply that all emanated and created things are in exile. In this way, the Kabbalists were able to disseminate their doctrine: namely, that the historical exile of the Jewish people is none other than the most striking symbol of that state of the universe in which there is no *tikkun* or harmony, and by which every thing is damaged and harmed. Exile and redemption are thereby transformed into powerful symbols, acquiring the background of a cosmic myth. This may explain the tremendous attraction of these ideas until the period of the Enlightenment.

Regarding another cardinal matter of the new Kabbalah, as well, one may see the same direction and the same bitter taste of the terrors and fears of exile: the doctrine of *gilgul* or metempsychosis, which began to be developed in full force in Safed, saw in the transmigration of souls different stages of the exile of the soul parallel to the exile of the bodies, an inner exile parallel to the outer exile. Due to the strong propaganda of the Kabbalists, this doctrine became widespread among broad sectors of the people amongst whom it did not have any appreciable following prior to the sixteenth century. Not only did the totality of the universe require redemption and *tikkun* because of the disturbance of its order which took place at the beginning, but also each and every soul needed to undergo numerous transmigrations and different forms of being in order to purge the stain of the sin of Adam and to restore itself to the full image of God which had been distorted by sin. The most terrible punishment which can befall the sinner is that of the lot of the banished or disembodied souls which are not allowed to transmigrate, and do not even deserve to enter *Gehinnom*. In this manner, the destiny of the people in exile was transferred from the historical arena to the psychological one. The pains and horrors of exile are reflected in the suffering of the wandering souls.

Under the influence of the movement originating in Safed, the Kabbalists became the bearers, not only for the limited circles of Kabbalistic practitioners, but for the entire people, of a mystical messianism embodied in Lurianic doctrine. The ideal type praised by the ethical works of the Kabbalah is the ascetic who carries in his heart the vision of redemption and who attempts through all his actions to bring about the correction of the fault of the world. In the Sabbatian movement of 1666 and the perplexities of Sabbatian faith during the years that followed, the power which had been stored up here broke forth with a power unknown in other messianic movements. Following the crisis of the Sabbatian movement and its transformation into a destructive force, only two paths remained open to Kabbalah: (a) to forget the masses and to return to the path of an esoteric faith for select individuals; and (b) to develop the popular tendencies inherent in Lurianic Kabbalah to their fullest, while rejecting the dangerous element which was full of the revolutionary tension of messianism.

The first path was adopted by those committed Kabbalistic masters who did not join the Sabbatian heresy. These had two important centers during the eighteenth century: the Klaus connected to the *bet midrash* in the town of Brody (Brod, in eastern Galicia), and Yeshivat Beth-El in Jerusalem. The latter served as a center of Kabbalah for Jews from the Eastern lands for some hundred and fifty years, and its influence upon Sephardic and Oriental Jews extends nearly down to our own time. The second path was that followed by the Ḥasidic movement during the second half of the eighteenth century, which strongly emphasized the elements of mystical ethics in Kabbalah and which aspired to interpret its doctrines along these lines. Once again, mysticism appears here as a decisive factor in the creation of a social ethic and in an original interpretation of its values. In Ḥasidism, the thoughts of the mystics reached the masses, albeit in a popular manner and with certain changes. Characteristic of these tendencies are the books of Rabbi Elimelekh of Lyzhansk and of Rabbi Naḥman of Braslav, but especially the Kabbalistic systems of the Ḥabad Ḥasidim (i.e., the disciples of Rabbi Shneur Zalman of Lyady), in which Kabbalah sloughs off its theosophic form and acquires the form of psychology, old-fashioned in language but new and even modern in its contents. The profound influence of Ḥabad teaching and its path in the interpretation of the Kabbalah is also reflected in the writings of the late Rabbi Abraham Isaac Kook, Chief Rabbi of the Land of Israel, in whose original personality there were once again incorporated in our own generation the holy lights of Jewish mysticism.

Chapter Eighteen

Memory and Utopia in Jewish History (1946)*

The issue of the continuity of the generations is bound up with that of the tradition of the past: i.e., the passing down of the past and its relation to this tradition. The problem is that of the ongoing presence of the past: how does one find the past in the present? This issue involves two separate questions: (a) In what sense is there continuity among the generations? and (b) Does it obligate us?

The vital forces within the Zionist movement answered the former question in the affirmative, while giving a resounding no to the latter.

That outlook, which is at once very understandable and very dangerous, which saw in Zionism a revolution directed toward the renewal of the character of the nation, quite validly adhered to the view that, in order to save anything, there was a need for negation, for criticism, for a break with the past. This revolutionism was quite convenient to all of us, so long as there was someone against whom to rebel. Today, following the great disaster which has befallen our people, our situation has been tragically altered: the revolution finds itself in a vacuum from the national viewpoint; the nation is no longer the great reservoir assuring the continuity of that against which we rebel. Thus, we ourselves need to worry about both sides of the coin.

* Delivered as a lecture at a gathering of youth movement leaders and teachers held in Jerusalem, March 6, 1946. Transcribed from shorthand transcript of that lecture. Revised and edited by Avraham Shapira. Published in 'Od Davar, 187–98.

Consciousness of historical continuity is not at all unproblematic; it comes under question at every historical moment. At every moment, history is challenged by both vertical and horizontal impulses. At any time we not only see the result of the historic causality of earlier doctrines; we also see the causality of the present, and this operates upon us and upon everything that we do, think, or want. All this has an influence, without us being at all able to know how or why or for how long. This fact can disrupt the sense of historical continuity.

Even if there is a constant encounter between historical consciousness and the impact upon us of the present, the historical consciousness itself is beset by tremendous inner contradictions. Reality is by its very nature dialectical and full of contradictions, so that it is no surprise that these same contradictions may also be discovered in the nature of our historical consciousness. As I mentioned earlier, the continuity of the generations involves consciousness of the past, historical memory. It is here that there begins the most difficult problematic; we attempt to draw a picture of the past on the basis of those symbols that have remained in the present. The monuments that stand out in our perception are those which we perceive as worthy of remembering, or which come into our memory involuntarily, by means of processes that are more powerful than our will. Our choice of the components making up our image of the past is made on the basis of intuition, on the basis of possibilities, of our power of awareness, of our interests. It is made through a certain mixture of memory and hope. These, in their various combinations, determine history in a manner that is subject neither to definition or analysis nor to full description.

We are accustomed to laugh at the early chroniclers—those forebears of historical science who did not know how to distinguish between great and small in the historical process; they recorded everything, without any guidelines or goals, and without taking part in the great game of the modern dialectician. The latter tries to analyze certain things among which he sees a certain relationship to hidden tendencies in the past, which he attempts to bring to light in terms of the present or the future. Yet our mocking of these early chroniclers is completely groundless and illegitimate, for that chronicler was the only person with a true historical intuition. It is he who holds that, in principle, it is forbidden that anything be lost to the future. And in truth, these petty, insignificant details which he recorded, and to which no one paid attention for thousands of years, have or will become at some point significant facts. This is proven by the history of economics and of social history. No one ever paid attention to the records of price differences from the days of Herodotus—or thought that there was any importance to such incidental information for the understanding of the historical epoch, of the great events. But in the final analysis, it is on the basis of these things that historians are able to build a true picture of the events. Today, to a great extent, we see in these small details a key for our own understanding, more so than those great events—descriptions of wars and all that they involve—which were at one time the subject of historical study.

The question is whether it is possible to write history from the viewpoint of the little person, from the perspective of the defeated rather than from that of the victors, where until now history has been written from their perspective.

The continuity of the generations is a dialectical matter. The images of the generations are liable to change; indeed, it is even necessary that they change with every development in our own consciousness, with every possibility of discovering new symbols (from the past) which have been forgotten or to which no one paid attention.

Yet these symbols are shaped, not only by the symbols of the past which are impressed upon our consciousness, or which can be elicited in our consciousness, but also by the hopes and utopias of the future. These, no less than the interest of the present or evaluations that are the result of sympathy or antipathy, have influenced us.

The past does not come alive without some utopian element, without a hope for something that stands behind our historical efforts to redeem something of the past. It is as if we will be able to understand the failures of the past in light of some new tendency which is to triumph in the future. We are interested in history because therein are hidden the small experiences of the human race, in the same way as there is hidden therein the dynamic light of the future. Within the historical failures, there is still concealed a power that can seek its correction. We choose out of all these. And we know that this choice always includes only a small portion of true human experience. There are very large parts of this choice which are sealed and invisible, which remain in question.

The historian sees himself, on the one hand, as appointed to preserve the memory of the past; but, on the other hand, for him the past becomes a tool in the battle of the future. Memory is the primary material upon which the historian draws. But memory also includes forgetting, and is no less important than memory itself. When I think of the history of Judaism and the Jews, it seems to me that forgetfulness is more important than memory—notwithstanding that we are commanded in the fundamental documents of Judaism to regard memory as a basic principle. To remember, to remember, to remember! Nevertheless, Jews' memory of the image of the Jewish past is extremely weak. I feel certain that Jewish history paid a heavy price for the messianic utopia. For its utopia, which constantly places it on the side of the defeated who shall be victorious in the future, the Jewish people paid with many productive energies. The tremendous power of utopia fills me with the hope that we no longer need be ashamed of our history. But, together with this, that utopia—that concentration upon future action—makes us obliterate the concrete things from our memory. People are in the habit of saying that we remember well. This is not true. We forget more than any other cultured nation. This forgetting is double: it contains elements of the future as well as elements of the past that have worn away, in which there is no longer vitality, and hence have sunk into the oblivion of forgetfulness. Forgetting is not only a lack. No less than the act of remembering, it is a real force. Forgetting contains that same infinite strength of symbols which will be revealed in the world of tomorrow. We remember things connected with the great crystallizations of the past. But these crystallizations are extremely dialectical; they are not only ideals. The great values in which the historical process is concretized are the result of victories, not of failures. Every crystallized value which arises in our historical memory is also to a certain degree questionable by virtue of the very fact of its being remembered, it being woven into history because it is the word of the victors of the generation. We remember what we wish to remember, not what we should have remembered.

I would like to emphasize two other things: there is an index to the past for the person who looks upon it from the present. It contains two contradictory signs: (a) on the one hand, the past is incomplete, it is lacking in something. It is enclosed within itself. It always contains unrealized tendencies; there were always things that we would have wished to know—and perhaps these are the subjects of our dreams—and which did not attain their full crystallization. This fault-in-principle of the past is highly visible, and man's desire to correct it in light of the picture that he combines with it is an elementary wish. (b) The past has the character of a symbol, which stands in contradiction to its dimension of vulnerability and non-completeness.

Talk about the past is false, for the past was never completely past. It is still with us, it still has a small opening to the present, or even into the future or the redemption. Together with this, I would say that the past has the character of a symbol. It may not necessarily be a symbol of a complete thing; perhaps there are symbols for lack of completeness. But it is completely clear that, in our consciousness of the past, history constitutes a symbol of constant failure. On the one hand, Jewish history seems to us like a failure whose flaw needs to be corrected. On the other hand, in retrospect the historical past appears arbitrary. There is contemplation of a symbol of reality which was whole within itself—and as a symbol of reality it has power. The symbolism of history is essentially the decisive power inherent within it. The picture which we piece together from the different symbols into one big symbol enlightens our path to something—and we draw from it our attitude to the events and situations of the past.

As follows from my words, our relationship to Jewish history cannot be simple. Our picture of the past is constantly changing, and we must ask ourselves: what can be learned from it or, indeed, can anything at all be learned from it? Jewish history can be put together in a completely different way than that which our ancestors saw in it. Its pictures and images have already changed innumerable times, but still are in transition. Today we seek a picture of the past in order to transmit something to the next generation. We feel a need for this. The vital interest that we all feel to be revealed in the actualization of Jewish history involves a great danger, the danger of tendentious subjectivism. I already said that I do not believe in a contemplative relationship to history, but this does not imply that the person with an historical consciousness is allowed to deal with historiography or history in a tendentious way. The great danger is tendentiousness of choice—against which the only safeguard is the desire for truth. Man needs to seek truth even though he knows that it is far beyond him (for even if he makes full use of everything, he can only write from the givens of his time and from its memories, etc., etc.). If he begins to put together whatever combinations come to him—and there is a very real danger of this in the Land of Israel and in the Jewish people at the present historical moment—then we are lost from the outset.

The issue of the consciousness of the continuity of the generations is, as I have said, a religious question. The Jewish memory of history is a religious memory. There is no avoiding this; it is an elementary fact of our tradition, and we ask ourselves: Can the historical consciousness of the past change this fundamental fact? Can everything which Jewish history encompasses in its principal values, all that which it teaches, be stripped of its religious form and contents? The issue is clear: we are in a far more radical situation than other nations, as not even the revolutionaries among them denied their past as we have. The Englishman does not deny the Christian tradition underlying his history, even if he does not accept responsibility for its barbaric acts or for all its corruptions and failures. Even if he does not accept Christian dogma, he does not turn his back on it. The same holds true for almost every other nation. In this respect, we have entered into a dead end and we cannot but state it explicitly. Thus, the question of our continuity with the generations of our forefathers is a very difficult one precisely because it requires a decision: are we prepared to deny any cultural form which has a religious form, because we are perhaps unwilling to accept its rules, or may we perhaps turn things around and say that the great suffering of past generations obligates us as well? This is a fundamental question, particularly in our secular lives. It is a simple matter for the religious Jew, but for the present the religious Jew does not determine the overall character of the generation. The question is: are we able to continue even though we deny many of the religious values of our forefathers? One must ask whether we are able to utilize critical methods regarding our memory or memories even as it pertains to religious issues. Here the secularization of education is unlikely to be of much use: it entails a considerable degree of dishonesty, of self-deception. We begin with the assumption that the documents which we teach in school are non-binding national documents—and this is perhaps the essential difference between ourselves and other nations. The documents upon which we base our education are religious documents. It is clear that, in our making them into secular documents, we are altering them in principle, we are discovering and emphasizing aspects which their authors did not consider important. At times, we teach the Bible as a text with a certain Berdichevsky-like tendency: to show how positive and vital this nation was. Or we teach *aggadah* with the aim of demonstrating the great creative imagination of the people. We create a new picture out of the symbols of the past, one which is tendentious because we consciously remove from these documents those values because of which they were preserved and were considered worthy of remembering. I am disturbed by this. The question is whether we are able to do this legitimately; whether we are allowed to choose such a path for ourselves, whether Jewish tradition is possible without God. We constantly see that it is possible, but the question is, to where does this lead us? Does it lead to an enrichment of the vital contents of these documents and a resolution of their vital problematic? Or must we forgo them if we are unable to relate to the documents of the past with proper reverence? It is this question which I should like to ask you. Here in Israel, the teacher tends to obscure the severity of the religious problem. But what we obfuscate today will burst forth with greater force tomorrow, in a different way. One cannot tell where the religious problem, which is inherent in our historical memory, will reemerge tomorrow or the day after. It is impossible to predict. It is very difficult to discuss the possibility of historical continuity in Israel if we deny this problem.

I am not an Orthodox Jew and I am unable, nor do I wish, to teach people to believe as our ancestors believed. Nevertheless, I ask myself what purpose there is in the study of these texts if they are not pertinent to me, if I do not need to respond to them, if I do not at least attempt to look at them honestly and without distortion, in the same light that I am able to discover therein. At this point, it seems to me that we must attempt to enter into the thick of the problem of religious matters in education.

The question that must be clarified is the following: to what extent may we hope for a continuity of our history if our children are not confronted with the issue of the past? It may be that each one of us will do as the new experience shows him. I am not a prophet; I do not know what form faith will acquire in the next generation. But I do believe in the historical necessity to pose the matter to the next generation. I think that to teach the Hebrew Bible and not to clarify the fundamental issues involved in it is not a fruitful approach. There is something sterile about it; by doing so, we encourage people to engage in denial and to run away. In light of such paradoxical matters, we cannot simply pretend to our contemporaries. One of the most difficult things, which most spoils the teaching of *Tanakh*, is: how do you arouse or elicit the questions of man's standing before God without clarifying the matter of man's smallness in his own existence. To put the question differently: is it really possible to interpret *Tanakh*, Talmud, the prayer book, *piyyut,* religio-ethical works—that is, our entire treasury of religious literature—without dealing with their contents? Is such a revolutionary approach at all possible, and if it is, can it bring any blessing to our existence here? I am, of course, extremely doubtful. I often ask myself, when I teach my own subject to seminars of Youth Aliyah—what do these good children, who will tomorrow be teachers, think? Is it interesting or is it not interesting? And if it is interesting—why is it interesting? Is it interesting because it involves absurd things and great failures and dreams which were once dreamt? And in that case, then is it not ours essentially a literary, belletristic interest? I have always emphasized that we do falsehood to ourselves with regard to several problems of our past: the issues are actually highly contemporary and people see in them a kind of hidden contemporaneity, even though they attempt not to see them in the guise of the religious problem from which they sprang. It is difficult for me to bring myself to the belief that it is possible to strip things of this garb without forgetting the past. Without its religious problematic, our past will be forgotten, would need to be forgotten. Indeed, it is not worthy of being remembered, because the heroism of the Jew is very questionable from an historical viewpoint. The moment the question of religion is not present to the Jewish historian, together with the clarifications of these questions by recent generations—our history will become sterile.

Socialistic education was able to present the new generation with a tremendous human possibility: a history that was not written by the victors. The history of other nations of the world was written by the victorious rulers, while our rulers were not great rulers, and insofar as they were rulers were not important. Insofar as our history is of any interest, this is due to its hidden appropriateness to the ideas of the future, to the people's great choice to pay the price for the messianic direction of its history, that same messianic direction which is guilty of the failures of Jewish history. Why is all of our history antipathetic? Were it not for the fact that these Jews had religious illusions, they could have corrected their situation seven times over by their own power, without linking it to the idea of redemption (for which they paid a tremendous price). Here, the Jewish socialist actually has a great interest at stake: do we now face a unique opportunity to change the history of a people which has consisted entirely of failures, of possibility, of the problem of the future—into one of making a life in the present?! Or may there perhaps be hope for change in an allegorical reinterpretation of these symbols, so as to fit a new secular interpretation? The question is whether we consider this possible, and whether we will need to teach and to explain the destruction of our brothers and sisters in Europe to the next generation without asking the question: Why did such a large part of our people allow itself to be killed? Why did they "sanctify the Name," as it is called? I am very skeptical whether we indeed wish to bind ourselves, as people proclaim from every hill and mountaintop, to the memories of the millions who were killed in Poland and Lithuania, etc. I am very doubtful as to whether this is possible without directly confronting the great problematic of our life. We must confront the reality which forces us to interpret an unparalleled catastrophe. We do not know what answers we can give, but there is no way to escape the question. Even the most radical attempt to deny the reality of the question of transcendence in our lives, even the most radical will, encounters here in a terrible and concrete way, in the attempt to explain the lot of the fathers to the children, the questions of religion. I do not know how you resolve this question in your work. Certainly there is a fixed routine to this thing, as to how one avoids the question or how one asks or does not ask. At this moment I wish to say: first of all, do not avoid it, but ask it. I think that this is the only possible way to create an historical connection between ourselves and the previous generations—to deal seriously with the questions that were raised here. I am certain that this will not make us Orthodox. We wish to educate toward a positive attitude toward the past of a nation with all its failures, for the sake of its future. And, as we said, this is impossible if we do not attempt to again pose the painful question of the unique nature of this nation.

If you ask whether, based upon this, I would say that there is a fixed essence of Judaism that may be learned or in which we need to stand in relation, my answer would be: No. As an historian, I do not believe that there is one Judaism. I have been unable to find it during all the years that I dealt with this problem. The Judaism of each and every period is more similar to its own world than it is to the Judaism which followed it. I am certain that the Judaism of Maimonides was closer to the Christianity or Islam of his contemporaries than it is to the Judaism of the contemporary Jew. I believe this completely. I am certain that our faith today, if we have any faith, is closer to what the Gentile nations believe at this moment than it is to the faith of our own past generations. I do not believe in one essence. I am certain that there is something unique which forces Jews to ask questions and to seek answers, and I am certain that this same substance in one form or otherwise will take form anew in a different guise. But this substance of Judaism is not subject to definition; it is one of those total, all-embracing things which defies formulation, but is present in reality.

We have a shared past that is not subject to definition. This substance, which is continuous in the historical perception of the Jewish nation, cannot be properly understood if we do not attempt to face the unique intention directly, the unique pain, involved in the questions which we have raised. I advise not to flee from these questions, not only here in this discussion among ourselves, but particularly in relation to those whom we have come to teach.

A Brief Response (To Questions Asked in Wake of the Lecture)

My lecture does not imply the negation of historical continuity. One might compare this continuity to a continuous line without any direction: one may also use the tangent line in geometry as a metaphor, for there too there is continuity with every point, while there is no continuity at any point.

The simplistic attitude to the problem of religion to which we have become accustomed over the course of generations is inadequate. The secular interpretation of religious concepts is problematic. Just as we may not make an absolute distinction between secularism and religion, so we may not obscure the unique nature of religious problems by means of philosophical answers. One must be very precise in one's use of the terms "secularity" and "religiosity." Clearly, there is secularism which is not at all connected to religion, but one must also note the fact that sometimes secular phenomena appear in religious garb. But even an exact historical analysis cannot resolve the riddle implicit in the unexplained nature of religion.

The positivistic explanation claims to refute religion by a rationalistic explanation of the absolute. Positivism is theology with a minus sign. Its fundamental principle, that all phenomena may be explained in such a way as not to leave any remaining questions—is one that arrogates to itself the status of an absolute principle.

The same holds true for Marxist explanations. It is neither an explanation nor a critique of religion when one explains the way in which man places above himself an absolute authority, to which he bows and bends the knee. This explanation may be useful for understanding the sociology of certain religious problems, but it does not touch upon the central problem of religion. None of the exegetes of religion in the previous century—Feuerbach, Marx, Kierkegaard, and Nietzsche—succeeded in explaining the basic concept of the Torah, "the image of God," an idea which is simple yet earth-shaking in its profundity.

This avoidance of the religious problem inherent in the Bible is likewise reflected in the different approaches to the teaching of *Tanakh* here in the Land of Israel. It is incorrect to say that one is effectively helping to revive this book by attempting to explain it as a national epic or a document like other folkloristic documents of the ancient Near East. In such a manner, the central document of the Jewish religion is transformed into a rather trivial document, emptied of the life that pulses within it. Those who ignore the problem itself do not uplift the Bible, but rather diminish its value. They shall ultimately dissipate its contents rather than passing it down to the coming generations.

The secular explanation hangs upon a thread, and we must examine the concept of secularism closely before choosing it as the only possible explanation. Secularism is no more than a narrow transition from one religious dogma to another. Secularism is good, so long as one is not required to bring sacrifices upon its altar; it disappears the moment people are asked to die for something.

The concept of "humanism" is closely connected with the concept of secularism. We are used to championing humanism as the opposite of religion, as a complete substitute for religious faith. But never in history were people killed in the name of secularism, nor are they killed today. Human beings will only sacrifice their lives for a value which they consider absolute. (One cannot deny that the vital kernel of Communism in Russia is one whose religious aspects stand out more and more.) Likewise, Germany fell to the Nazis because the German Social-Democrats were unwilling to be killed for their belief in the ideal of humanity.

When humanism struggles with the problem of its own future, it too discovers the need for religious concepts. In such situations, it tends to revive a religious system with absolute value, albeit in concealed form. The contingency of the events of life brings man to pose questions which are necessarily religious (however, we may designate them) and which are raised above human life, requiring of him a precious sacrifice.

Regarding the claims concerning religious reaction, it should be noted that this distinction is not based upon a precise understanding. While it is true that people have distorted or falsified the true face of religion, and there are no lack of historical examples of this, this does not mean that such falsification is the unique prerogative of religion. Any value can be distorted—and let us not forget the example of the totalitarian movements which championed socialism. The moral catastrophe of the distortion of socialism in our day should teach us a lesson—namely, that falsification is not inherent in the nature of one or another value, but in the external form which it assumes. When a certain value makes absolute demands for itself, extending over all and dominating all, only then are the dark and corrupt aspects of this guise revealed.

There are also historical examples of the opposite kind. In every official religion, there were holy revolutions against the dominant line, and there were always those who struggled to renew the religion once its form was emptied of healthy, living contents. Those who have a proper sociological understanding of history inevitably arrive at a perception of religion as a progressive, militant, and purifying force. Nor is Jewish history lacking in this progressive kernel. While it is true that our history has been that of the defeated, nevertheless our religious documents reveal to the historian a powerful hidden revolutionary stream. In its essence, this revolutionary will is connected with a supreme value, and the revolution is a religious revolution. It seems to me that the events of our own time once again confront us with a truer understanding of the significance of religious concepts. The slaughter which took place in the European Diaspora is an event unequaled in Jewish history. Essentially, we have no appropriate concept or expression for that which has occurred before our eyes. Examples from the past are inappropriate to the present situation. Bialik's response to the persecution of Jews—"The City of Slaughter"—no longer satisfies us, and can no longer serve as an example. This problem forces us to reflect within ourselves and to find our own solutions. The answer to the question of the "image of God" can no longer be evaded by belletristics nor by ideology. The sociological explanation does not respond to the ethical and human dimension of the terrible slaughter. Once our eyes have seen the great crisis and destruction, we can no longer fall back upon this routine solution. Disbelief is not passed down as an inheritance. We cannot conceal the religious problem from our children and our young people, and we are not justified in thinking that we will spare them difficulty and pain to their souls by offering them the comforts of secularism. This evasion of the religious problem entails a very great danger, as we cannot know how it will break out and in what manner it may destroy the soul which was given easy solutions and denied a religious revolution.

Modern socialism wished to fix the framework of the revolution, being certain of the transitional period which is approaching us. However, that history in which people longed for their redemption—so long as man's soul is as it is—does not recognize any transitional periods. At every hour, so long as religion constitutes a living force within him, man is about to bring about the revolution of redemption, and is even called to bring it about.

Chapter Nineteen

The People of the Book (1975)*

What I have to say here concerning the Jews as the "people of the book" will certainly surprise many of you, nor is it without a certain degree of current interest, albeit in a paradoxical manner. This term, perhaps the most complimentary among an abundance of vicious ones we have been called, originated among none others than the Arabs! It was Mohammed, the founder of Islam, who used this term in many passages in the Koran specifically in reference to the Jews. This acknowledgment of the fact that the Jews were the possessors of a fundamental book which, at least to a certain degree, corresponded to the one book which God has in the heavens, or stemming from it—this, in the mouth of Mohammed, who held a deep grudge against the Jews of Arabia who refused to believe in his prophetic mission, was the greatest compliment which he could have given, albeit very much against his will. He had actually hoped, by means of the revelations in the Koran, to convey this title upon his own people. The Arabic text speaks in this context of "the people of the writing" *(ahal al-katab)*—that is, a group of human beings who possess holy writings. But one may also come from this to "the people of the book," found in many translations of the Koran, and it is that phrase which took root several hundred years ago in the languages of Europe.

This same people of the book appears with a certain degree of ambivalence in the eyes of Heinrich Heine, who wrote some one hundred and

---

* Based upon a lecture given by Scholem. The Hebrew manuscript was prepared for publication by Shlomo Zucker; published in *'Od Davar*, 153–61.

thirty years ago: "As a ghostly spirit guarding a treasure which was placed in its care when it was still alive, so did this murdered people sit, this people of ghosts, in the darkness of its ghettos, and preserved the Hebrew Bible."[1] From there—he goes on to say—Johannes Reuchlin and his friends took it and passed it on to Martin Luther. One may argue whether the Jews were in fact a ghost people, as Heine put it; indeed, he himself never completely recovered from that same state of ghostliness, being a part of them. But there can be no doubt that they were not only the guardians of the Bible and its saviors, but the people of the Bible in the noble sense, and as such eminently deserving of the title "the People of the Book," because they not only preserved the book, but also lived by it. If it was a treasure that had been placed in their hands, then they, by their magical contact, altered it and placed it in a new light, by which it served as the fundamental book constructive of their existence as a nation. One may say that, in terms of the function of the Jewish people in world history, they were shaped by the book. The Book of Books underwent no less change in their hands than they themselves underwent.

Archaeologists, ancient Near Eastern experts, and Bible scholars have shed light upon the struggles which took place within the Jewish people from its earliest days until the Babylonian exile, where there took place their development into the people of the book. The nation became such from the days of the Return to Zion in the sixth and fifth pre-Christian centuries. However, the consciousness of obligation toward the book of holy writings as a document of revelation did not become the heritage of the entire people so long as they dwelt within the land and underwent a history of numerous changes. But the process of transformation of the people, which took place by virtue of the tremendous power of the monotheistic idea of God and the worship of an imageless God, is not the subject of our present study. We are specifically concerned with the outcome of that process by which, two and a half millennia ago, the Jews were turned into the people of the book. What was the significance of this change for the spiritual and historical image of the people? What happened when a book was placed at the center of the experience of a nation? What function did the book fulfill in its life, and what were the powers that were freed by it, or that were chained and restrained by it? From what perspectives was it possible for a book to fulfill such a function? Concerning all these questions, the Jewish literature and traditions which accompany the canonization of the Bible give us an abundance of information, pulsing with life. I will attempt to define here only the crucial points.

When one speaks of the "book" as such, one must distinguish between two different intermingled approaches. The book *par excellence* was the Pentateuch, or Five Books of Moses, which was given to the Congregation of Israel as the principal document of revelation, as the binding word of God. The Torah enjoyed a position of preference and supremacy as compared to the other writings which, together with it, constituted the biblical canon—prophecies, or historical, didactic, and liturgical writings. Already in the Talmud these writings were designated, as opposed to the Pentateuch, as "received words" *(divrei kabbalah;* i.e., in the sense of a tradition transmitted from generation to generation), a term which cannot at all be compared to the meaning of the word *Torah*, which positively radiates authority. We are not interested here in the question as to precisely when the collection of holy writings was fixed as a comprehensive document embodying religious authority—whether in the third century B.C.E. or, finally, only in the last quarter of the first century C.E., during the generation following the destruction of Jerusalem. The fact is that, with the closing of the biblical canon, there began a process whereby the concept of the revelatory nature of the Torah began to encompass the other books of the Bible as well. This process involved a variety of nuances, and essentially never ceased. One may nevertheless say that the unique stature of the Five Books of Moses was preserved in the consciousness of the Jews. However, it seems quite certain that the prophetic books of the Bible, which are found in whole or in part in the extant writings, were already read in the second century as documents of divine revelation. For this reason, each generation could relate to them as if to a revelation of their time. This process was strengthened following the destruction of the Second Temple, when the majority of the Jewish people lived in Diasporas and the *Tanakh* functioned for it as a kind of "portable homeland." With the destruction of the physical center, the spiritual center became increasingly brilliant.

Once the Bible had ceased to be the provenance of priests or sages alone, but penetrated to broad circles within the people, it became thought of not only as sacred writings, but as the book of the people *per se*. There was thereby created a common platform for the different levels of society. It was not for naught that the school, which for more than two thousand years was attended by most of the youth of the male sex, became known as *beit ha-sefer* (literally, "house of the book")—that is, the house in which the book is studied and read. By this means, the community and the public were exposed to the influence of the biblical texts, and a fertile soil was created for its absorption and creative renewal. The words of the Sages and scribes were those heard in the early books, and they took a decisive role in the influence of the book, but under no circumstances they alone. Following the destruction of the Temple, the obligation to support the priestly caste was completely nullified. The public was likewise not required to support the Sages *(tannaim)*, who supported themselves through various crafts rather than making their knowledge of Torah "a spade with which to dig" (to use the phrase of the ancient saying in M. Avot 4:5). This fact was sufficient to prevent the creation of a separate caste of the learned, whose livelihood was imposed upon the other sectors of the people. The commandment of the Torah, "and you shall teach them to your children, and speak of them, when you sit in your house and when you walk in the way, and when you lie down, and when you rise up" (Deut. 6:7) was fulfilled in reality to a very great extent. An expression of the popular nature of Torah study and the power concealed therein is reflected, for example, in the touching words preserved in the Midrash, cited in the name of a certain "Daniel the Tailor" (ca. fourth century), of whom nothing is known apart from the homily cited here. Kohelet's words protesting against "the tears of the oppressed, who have no one to comfort them," is explained as referring, not to the tyrants and oppressors of this world, but to God Himself, due to the hopeless situation brought upon a certain group of people by one of the commandments in His Torah.[2]

The "book" included everything which life is likely to bring, if one would only know how to learn it properly. Here there emerge two important aspects, from whose dialectic there follows that "spiral advance in the spiritual life of the Jews" which constantly surrounded the Bible with new circles—as formulated by an inspired observer, Aharon Steinberger. What were these two aspects? On the one hand, one may see the book as carrying a stable and unified meaning that guides life. On the other hand, precisely because it incorporates the word of God, one may consider the book as infinitely plastic, containing therein infinite levels of meaning. The tremendous effect of the Bible upon the Jewish people is connected with the living interplay between these two tendencies.

With the acceptance of the Holy Scriptures as a document of Divine Revelation, it was inevitable that in the course of history two approaches emerge regarding the nature of this revelation—approaches that simultaneously differed from one another but nevertheless complemented one another. The word of God as revealed to His people encompassed a unique statement of specific content. The Sages wished to precisely examine and determine this content, in its aspect of that which shaped the life of the Torah-observant Jew. By this, there began the process of constitution of the Tradition *(Masorah)*, whose significance was the understanding of the Bible in relation to every concrete situation in which the society thereupon based might find itself. Importance was attached, not only to the question of how the given concrete contents of the book should be preserved and passed down; rather, there also arose the broader question of the possibility of application of this revelation on the historical plane. The people of the book became the people of the commentary. Holy Writ is examined, not only in order to establish the norms contained therein, for the shaping of life according to the Torah—that is, the fixing of the Halakhah—but also for what they contain beyond the normative—for that "expression" known as *aggadah*. The literal meaning of Midrash is the searching out of the halakhic and *aggadic* meanings of the biblical text. Over the course of a thousand years, Midrash was the authentic form of Jewish literature, as embodied in the two Talmuds and in the midrashic works.

Over the course of generations, commentary became the first ranking form of Jewish creation. In a society based upon the acceptance of a truth which had already been revealed in a written document, originality could not be a central value. The truth is already known. We have naught to do but to understand it, and what is perhaps more difficult, to pass it down. In other words: originality and the creative impulse which acted here did not declare themselves as such, but preferred to manifest themselves in a form which was less pretentious but in fact was no less creative—namely, that of commentary. By their very nature, the commentators were modest in demanding authority for themselves. Their authority underwent changes and at times even went unchallenged, but the theological demand implied in their words was fundamentally radical: the Divine Revelation was interpreted through them to the human intellect. The voluminous exegetical literature reflected not only the Jews' understanding of the book, but their own self-understanding. For most of the Jewish people over the past nine hundred years, the name of Rashi—Rabbi Shlomo Yitzḥaki, the great eleventh century commentator, a native of Worms on the River Rhine in Germany who studied Torah in the city of Troyes in France—was a kind of embodiment of exegetical genius.

But it was not only in the realm of exegesis that the Jews proved themselves the people of the book. One might say that their geography and history was also that of the book, and that which happened outside of it did not touch their hearts. Their geography was that of the Bible, rather than that of the environment in which they found themselves. They saw places in the Holy Land as being the source of their lives, in which they were rooted, even when over the course of time that rootedness became—or seems to have become—fictitious. Historical events that took place within the book had nothing in common with the secular events which took place around them. The feeling of reality was changed. Reality was to be found in the Bible, and not in that which disguised itself as concreteness. In the eyes of Rabbi Moses ben Maimon, involvement in the chronicles of secular life was a mere waste of time, just as it was considered in the eyes of the Ḥasidim in Poland, some six hundred years later. Chronicles describing events involving kings and their battles are depicted as the nadir of emptiness. And when contemporary events did have relevance (albeit generally speaking disastrous) for the Jews, they took their example from the Bible. "The deeds of the fathers are a sign for the sons," was the talmudic rule. The Midrash, which also includes such typological exegesis of the Bible, frequently serves a political function, alongside its spiritual function, from the middle of the second century B.C.E. (and perhaps even earlier) until our own day.

Moreover, the lives of the Jews were checkered with or—if one can say so—implanted with phrases from the Bible. In later times, even their everyday experience could find expression through the world of images and metaphors of the Bible. Over the course of centuries, Jewish children already began going to school in the fourth year of their lives, where they learned to read the Torah and to translate it into the vernacular. Let us try to imagine the meaning of such a thing. The images and impressions from the dawn of childhood are impressed upon the soul of the child. The very first thing that the child received from the Jewish heritage was "the book," and the associations which it elicited, from the Bible and from the *aggadic* tradition associated with it, were the same from Yemen and Bukhara to Amsterdam, Leghorn, and Venice, to Vilna, Lemberg, Prague, and Frankfurt. Thus, as I said at the beginning of my remarks, the book was not only a matter for the learned or for those whom we are accustomed to calling intellectuals, but was the heritage of the entire people. And this heritage was not closed and sealed, but something organic and constantly developing. Jewish history was impressed by its stamp, as was also its folk legend and the Jewish way of life. The Bible and its profound message are the guarantee that creation and history have one meaning.

I spoke previously about the two aspects in which the Bible fulfilled its function in the spiritual life of the Jews. Thus far I have spoken primarily about the first aspect, of the book of Holy Scripture as the stable carrier of significance that guided our lives. This is certainly a basic element for understanding the idea of the "people of the book." But we also need to turn our minds toward the second aspect, which follows of dialectical necessity from the conviction that the Bible contained the living word of God which was inscribed in writing in a book. Already from ancient times the Torah was identified with wisdom; that is, with Divine Wisdom—the Sophia, the divine cosmic understanding woven within creation as a whole, as is already implied in the book of Jesus ben Sira, from the third pre-Christian century. But by this the book turns into something more than a book, as Leo Baeck once said. The book here becomes a cosmic power, which is not only the source of every crystallization of future image and form, but from which there also flows its continual change.

> This community of the book also ascends to another world; it becomes something which has existed since the Creation. The universal extension of the book finds its parallel in the function of the congregation, of the people of the book—this is a function that goes constantly further and transcends into the realm of the mystical. Its place is within the world, but its mystical spread touches the realm of the cosmic, to which it belongs no less than to the world itself.[4]

As against the thesis of revelation documented in the Bible as a definite system of positive meaning, which is to be studied and transmitted as a tradition, there is raised the other thesis, which was very widespread and developed in a fundamental way in the writings of the Kabbalists—namely, that concerning the infinite wealth of meaning in the divine word. The underlying inner logic of this approach is clear: if there is a divine word, then it must be utterly different from the human word. It encompasses and includes everything, and cannot only apply to a specific meaning context, like the human word. It becomes plastic and of infinitely multiple meaning, as if it is meaning itself. Indeed, by this we have gone far beyond the original historical outlook regarding revelation and Holy Writ as conveying some specific content, of which we have spoken until now. The very fact that the written word is subject to endless exposition—as opposed to that which is known as "the simple/literal meaning of Scripture," which is no more than an external garment—is indicative of its divine nature. An infinitude of lights shines in every word of Scripture, and the primordial light that illuminates every word is broken into multifaceted meaning. From this there followed the aphorism, "there are seventy faces to the Torah," that is, seventy different levels of meaning. The number seventy represents that inexhaustible and meaningful comprehensiveness of the written language. The later Kabbalists derived from this an idea that became quite widespread, namely, that the Torah addresses every Jew with one of its faces or aspects that is intended for him alone, and which may be understood by him alone. The subject of the transmission of the word of God consists in this: that each individual will find in the Torah an aspect intended for him alone, and include it in the great tradition. The chain of the tradition will not be broken, because it is the translation of the inexhaustible word of God into the human realm, and to that which may be comprehended by the individual. In it, that voice which was uttered from Sinai in infinite tones and possibilities is translated into the division and vocalization of letters and the articulation of speech. Every generation and each individual therein is required—at least in principle—to turn his ear toward this voice and to what it demands or expresses from generation to generation. The main effort of the one who seeks truth is not to find something new, but to connect himself to the continuity of the tradition of the divine word, and to that which reaches him from there appropriate to his own time. In a homily on the verse, ". . . Now Moses diligently inquired" (Lev. 10:16: ". . . *darosh darash Moshe"; which may also be read "Now Moses thoroughly expounded"), based upon the masoretic tradition that the space between the two words *darosh darash* marks the precise "half-way point of the number of words of the Torah" (B. Kiddushin 30a), R. Moses Ḥayyim Ephraim of Sudylkow (grandson of the Ba'al Shem Tov, founder of the Ḥasidic movement), wrote in his book, *Degel Maḥaneh Efraim:*

> And one needs to understand what they meant to say by this, and what it implies. And one may say, according to my humble opinion: That it is known that there is an Oral Torah and a Written Torah—all is one, and neither one is separated from the other at all, for it is impossible to have one without the other. For the Written Torah without the Oral Torah is not a complete Torah, and is only like half a book, until the Sages came and expounded the Torah, and illuminated our eyes to reveal its mysteries and things which were hidden and unknown. And at times they would uproot the words of the Torah, as in the matter of stripes [i.e., corporal punishment], of which it is written, "Forty stripes you may give him" (Deut. 25:3), yet the Rabbis came and reduced it by one [i.e., they fixed the maximum at thirty-nine stripes]. And all this is in accordance with the manifestation of the Holy Spirit, which the Master, blessed be He, made appear to them . . . and it was concerning this that the Torah hinted . . ."half"—that is, a part and not a complete thing. And in the *derush* (i.e., expositions) of the sayings of the Rabbis, the Torah was completed, to become a whole book.[5]

In these comments, this Ḥasidic author expressed the sensitivities of many generations.

The Jews, who in terms of biological existence are hardly deserving of more attention than any other nation of the ancient Near East which has long since disappeared, appeared on the historical scene together with their book. The people and the book were combined together in the self-awareness of the Jews and in the consciousness of the world. In world history they were characterized by the stamp of their writing, which greatly affected them. The connection between the people and the book was so strong and so organic that it could not be undone by the tempests of history. And they are still the people of the book, so that even in the secularization of the holy book and its transformation into a kind of epic of the Jewish nation, their claim is preserved and there still echoes something of the call that emerges from it. Whether this people will continue to exist after the undoing of this knot—which still exists and is reflected even in the cult of archaeology, which so many people in Israel today follow in their quest for themselves, and behind which in the final analysis there stands the frightening giant of the book and its voice—remains a profound and fateful question. A hundred years ago, one of the upright thinkers of the German bourgeoisie, Friedrich Theodor Fischer, wrote a sentence that today seems strange: "The ethical is always self-evident." Today, when the unethical seems so self-evident, does the Bible still address us with its call? And is the people of the book still able to do something with its book? Is it possible that a time will come when it will fall silent? I am convinced that the existence of this nation depends upon the answer to this question far more decisively than it does upon the ups and downs of politics.

Chapter Twenty

Three Types of Jewish Piety
(1969)*

I

Let me begin by quoting a talmudic story:

> Rabbi once opened his storehouse of victuals in a year of scarcity, proclaiming: "Let those enter who have studied Scripture, or Mishnah or Gemara or Halakhah or 'Aggadah. There is no admission, however, for the ignorant." R. Jonathan ben Amram pushed his way in and said: "Master, give me food!" He said: "My son, have you learnt the Scripture?" He replied: "No." "Have you learned Mishnah?" "No." "If so," he said, "then how can I give you food?" He said to him: "Feed me as the dog and the raven are fed." So he gave him food. After he went away, Rabbi's conscience smote him and he said: "Woe unto me that I have given my bread to a man without learning!" His son ventured to say to him: "Perhaps that was Jonathan ben Amram, your pupil, who all his life has made it a principle not to derive material benefit from the honor paid to the Torah?" Upon inquiry, it was discovered that it was so; whereupon Rabbi said: "All may now enter."[1]

---

* Reprinted in *Ariel* 32(1973), 5–24. Also reprinted in *Devarim be-go,* 541–56. The notes to this essay, except where otherwise specified, are by Scholem.

One can talk about a religion and its specific world in many ways. One can describe or analyze its theology and dogma, that is, its teaching about God and Creation and the place of man in the scheme of things. One can also describe its ritual and way of life *(Lebensordnung)* and, in particular, I would say that often the liturgy, the order of prayers, and the life reflected in them serve as a true mirror of the spiritual life of a religion. Some of the best works on Judaism or Christianity have brought out the particular color and life of such groups by looking closely at liturgy. But this is not what I propose to do this time. I wish to talk here about the basic attitudes, about the ideal human types, which the history of rabbinic Judaism has evolved and I should like to discuss the tensions that are possible among them. The basic tension in the religious society of Judaism is that between intellectual and emotional factors, rational and irrational forces. The ideal types formed by such a society will necessarily reflect this tension.

Let me put it another way: How did the Jews see themselves, what were the ideal Jewish types of piety which Judaism knew in its classical forms over the last two thousand years? Such human types represented embodiments of a scale of values or of more or less autonomous highest values which have been offered as an example for imitation or to be striven for by other people. Such ideals of highest values realized in human lives will allow us an insight into what living Judaism meant for its people.

Now I do not think that there can be any doubt as to what these types of the ideal Jew are. They are, if you will allow me to use the popular Hebrew terms, the *talmid ḥakham,* the rabbinic scholar; the *tzaddik,* the Just Man; and the *ḥasid,* a term which it is not easy to translate even though its meaning will be made quite clear to us. Everybody has heard about these types in a more or less vague way, but we shall try to take a somewhat closer look at the meaning of each of them. Let me say at the outset that I am not discussing here biblical religion. I am discussing Judaism as constituted in its talmudic and rabbinical forms, to which Jewish philosophy or, for that matter, Jewish mysticism have added other dimensions without basically changing its substance.

That is the reason why I am not speaking in this context of the prophet as an ideal type. Prophecy as seen in Judaism is not something for which one can prepare oneself, which can be made the ultimate aim of a religious path. The prophet is a man chosen by God for a mission to his people whatever his preparation or lack of preparation for such a mission may be. You can neither educate your pupils for such a state nor can you set it as your own aim. It depends on something utterly beyond you, not to be foreseen and not to be sustained in a continuous frame of mind or as an attainment available *ad libitum.* You may argue that in early biblical times we hear about schools of prophets, but they have no relation to Judaism as an historical phenomenon as it crystallized after the Babylonian exile. For the philosophers of Judaism, such as Maimonides, prophecy was indeed a highest spiritual state, but not one to which we may aspire in our time and place. It was something belonging to the past, to the creative periods of Revelation, in other words: something belonging to biblical theology but not to the concrete requirements within the framework of our own life as Jews.

I mentioned in the first place the figure of the *talmid ḥakham,* the rabbinic scholar, or, in the literal translation of this extremely modest term: "the pupil of a sage." Now what is meant by this term? It is, above all, an intellectual value and a value of a life of contemplation. It has no essential relation to an emotional scale of values. What is asked of the scholar? A rational effort of the mind and its concentration. He is a student of Scripture and tradition who has fully mastered the ways and means by which these two spheres—or should I say sources of the religious life of Judaism?—are connected. Let us pause here for a moment. Judaism, like other religions based on the principle of Revelation, has a canon, an established collection of sacred Scripture, and the Holy Writ contains the truth about human life. The basic assumption of a religious constitution based on Revelation and tradition, as historical Judaism obviously is, can be formulated in a simple and yet far-reaching way which has profound implications of its own. The truth is given and known once and for all. It has not to be discovered. It has been laid down. The great task is to pass it on and to develop its meaning for every subsequent generation.

Modern man is prone to think highly of originality. Now, I would stress the fact that originality is not a value highly considered by the great religions. They do not think the truth has still to be discovered. It is there, in Revelation, for all to see. It is the tremendous conflict between the modern and the traditionalist mind that they clash over this evaluation of originality and the discovery of truth. But even within the old framework there is still immense room for the exercise of originality—but of an originality that does not acknowledge itself as such. Rather, it hides behind the unassuming name of commentary, as though all that remained to be done was to elicit and to develop what is laid down, perhaps only in a general way, in the documents of Revelation.

The tradition of rabbinical Judaism constitutes a method of exploring the meaning of Scripture. It has gone to great lengths, sometimes in highly colorful and paradoxical ways, to stress this point—namely, that whatever a confirmed and genuine scholar of Scripture can say about its meaning and application at any given time has been somehow hidden away in

Scripture itself and is a part of Revelation in its more general sense, comprising what in Judaism is called the Oral Law, *Torah shebe'al peh.* Let me illustrate this by a famous story told in the Talmud about Rabbi Akiva in the second century, that is to say, about a man who was always considered as the perfect embodiment of the type of which I am talking and who did more than any other single great teacher in Judaism to bring about the crystallization of rabbinical Judaism into a system of extraordinary vitality. The story, for all its simplicity, is not without sublimity and depth or a twinkle of irony.

> When Moses ascended on high he found the Holy One, blessed be He, engaged in affixing coronets to the letters. Said Moses: "Lord of the Universe, who stays Thy hand?" [That is to say: is there anything wanting in the Torah that these additions in the form of coronets are necessary?] He answered: "There will arise a man at the end of many generations, Akiva ben Joseph by name, who on each tittle will expound heaps and heaps of laws." Said Moses: "Lord of the Universe, permit me to see him." He replied: "Turn thee around." Moses went and sat down behind eight rows [of Akiva's disciples]. He was unable to understand their arguments, and this made him alarmed [because he was unable to follow the discourse on the Torah given by himself]. But when they came to a certain subject and the disciples said to the Master: "Whence do you know this?", and he replied: "It is a teaching given unto Moses on Sinai," he was comforted. Thereupon he returned to the Holy One, blessed be He, and said: "Lord of the Universe, Thou hast such a man and Thou givest the Torah by me?" He replied: "Be silent, for such is My decree."[2]

The genuine *talmid ḥakham,* in the eyes of tradition, cannot say anything utterly new, but only what was always known and contained in the source of Revelation. His specific task in the world of Judaism is, then, a twofold one. First of all, he brings out what was implied in the Torah, he is in full command of the art of reading and interpreting the sacred text. Secondly, he is able to apply his interpretation to the changing needs of the community. All this leads to one more point: the real sage who is so unpretentiously called only a pupil of the sages is the teacher of his community. His is not a prophetic quality; what is expected of him is not any novel revelation or truth of religion. The decisive qualities expected of him are his sobriety and rationality, by which he is able to expound the values that have come down and been upheld by tradition, and his clarity of mind, which makes him an educator, handing down those values to the next generation. He need not be ashamed to call himself what he is. We would think it pretty strange if somebody came along announcing: "I am a *tzaddik"* or "I am a *ḥasid,"* and the very statement would in our eyes disprove itself. But the Talmud says: "If you come to a foreign place where you are not known, it is proper for you to say: 'I am a pupil of the sages *(talmid ḥakham)'"* (b. Nedarim 62a). It is a measure of the sobriety of which I have spoken, of the reticence with which this type is described, that for many generations, in European Jewry, the highest praise you could pay to somebody was the deceptively simple sentence, *"Er kann lernen"* (He knows how to learn). No more modest formula could be found to express the highest valuation. The little verb *lernen* (to learn) has an enormous implication. *Lernen* does not only mean studying; it means complete mastery of the intellectual tradition of the Talmudist's world. He of whom this can be said is at the same time the teacher of his generation.

The scholar, in the sense in which I have tried to describe him, is at the same time a goal of education; I might say, the highest goal of education for Jews over the last two thousand years of their history. I think that it is a tremendous thing, speaking for the extraordinary vitality that has gone into the making of this type of Jew, that it has been able to maintain its unbroken power over such a period and in the face of all the vicissitudes of Jewish history. It is an ideal toward which you can educate people and develop institutions that might produce it. And it is an ideal that held equally for Jews wherever they lived, whether in Yemen or Russia, in Babylon or France. Even today the power of this ideal has not been broken, although the last generations have made heavy inroads into the traditional ideals of Jewish life and we are witnessing revolutionary changes, both in Israel and the Diaspora, affecting the basis on which this life was built. But still, it might be said that the number of students in Israel studying in the yeshiva—that institution which is intended to develop this particular ideal type—is approximately as large as the number of students in institutions of secular higher learning. At the same time it is indicative of the depth of the crisis in which we live that these institutions have to a great extent ceased to fulfill that central social function which was one of their greatest claims to fame in our history. The *talmid ḥakham,* as I have described him, fulfilled a central function in the Jewish community; he had authority in the world of tradition, but he did not evade his responsibility for the application of the Old Torah to his own time. It is this evasion, this shying away from taking on responsibility, which is one of the more distressing facets of the clash of ideals that we are now witnessing in Israel.

I said that the figure of the *talmid ḥakham* had a deep rational significance. But its aura has pervaded Jewish society far beyond rational limits. The magic of the names of the great representatives of this type spread far and wide and became household words to millions. The Gaon of Vilna, or Rabbi Yitzhak Elḥanan, the Rav of Kovno, to name only two outstanding figures, were such archetypal representatives of the ideal *talmid ḥakham*.

Controversy about the value of this phenomenon has not been lacking since the early days of Christianity. It was open to attack, I might even say it invited attack, from a more emotional point of view and from those who sought the center of religion and religious life in other spheres of a more emotional character. It is not for me to take sides in this discussion. What I wish us to understand is the structure, the build-up and the meaning of this type which, after all, has given to the Jewish people that particular class of intelligentsia for which they have been, rightly or wrongly, praised or condemned.

II

When we come to speak of the two other ideal types, the *tzaddik* and the *ḥasid*, we enter an entirely different sphere. The values represented by the "pupil of the sages," the rabbinical scholar, belong, as I said before, to the sphere of contemplation. The scholar moves himself into the world of the Torah, which for him is a vehicle to a purely spiritual life. He studies actions, but not in their active quality; he transforms them into subjects for contemplation, intellectual concentration, and judicious penetration. The *tzaddik* and the *ḥasid*, however, are not judged by the perfection of their intellectual penetration, but by the way in which they discharge their religious duties in practice. They are, to put it briefly, ideals of the active life. Of course, the types are not mutually exclusive. A scholar may wellnigh be a *tzaddik* or a *ḥasid* at the same time, and vice versa. Each is to be judged by his own scale of values. If the *talmid ḥakham* represented an intellectual value in its perfection, the *tzaddik* or the *ḥasid* represent what we would call ethical values, values of the heart and of the deeds of man.

In popular parlance and even in some parts of the old rabbinical sources, there are no clear-cut distinctions and separations between the two conceptions. There is a tendency to speak of the *tzaddikim* and to ascribe to them the widest range of virtues and qualities, and very often the terms could be exchanged. The great figures of biblical literature are characterized almost throughout as *tzaddikim*. On the other hand, if the Talmud tells some extraordinary story about a feat of religious performance or a miracle vouchsafed to a pious man, it generally opens: *ma'aseh beḥasid eḥad*—"there is a story of a *ḥasid* . . ." But we may safely say that, for the religious consciousness of Judaism as it developed from talmudic times and crystallized in the Middle Ages, the difference between the two types and their specific characteristics became more and more distinct and significant. Particularly, we have a very large literature on the ethical behavior and the moral ideas of Judaism, a literature which stretches over almost a thousand years and which was not so much destined for the use of the scholar, but which appealed in general to the common reader with a moderate or even less than moderate knowledge of things Jewish. It was this literature, in contradistinction to the proper halakhic or talmudic literature, which not everybody had the prerequisites to understand, that was most influential in bringing the message of Judaism to the widest circles. It is in such sources, but also in many other documents of Jewish life from those times, that the distinction between the two types becomes crystal clear. They may still be mentioned together as a kind of formula (as in the benediction in the *Shemoneh 'Esreh* prayer, opening *'Al ha-tzaddikim ve-'al ha-ḥasidim)* but, rather than being understood as some kind of synonyms, they are now perceived as two basically distinctive qualities.

The term *tzaddik* originates in forensic language. A *tzaddik* is somebody who has been before the courts and has been found "not guilty." It is in this very sober vein that the term has entered Jewish ethics. The *tzaddik* is the Jew who tries to comply with the commandments of the Law. He would be a *tzaddik* in the eyes of God if, brought before His court, it would be found that he has fulfilled his duties at least more than fifty percent. If the scales of the balance swing slightly in his favor, he is reckoned among the *tzaddikim*. We mortals, however, do not know how the scales of God's justice work. In the eyes of his fellow man, the *tzaddik* is one who tries his best to fulfill the Law insofar as it lies within his power. For him, all commandments, all duties put upon him by religion are of equal importance; he tries to pay attention to all of them equally without stressing any particular part of them. No special grace is required to accomplish this. Everybody is called upon to do his duty to the best of his capacity, and everybody is equipped with sufficient strength and innate judgment to try and succeed. He may not succeed fully, for there are many pitfalls in man's way. But the *tzaddik* does not lose sight of the goal; he may stumble seven times, but this will not prevent him from going on and dividing his energies among the manifold tasks which he is called upon to fulfill. He is the man who puts harmonious order into his life, or at least tries to do so and essentially succeeds. This order is the order of the Torah, an all-comprehensive ideal of harmony in the deeds and activities of men that leaves no room for extravagance. The *tzaddik*, as the Talmud says, is not expected to be a man of words, he is to be a man of deeds. He may be a great scholar in the sense that I have described, but even though he may be devoid of intellectual attainments, if he were a simple and unsophisticated man, he could still be a *tzaddik*. And even if he fulfills his task fully and is as successful in its realization as could be wished, he is still a *tzaddik* and nothing else. And indeed, in the eyes of Jewish ethics this is a great deal. The *tzaddik*, to put it in a sententious way, is the ideal of the normal Jew; if he fulfills all that he sets out to do, he is still the embodiment of the normal Jew at his best. This is the main point, stressed by the tradition of our moralist literature.

In the moral sphere, indeed, the ideal of the *tzaddik* contains a common element with that of the scholar. This is the sobriety of the ideal, the absence of emotionalism. The Just Man is balanced in his actions: there is something deeply composed and cool-headed about him, however intense may be the passion to fulfill the divine command that drives him. He does not lose control of himself. And this is of course the reason why righteousness, the quality of the *tzaddik*, is generally considered in Jewish tradition as something that can be taught, for which one can be educated and trained. The classical manuals of Jewish morals describe such training for the state of *tzaddik*, none more stringently than the famous treatise *Mesillat Yesharim* (The Path of the Upright) by the Italian poet and mystic Moses Ḥayyim Luzzatto (1740), no doubt one of the noblest products of Hebrew literature. The author, who tried to combine the two ideals of the *talmid ḥakham* and the *tzaddik*, set out to teach the beginner, step by step, how to achieve these goals, which are within the rational grasp and within the power of goodwill implanted in all of us and open to systematic development. Or, as another moralist, Baḥya ben Asher, defined it five hundred years before him:

> The main principle of the Torah and its foundation consist in the command that a man should break his passions and his natural drives and subjugate them to the domination of his rational soul. Whoever accomplishes this and makes his intellect the master of his passions and subdues his animal soul is called a *tzaddik*.[3]

This harmonious and judicious function of the *tzaddik* who tries to dispense justice by his actions is maintained widely and has been greatly stressed by the mystics of Judaism. About seven hundred years ago, one of the great Kabbalists, pursuing the line of thought which I have just indicated, said:

> For this is the reason why the *tzaddikim* are called Just Men, because they have put everything in the world, both in the inner and outer world, in its rightful place, and nothing oversteps its prescribed limits, and this is why they are called Just Men.[4]

This definition dominates the spheres of Jewish ethics, especially in the ethics of the Kabbalists and the Ḥasidim. The *tzaddik* puts everything in its proper place. This appears to be a very simple sentence. But the simplicity of this definition should not deceive us as to the messianic implication and the utopian power lodged in such a sentence. For, in the eyes of Judaism, a world where everything is in its proper place is precisely what is meant by a messianic world, a world redeemed. The idea of the Just Man is thus linked with the messianic idea. The *tzaddik* who puts everything into harmonious order and causes things to dwell together in this world undisturbed and undivided brings about the revelation of God's unity through the harmonious unity of the world. The disorder in the world is at the heart of injustice, the objectionable and reprehensible are connected to disorder. Therefore, the Just Man, for whom the Torah is a law of order and the guide to order, is concerned with putting the world in order and keeping it so. There is a messianic spark in his activities.

III

In speaking of the *tzaddik*, I have described the ideal of the average Jew, I might even say, the ideal *ba'al-bayit*, the family man and citizen of the community. He measures his steps, he weighs his actions, he considers the demands made of him, and by doing so, and in combining his efforts with those of his like, he as it were creates the Jewish community in its highest form. Of course, he will be called upon to resist temptation, to prove his worth, and to overcome great difficulties, but nothing essentially extraordinary is asked of him. The *ḥasid*, whom I am going to discuss now, represents a very different type, is in fact at an opposite pole in the world of human values. In the ethical literature of Judaism and in general, wherever the terms are used with more or less precision and a sense of discrimination, being a *tzaddik* always means distinctly less than being a *ḥasid*. Whereas the *tzaddik* is the ideal embodiment of the norm, the *ḥasid* is the exceptional type of man. He is the radical Jew who, in trying to follow the spiritual call, goes to extremes. The kind of extremism practiced by such devotees has changed considerably in the course of time, but its nature has not. The *ḥasid* does not, like the *tzaddik*, do what is demanded of him, but goes beyond it. He is never content with the middle road, he does not count his steps. He is the enthusiast, whose radicalism and utter emotional commitment are not to be deterred by bourgeois considerations. The self-restraint characteristic of the behavior of the *tzaddik* is foreign to his nature. Whatever he does, he does in a spirit of spontaneous exuberance and of supererogation, that is to say, far beyond the requirements of duty.

The Hebrew word *ḥesed* is not easy to translate. It combines the meanings of charity, lovingkindness, and grace. When we speak of God's *ḥesed*, in contradistinction to His justice and rigor, we indicate the quality of His boundless generosity, the exuberant and spontaneous nature of His benevolence and grace. The usual translation of *ḥasid*, "pious," does not really render its meaning. When the Psalmist says of God that He is a *ḥasid* in all of His deeds, he does not refer to His piety but to those qualities which I have just described. And the human *ḥasid*, in his own limited sphere, still represents the same basic qualities which he has made the cornerstone of his moral being. He adds to the severity of the prohibitions by forbidding himself things which even under the Law are permissible, and he adds to the commandments by doing a lot of things which under the Law he is not required to do. He demands nothing of others, everything from himself. The "Sayings of the Fathers" in the Mishnah have the famous definition of the four qualities in man:

> He who says: Mine is mine and thine is thine, he is the average man, and some say, it is the quality of Sodom. Mine is thine and thine is mine, that is the ignorant. Mine is thine and thine is thine, that is the *ḥasid*. Thine is mine and mine is mine, that is the wicked.[5]

The *tzaddik* follows a law valid for all. I would say that he is the Jewish disciple of Kantian ethics. The *ḥasid* follows a law that is valid and binding only for himself. That often makes him an extravagant figure, bound to arouse antagonism and opposition by the very radicalism of his doings. There is something non-conformist and even an element of holy anarchism in his nature. It is true, in his outward behavior he submits to the established law in all its rigor, but he transcends it by his spiritual fervor. In rabbinic usage, the term *ḥasid* never means or implies an attitude of mind alone, it always carries the connotation of the practical application of such an attitude. The old talmudic phrase significantly puts together the two terms: *ḥasidim ve-anshei ma'aseh*—"*ḥasidim* and men of action."

This element of radicalism is always present when the great authorities of Judaism speak of the *ḥasid* and of his quality called *ḥasidut*. Maimonides explains[6] that a man who gives equal attention to every mitzvah or commandment is a *tzaddik*, but a man who singles out one mitzvah in order to exalt it, to go to extremes in its performance and thus leave the middle road, is a *ḥasid*. It is clear from all this that there is a peculiar emotional element in the *ḥasid*. The intensity of emotion which he pours into the execution of the special duties that he has taken on himself makes him an enthusiast. Over and over again we hear of *ḥasidim* who take one of the 613 commandments and make it a life task. They elaborate it in richest detail. If they are scholars at the same time, they try to work out all its ramifications and combine sophistication with enthusiasm. If they are unlearned—and, a famous saying of the Mishnah notwithstanding, a man could be a Ḥasid quite independent of learning and even innocent of learning—they think out the widest application of the one great mitzvah for which they live. There were among them specialists in chastity or in charity, in walking in the fear of God or in the application of love.

If a man decides to take the path of *ḥasidut*, he has to suffer for it. It is even said that he gets a special angel to guide him on the way of suffering, to enable him to stand up to the tribulations of his career. There is thus a basic element of self-denial and asceticism in this figure and this, in my opinion, explains a phenomenon of great importance on Jewish history. For all the high evaluation of the ḥasidic type, there is at the same time a noticeable reservation toward him or even a certain distrust. This fact finds its expression in the notion that, throughout a period of at least fifteen hundred years, no organization of *ḥasidim* as a group has been allowed to come into being. This is all the more remarkable as there was no lack of books propagating the ḥasidic type as something of the highest value, both among Spanish and German or Ashkenazic Jews.

One of the most famous works of medieval Hebrew literature is a rather extensive book called *Sefer Ḥasidim* (the Book of the Ḥasidim).[7] It was written during the twelfth and thirteenth centuries in Germany and expressed the ideals of a religious movement called German or Ashkenazic Ḥasidism. Here the virtues and qualities forming the true *ḥasid* were lauded: the renunciation of profane pleasure, the conquering of the temptation of ordinary life, imperviousness to insult and the bearing of shame without flinching, the acting in every respect within the line of strict justice, and the like. But even though there was a tendency to put the highest value on such qualities, the *ḥasid* remains always an exceptional, an unconventional case, a highly individualistic and strange phenomenon in his milieu. No advice is given as to how to organize such people into a common framework; on the contrary, it is taken for granted that every one of them would be active only within the framework of the community of the common people and not strive to build a community of their own. We therefore find such Ḥasidim here and there in large and small places, but it is obvious that the tendency of the rabbinical authority was to integrate them into the general Jewish community and not to encourage separatism.

This is in marked contrast to similar tendencies within Christianity, in which parallel tendencies of Christian radicalism found their expression in the discipline of monastic life, where much of what we would call ḥasidic behavior was preached and practiced. Judaism has frowned upon such separate organization of the people of spirit, of a separate class which was expected to enact the demands of religion in everyday life and leave it to the rest to muddle through as well as they could. There is an essentially sober streak to Judaism which, for all its intellectual and emotional commitment to its religious tenets and demands, strove to prevent just this stratification of a religious society which we find in medieval Christianity. It tried, instead, to bind together the disparate elements into one community and to allot to each type, be it the scholar, the *ḥasid*, or the *tzaddik*, an organic function within this framework.

I have said that the *ḥasidim* were single figures. Let me illustrate this from an authentic source. We have lists of martyrs slain in many parts of Germany during the persecutions of the twelfth and thirteenth centuries. Many communities used to record their names for remembrance by subsequent generations and they were recited at the *Yizkor* (Memorial) service on High Holidays. Many of these lists have been preserved and published by historians. They mention the names of the men and women concerned and are extremely reticent in conferring honorific titles. They say that somebody was a scholar or a rabbi, and there are several men of this type in most communities, but only here and there, used very sparingly and obviously meant as the highest sign of distinction, do we find the title *ḥasid* or *ḥasidah* added to the name of a man or a woman. None of these Ḥasidim are at the same time characterized as scholars—and this at a time when the ideals of German Ḥasidism were widely propagated in these communities.[8]

Whether you are a *ḥasid* or not is basically a matter of gift and character. It is a propensity which you either have or do not. If you have it, you can develop it. But you cannot educate everyone to become a *ḥasid*, as you can in principle educate everyone to become a *tzaddik*. Rabbi Ḥayyim Vital, one of the great Kabbalists of Safed in the sixteenth century, offers the following explanation of the terms, which still clearly indicates the superiority of the *ḥasid*.

> He who conscientiously keeps the 613 commands of the Torah, who perfects his rational soul but has not yet made his good propensities part and parcel of his being and still has to fight for them against his evil inclination—such a one is called a perfect *tzaddik*. But when his good propensities have become an integral part of his own nature and come to him so naturally as to make him keep the Torah in loving joy without having to

fight his evil urge, because his body is purified as if the good were his nature since he came out of his mother's womb—such alone is indeed a perfect *ḥasid*.[9]

Even in that great manual of moral values which I have mentioned, Moses Ḥayyim Luzzatto, when starting to discuss the *ḥasid*, in contradistinction to the *tzaddik*, insists that all the advice or analysis which he can give is of no avail. The main thing is, according to him, that only those who have been vouchsafed a gift of Divine grace, who have a particular spark in their soul, may strive for the quality of a *ḥasid*. He embarks on polemics against the vulgar and easy use of the term to denote what he calls

> practices that are empty or against common sense or sound judgment, with constant weeping and excessive bowing and strange mortifications of the flesh, such as immersion in ice-cold water or rolling in the snow. But it is not on them that *ḥasidut* rests.[10]

But whatever Luzzatto's own lofty ideal of the *ḥasid*, which is largely identical with what we would call a saint, it is clear that he and his contemporaries had a very definite type in mind when speaking of *ḥasidim* and *ḥasidut*. There existed a pattern of common behavior which characterized the Ḥasid as a visible and a very pronounced radical in Jewish society, although there may have been quite a number of invisible though no less pronounced radicals. This pattern showed no basic differences in Turkey, Italy, Holland, or Poland.

I have tried to delineate three types which, together, give us a picture of the moral ideal of Judaism. In the course of history, all kinds of combinations and alterations have made their appearance. In particular, many examples could be adduced as to the popular usage of *tzaddik* and *ḥasid* in an imprecise way. But surely no stranger example can be found than the metamorphosis of the terms in the ḥasidic movement of the eighteenth century originating in Podolia and Volhynia and centered on the figure of Israel Ba'al Shem Tov, who died in 1760. It is in many ways a striking illustration of some of the points that I have made here, particularly regarding the organization of people of the ḥasidic type. For it was only as an organization in which all kinds of people gathered around a central figure who was of a genuinely ḥasidic type that Ḥasidism could maintain itself.

If the leaders had clung together and formed a body composed exclusively of people of their own type, the movement would have succumbed under the onslaught of old-fashioned rabbinical Judaism, whose antagonism it in any event could not fail to arouse. We would not be talking of a specific world of Ḥasidism, in the sense of the word as it is used with regard to this movement, some of whose ramifications are still with us, were it not for its success in placing the figure of the Jewish saint as a radical Jew into an organic Jewish social body.

A very curious metamorphosis of terms has however taken place here. It never would have occurred to earlier generations, either in literature or in life, to give the title of *ḥasidim* to people who admired *ḥasidim*. But this is precisely what has happened here. People who admire the living embodiments of hasidic ideals called themselves *ḥasidim*, a rather paradoxical, if not to say scandalous, usage of the word—while the true *ḥasidim*, those who live up to the ideal, now came to be called *tzaddikim*. This novel turn of terminology is surely highly confusing. A *tzaddik* in the hasidic sense has nothing to do with what the term meant in the traditional usage which I have tried to explain, but rather connotes the "super-*ḥasid*." It is beyond the scope of this lecture to explain the historical reasons for this change and the processes by which it came about. What we are concerned with is the understanding of the essential meaning of the three types, of the phenomena themselves, by whatever names they may be known.

Let me close with a remark about a figure of Jewish popular tradition in which the original figure of the *ḥasid* has reached a climax. This is the concept of the so-called hidden or concealed *tzaddikim* which, since the time of the hasidic movement, has held a place of honor in Jewish legend. Its roots are very old. The famous second century teacher, Rabbi Simeon bar Yoḥai, was credited with the saying: "The world never lacks thirty *tzaddikim* like Abraham."[11] These protect the world, just as Abraham did in his own time. Later on, another talmudic teacher maintained that in every generation the world has no fewer than thirty-six just men who are vouchsafed the vision of the countenance of God.[12] This is the source of the concept of the thirty-six hidden *tzaddikim* of popular legend, known in Yiddish as *Lamedvovniks,* after the Hebrew notation of the number thirty-six. It is on them and their merit that the world rests.[13]

There are two types of *tzaddikim:* those who are hidden and keep to themselves, and those who manifest themselves to their fellow-men and are working, as it were, under the public eye. The former is called a *nistar,* that is, "a concealed one," and the latter *mefursam,* that is, "known." The hidden *tzaddikim* are of the higher order, because they are not tempered by the vanity almost inseparable from a public career.[14] Indeed, some of them take it upon themselves to create an image in sharp contradiction to their true and hidden nature. They may not even be aware of their own nature and go about performing their good deeds in secret without knowing that they are of the elect. They are hidden not only from mankind but from themselves. Eastern Jewish folklore was indefatigable in elaborating these aspects and particularly their paradoxical side. Legend has it that one of the thirty-six is the Messiah and would reveal himself as such, if only his generation were worthy of redemption. You can never know who these highest bearers of moral standards are. One of them, and this is the final moral to which this idea points, may be your neighbor.

Part Five

Reflections on His Contemporaries

Chapter Twenty-one

On Kafka's *The Trial* (1926)*

If one can say that prose, in order to be renowned for absolute greatness, must necessarily shed light upon the theological contents of experience in the realm of language—then this book serves as a confirmation of this. After millennia, there has been attained anew, from an unexpected point of view, the linguistic world of expression of the Book of Job. Essentially, this work is without parallel, apart from the Book of Job. The situation of the hidden trial, within the framework of whose rules human life occurs, is developed in these two works to the very highest level. One may conjecture that never did any Jew attain such a fashioning of his world from such an inner and profound center of Judaism. Proof of this is found in the penultimate chapter, "In the Cathedral," where we find the peak of the theological capacity which may be attained by artistic prose. Many readers have certainly already listened to the voices which burst forth from this chapter, from these few pages. The parable which describes the guardian of the law is like a kind of summary of Jewish theology, which in its unique dialectic is not destructive but, on the contrary, radiates a powerful inner melancholy. Here the true talmudic thinking breaks its light into a rainbow of colors.

* An unpublished manuscript found in Scholem's *nachlass*. Published in *'Od Davar*, 337.

Chapter Twenty-two

With a Copy of Kafka's
The Trial—A Poem (1934)*

Have we completely separated from You
O God? In darkness
shall we no longer be overtaken by any whiff
of Your peace, of Your message?

Has Your voice been so extinguished
In the wastes of Zion? Or
has it not at all penetrated to here, to within
the kingdom of enchanted illusions?

The great deception of the world
has already been completed to the very rafters.
Allow to awaken, O God, the man
who has been severed by Your nothingness.

Only thus shall Your face be revealed, O God,
to a generation that has thrown You off
Your nothingness is all that is left
for him to experience of You.

* Published in the supplement to *Ha-Aretz* for Scholem's eightieth birthday, December 2, 1977; reprinted in *'Od Davar*, 338–39.

Only thus does there come to remembrance
A teaching, which splits the enchantment:
a heritage more certain than all
of the hidden judgment.

We have been weighed on the scales of Job
to a hair's breadth.
We are disconsolate as on the Judgment Day,
without comfort or knowledge.

In realms without end,
our image is reflected.
There is no man who knows all the way:
it darkens every eye.

The redemption brings no benefit
That star is too far distant,
Even should you arrive there,
You yourself, your body, stand in your way.

Exposed to the mercies of mighty forces,
who cannot be controlled by any oath
Nothing can live without
being gathered into itself.

Yet from the heart of the chaos
There sometimes bursts forth a distant light
But it cannot show the goal,
which the law has commanded us.

Since then, there stands before our eyes
the same melancholy knowledge;
Suddenly the veil is rent, O God,
from upon Your supreme glory.

On the earth your trial has begun:
Shall it cease before the throne of Your glory?
You have no defenders,
Here all the illusions burst.

And who is it that is accused—
You or the Creation?
Were a man to ask this question
You would be silent.

For is it possible to ask such a thing?
Is not the answer known?
Ah! One must live with all this,
until the day that we stand in judgment.

Chapter Twenty-three

Franz Rosenzweig and His Book *The Star of Redemption* (1930)*

Wenn aber stirbt alsdenn,
An dem am meisten
Die Schönheit hieng, daß an der Gestalt
Ein Wunder war und die Himmlischen gedeutet
Auf ihn, und wenn, ein Rätsel ewig füreinander,
Sie sich nicht fassen können
Einander, die zusammenlebten
Im Gedächtnis . . .
    selber sein Angesicht
Der Höchste wendet
Darob, daß nirgend ein
Unsterbliches mehr am Himmel zu sehn ist oder
auf grüner Erde, was ist dies?

* Based upon a eulogy for Rosenzweig on the thirtieth day following his death *(sheloshim)*, at the Hebrew University of Jerusalem, 1930, published in *Devarim be-go*, 407–25. Previously published in English in the conference volume of the Fourth Jerusalem Philosophical Encounter (1980), *The Philosophy of Franz Rosenzweig*, edited by Paul Mendes-Flohr (Tauber Institute for the Study of European Jewry. Series No. 8; Hanover and London: for Brandeis University Press, by the University Press of New England, 1988), 20–41. Translated into English by Paul Mendes-Flohr, with notes by the editor-translator.

Es ist der Wurf das des Säemanns, wenn er faßt
Mit der Schaufel den Weizen,
Und wirft, dem Klaren zu, ihn schwingend über die Tenne.
Ihm fällt die Schale vor den Füßen, aber
Ans Ende kommet das Korn.
Und nicht ein Übel ists, wenn einiges
Verloren gehet und von der Rede
Verhallet der lebendige Laut.
    Hölderlin

But when he then dies,
To whom beauty clung most,
So that a miracle was wrought
In his form and the heavenly pointed at him,
And when, an eternal enigma for one another
They cannot grasp
One another, who lived together
In memory . . .
Even the Highest averts
His face, so that nowhere again
An immortal is to be seen in the skies
Or on the green earth, what is this?

It is the sower's throw, when he holds
The wheat in his shovel,
And throws, towards the open, swinging it across
The thrashing-floor. The husks fall at his feet,
But the corn reaches its end.
No harm, no evil it is if some of the speech
Is lost and
The living sound subsides . . .[1]

In his short life Rosenzweig accomplished much. He came from the deso-
late Jewish wastelands in Germany, of which the word assimilation gives
only the slightest hint, and grew up and developed his vast talents without
Judaism and without Torah. His first accomplishment was in philosophy
in the academic sense. Wholeheartedly he entered the grove of German
idealism, wherein he came upon one of the decisive discoveries in the history of its development—the discovery of the earliest outline of the idealist
system, namely, a manuscript in the handwriting of the young Hegel but
which according to Rosenzweig actually recorded the ideas of the young
Schelling.[2] It was to Hegel that Rosenzweig devoted his first major book,
Hegel und der Statt (1920) (Hegel and the State), a book that superbly combines a profound descent into the world of dialectics with strict philological work. Hegel, who laid the cornerstone of idealistic philosophy and who

became the standard (and at the time the stumbling block) for the philosophizing of all those who came after him, drew Rosenzweig too into his charmed circle. Even after Rosenzweig freed himself from the spell of Hegel's philosophy, it left its impress on him for a long time, as the firm and inner style of his second book, *The Star of Redemption* (1921), testifies.

It was Hermann Cohen, Hegel's *locum tenens*—even if unwittingly and unwillingly—who drew Rosenzweig to Judaism, or more precisely, who led him to the great awakening for which a language was found in his book *The Star of Redemption*, about which I shall have more to say later. The chance meeting between these two men—as Rosenzweig related it, he went to one of Cohen's classes at the Hochschule für die Wissenschaft des Judentums in Berlin merely out of curiosity and without any vital interest—led not merely to a friendship, but to a richly consequential love between the old man of seventy who was then about to rediscover Judaism, and the youth of twenty-five, who had then only just begun to formulate his view of the world. That encounter became a great event along the road of the Jewish people's spiritual history. Cohen's noble personality, which had as if transmigrated and reached us from the days of antiquity (all of us who still sat at his feet felt that way), and his talks—not Cohen's philosophical system but, if I can be precise about the intention of this word, the system or method of his thought, its inner flow and flux—made a deep impression on Rosenzweig, which is discernible in everything he wrote subsequently, up until his very last days.

During the First World War, while serving on the Macedonian front, Rosenzweig issued his famous appeal for the establishment of an Academy for the Science of Judaism as an organ for the renewal of Jewish life in Germany. All of us who were then in Germany remember how great a resonance the appeal, contained in his open letter to Hermann Cohen, which appeared under the title *"Zeit ist's"* ("It Is Time"), had for many.[3] He called for a new form of Jewish education and for an institution that would engage in the training of teacher-scholars who would combine precision of discernment and depth of knowledge with an alertness to the contemporary demands of a living education. The Academy for the Science of Judaism that was founded in Berlin in 1919 was the fruit of this first call by Rosenzweig, even though he tended to disavow his creation after it had strayed from the path he regarded as its very raison d'être: the path of a bold association between pure scholarship and the work of educating the Jewish public. In the last years of the war, as a soldier on the battlefield in the Balkans, he began his great book, the formulation of his *Weltanschauung*—*The Star of Redemption*. After the war he searched for a new way to fulfill his longing to study and teach. Cohen's spiritual heir, whose later introduction to Cohen's writings taught us to see and understand the fundamental revolution that had occurred in Cohen's spiritual world in his last years,[4] became once again a pupil and learned Talmud from the late Rabbi Neḥemiah Nobel,[5] the "Kabbalist" among the rabbis of Germany. Rosenzweig then founded the Freies Jüdisches Lehrhaus in Frankfurt, where, as director, he was the first of its pupils and where I and many of my early colleagues at the Hebrew University had our initial experiences as teachers. About all of this—his activity and great influence on our elders and youths in Germany, who at that time flocked to the rooms of his school from all camps and all parties in Jewry—much can be said, but it is not in this that his greatness should be seen. Nor do I have anything to say in explanation of the secret of his personality and the attractive force that emanated from him then, in the brief days when he had his health. His books will testify for him; I have already dressed my feelings in the words of the great German poet Hölderlin, with which I have prefaced my remarks. We who had the privilege of knowing Rosenzweig regarded him as one of the most sublime manifestations of the greatness and religious genius of our people; he already exemplified for us the truth of the sages' definition of religious genius: "For wheresoever we found his greatness and majesty, there we found his humility."[6]

I set out to address myself to what I called Rosenzweig's distinctive activity in theology. This theology was indeed new, and if I add that in his article *"Das neue Denken"* ("The New Thinking"),[7] one of his most distinguished pieces, he called the content of *The Star of Redemption* a philosophical system, it will be appreciated that we must establish the place of this great book, which appeared two years after the conclusion of World War I, in relation to the spiritual world of the generation that experienced that war. *The Star of Redemption,* written with an exemplary precision of thought but nevertheless in the style of that generation, was considered in Germany among Jews and Christians, believers and apostates, to be one of the most difficult books in the philosophical literature; one can be certain that Jewish theologians (if there be such) either have not read it or, if they have, have given up on it. This book, which tries to set out a new way of thinking, is not one of those books of which one can readily say, I have understood it. There is no hope of encompassing the content of a book as rich and profound as this in a brief essay, and certainly no hope of interpreting it; all I try to do is outline some of its major features. As for the historical status of the book, it can be grasped from three perspectives: philosophy, the general situation of theology in Rosenzweig's day, and the status of theology among the Jewish people in that period.

In reference to philosophy, Rosenzweig himself described his point of departure and formulated it very sharply in his lengthy introduction to the first part of the book, called "On the Possibility of Knowing the All" *("Über die Möglichkeit das All zu erkennen"),* which was intended as lethal criticism, as a war to the finish against idealism. For that is the demand and pretension of philosophical thought—to know the All, or the Whole. That was the demand from Parmenides to Hegel, "from Ionia to Jenas," as Rosenzweig put it. Never in the history of philosophy did this aspiration receive more extreme expression than in the doctrine of Hegel. It and all those resembling it, including the teachings of Hermann Cohen, were considered ripe fruit on that Tree of Knowledge called independence or "autonomy" of thought. When, in Hegel, philosophy encompassed its own history and made it too a part of the system of pure thought, when it also included God in the Whole, in the one All of its own thought, it reached its summit and came to its end. For in truth, what step could it still take without falling from its haughtiness? Pure autonomous thought brings forth *(erzeugt)* its content by itself and from itself, and this content is being *(das Sein);* the thought that thinks itself thinks the world, thinks the Whole. The unity of the Whole, the wholeness, is assured by the unity of thought. For, asks Hegel, what assures us that there is only one wholeness in the world? And Hegel replies, only the presupposition that the world can be reckoned in thought. Against the multiplicity of contents of cognition, the unity of thought maintains its identity with pure being. This indeed is a very proud and distinguished world: *hen kai pan* (one and all). Philosophy pretends to know the essence of the world and does not admit that something is missing from the wholeness it thinks. But can everything be grasped by thought? Is that philosophy's consolation to a flesh-and-blood individual who trembles with the fear of death, that it says to him we have already prepared for death and have overcome it by thinking? Does this consolation of Plato's really console us? Is not that answer a deception? It is this question of death that Rosenzweig placed at the very opening of his book, and truly there is no more apt point of departure than that for theology. This was, of course, not really the beginning of the rebellion against idealistic philosophy initiated by Kierkegaard's opposition to Hegel, and Nietzsche's objections to Schopenhauer, a rebellion later extended by Leo Shestov, who, when Edmund Husserl—perhaps the keenest mind to emerge from German Jewry—raised the Hegelian banner in his famous article "Philosophy as a Rigorous Science," came forward with his "Memento Mori," his remarks cutting to the very core of idealism.[8] It is not at all surprising that Rosenzweig and Shestov produced their works at the same time, during the First World War. The living present I, not the I of the doctrine of the transcendental subject of idealistic deduction and not the general I, the idea of the I, but the empirical I occurring in experience, the I that has a first name and a last name: that man Søren Kierkegaard and that man Friedrich Nietzsche asked about their place. For their very real afflictions, which idealism denies by not acknowledging them, there is no remedy in the system that is in a great hurry to pass from the wretched I that is no more than a "given" to the loftiness of the ideal subject. I wonder if anyone can read the modern idealists on the "given" as no more than a methodological principle, without despairing over the extent of this deception. In the world of idealism nothing is more contemptible than this "given" which, as it were, comes to the idealist as a reminder of sin, of the conjoining of being and thought involved in a rape, the groaning of the ravished I disturbing the repose of the noble philosophers. This empirical I has stepped outside of the philosophers' "Whole," finding itself beyond all-embracing thought, or more precisely: in the thought by which it thought itself it could not think anything else, not the world and not God. The unity of thought, and within it the unity of being, the All or Whole of philosophy, were shattered. And along with the I's departure from the fortress of the All, the divinity too left, and among the broken fragments of the pan-logical cosmos, among the "breaking of the All," philosophy searches its way. This "breaking of the vessels" of idealism is what Rosenzweig came to repair in his book.[9] Theology builds for him this restored world. The autonomy of thought has broken down, and henceforth it, thought, will not create its subjects but will find them. This heteronomy of thought has other aspects as well: although each thought will think its own "Whole," it cannot link the various Wholes it will think. I will return to this topic later.

As for theology, the discipline—I dare not say science—that deals with man's innermost and darkest needs, that seeks to bare the riddle of his concrete existence and to show him the deed he must do in order to uncover the path leading from creature to Creator: theology is not a science of the essence of the divinity beyond creation but consists rather of the eternal questions of love and will, wisdom and ability, judgment and mercy, justice and death, creation and redemption. Theology has concrete questions. In time this theology took on an alien cast, in our times astoundingly abstract and pallid, as if abandoned by its subjects which went off in search of another field. The weakness of theology in our time, of which everyone is aware, undoubtedly has deep roots, but this is not the place to examine them at length. Theology became impoverished when in the last century it consented, equally among Jews and Christians, to position itself at philosophy's furthest boundary, a kind of ornament bedecking the roofs of philosophy's vast structures, rather than insisting on its own; so theology suffered the same dismal fate as philosophy, its most important issues abandoned by it. These issues were to find refuge for themselves elsewhere, I will not say forever but certainly for a long time. In sociology and psychology, matters of the divinity and of man, theology's eternal subjects assumed a secular form. What was left as theology's legacy was what no one else wanted, and theology itself (disgracefully) was ashamed to inherit it and instead of extolling it concealed it in back rooms and clothed it in the tatters of scandalous allegory and embarrassing prattle. I am referring to the doctrine of miracle, which forms the mainstay of the second part of *The Star of Redemption*. The categories of faith hid themselves from the categories of science in the nineteenth century: the latter demanded for themselves the right of the mysteries of creation and the wretched experience of the "disenchanted" world, which they called *Erfahrung* (experience), set itself up as eternal.[10] All of us know how feeble were the protests of theology, which is only now beginning to stir, now that physicists in our generation have for their part, five years after the publication of Rosenzweig's book, come upon miracle as a possible category and leading scientists have begun to debate whether or not to allow miracle a place among the fundaments of physics.[11] The stone the builders spurned is become a cornerstone!

Is it at all surprising that with theology's status at its nadir, even problems no one could doubt belong to it have fled and have ensconced themselves in arts and literature? Dostoyevsky was already well aware of this in *The Idiot*. And if we consider undertakings of a clearly theological nature such as Marcel Proust's *A la recherche du temps perdu* or Franz Kafka's *The Trial* or *The Castle*, it is amazing that the theologians had no feeling whatever of *tua res agitur*—that their concern is taken up here—but rather have allowed this discovery to be made by discerning critics. It is obvious, then, that in our time theological issues have vanished from sight, have become concealed—lights that cast their light inward and are not seen from outside. The divinity, banished from man by psychology and from the world by sociology, no longer wanting to reside in the heavens, has handed over the throne of justice to dialectical materialism and the seat of mercy to psychoanalysis and has withdrawn to some hidden place and does not disclose Himself. Is He truly undisclosed? Perhaps this last withdrawal is His revelation. Perhaps God's removal to the point of nothingness was a higher need, and He will reveal His kingship only to a world that has been emptied, in the sense of "I gave access to them that asked not, I was found by those that sought me not." That is the abandonment and the question from which *The Star of Redemption* appeared to Rosenzweig, and to him as a Jew it appeared in its Jewish form, as a Star of David.

And what of the state of things in the Jewish world? We all know: ever since Judaism's association with and rootedness in the Eternal People was loosened in the decisive historical encounter between it and the riches of Europe in the last century, ever since the sorry attempts to turn its substance into nothing, to lead our reality into oblivion, ever since the ground of the people was taken from it, Judaism, having placed itself in a hopelessly vulnerable position, has of course suffered great damage. The fortification and forbearance needed today to read one of the theological works produced by the great thinkers of Western Jewry in the nineteenth century is well enough known. It is not for lack of ability to think precisely or lack of awareness of theology's unique perspectives, for it must be admitted that Reform Judaism certainly does not lack this ability, and undoubtedly the day will yet come when the life of thought buried in forgotten books such as Ludwig Steinheim's *Die Offenbarung nach dem Lehrbegriff des Synagoge* (Revelation According to the Doctrine of the Synagogue) or Moritz Lazarus's *Die Ethik des Judentums* (The Ethics of Judaism) will be discovered.[12] But this life is concealed, for it has no homeland or ground beneath it; it cannot be revealed because willingly and intentionally the authors of these books excised from themselves the life arteries of a full Jewish existence. As for the Orthodox theology constructed at that time by that exceptional person within Western Jewry, Samson Raphael Hirsch (1808–1888), the power of thought it contains is slight and frail. That can readily be appreciated if we descend one more rung in the analysis of this Jewish reality: if we ask what Jewish theology was, and where a full Jewish religious reality found living expression in thought during the centuries preceding the emancipation. The inescapable answer—so much to the displeasure of Liberals and Orthodox, secular and religious, that they fled in all directions so as not to hear it—is: in the Kabbalah. The Kabbalah in its last dialectical form is the last theological domain in which the questions of the Jew's life found a living reply; but in the period when panlogism totally overtook Western Jewry, this precious possession—a pitiful possession, perhaps, but a living one!—became a source of shame to those who inherited it, even in Orthodox Judaism. This Samson Raphael Hirsch, whose opponents were very much on target when they said of him, in derision, that as a mystic who did not make it to mysticism *(ein verhinderter Mystiker)* he kept himself from taking nourishment from its spheres and chose to create a new mysticism—unwittingly—so he would not be associated with any trace of Kabbalah. The Orthodox too severed the continuity with the most powerful religious forces at work in the preceding period, and the Kabbalah was forgotten among Western Jewry. The mark of this historical amnesia—induced by fear, opposition, as well as will—is impressed on all the attempts to express Jewish reality in the last century. Mystery does not sit well with the *derekh 'eretz* with which Hirsch enlightened (and some say deceived) Orthodox Jewry.[13] Mystery, the most national of all the domains of Jewry that Reform Judaism sought to "rectify" by a universal, abstract, and allegorical language, did not at all suit its aspirations. Finally, in our generation, the generation of Rosenzweig, this "amnesia" had already begot a new reality: it was no longer necessary to turn a blind eye to the reality of such a force, for it was not at all known to be such a "force," and it is not surprising that even Rosenzweig's remarks on the Kabbalah are like the words of a babe held prisoner among the Gentiles, unaware that his life is endangered.

This neglect of mystery as the ground of Jewish thought was shared by the early generations of the Zionist movement. And not only for the reasons I hinted at earlier, but also because the remedy of Zionism is itself the rub. The stirring new discovery that the nation has a reality and the rediscovered link between the individual and his world, namely, his people, have as it were drawn unto themselves all the problematics. The forgotten base level sometimes easily becomes the most important of things: here great problems have been uncovered that have not yet been solved because the ground from which they sprang was missing. The creation of the doctrine of Zionism, the attempts to portray the new world we Zionists have entered—the world of the living Jewish people and the Land of Israel and all the new riches we discovered in them—these have attracted and absorbed the best of our people's spiritual forces. Theology stood, as it were, outside the bounds of this new world, and as it is written, the poor man's wisdom is despised. Nobody needs it, and why should we, who in our new discovery of nationhood are making Judaism secular, who are taking the path of *saecularisatio,* have any need of it? However, questions about the eternal life of the Eternal People before the eternal god are not of the sort that can be forgotten. After the Zionist movement has set itself to the work of implementation, the question must arise with redoubled force and with the almost frightening vitality that attaches to every authentic question, that is, a question that time makes pressing, the old question that the Jewish people are not free to rid themselves of or ignore: Where are we headed? And with it comes the old answer: toward "the star of redemption."

In the generation before World War I, one person did awaken and discover this world from which both philosophical thought and the concatenation of our people's history had banished us. It was Hermann Cohen, who in his last book, *Religion der Vernunft aus den Quellen des Jüdentums* (Religion of Reason out of the Sources of Judaism)[14]—written when he was seventy-five—broke through into that world here called the-

ology and established the heteronomy of thought, not because he wanted
to take this step but because he was led to it by the idealistic dialectic of independent thought. What Rosenzweig said about Cohen's book was indeed apposite: today we all know of the errors in the plan Columbus
presented to the professors of Salamanca, but America was found by
means of this plan; until his dying days Columbus thought he had
reached East Asia, but he had "only" discovered America. Cohen, for his
part, thought he remained on the ground of the German idealism that
had so thoroughly suffused its perspectives in his system. He believed that
his last book was no more than an embellishment to his idealistic philosophy, especially to his ethics; he did not even acknowledge the systematic independence of religion, but merely accorded it a unique character
(Eigenart). He did not know that he had discovered the paradise from
which he had been banished because of the rebelliousness of autonomous
thought. Others too, among them the great of our generation, have discovered the way of the Tree of Life, although not in the language of Jewish
theology; here it suffices to mention two Jews who have done so, Martin
Buber and Leo Shestov, the great Russian-Jewish philosopher. But this new
thought, the thought of the generation that experienced the hell of the
First World War, is nowhere expressed with such full awareness and clear
grasp of the perspective that had here opened up as in Rosenzweig's book,
which expresses it in the old words of the Torah of Israel.

Rosenzweig's book is a philosophical system, as can be seen from its
form—its architectonic, tripartite division, the classic trichotomy that Kant
established for a system. But how different this threefold division is from
that found in any "proper" philosophical system: logic and the theory of
knowledge, ethics and political philosophy, aesthetics and the theory of art.
We vainly search for this division in *The Star of Redemption,* a book that begins with death and ends with a theory of knowledge. The subjects of the
standard parts, logic, ethics, and aesthetics, are discussed here, with much
attention paid especially to logic and aesthetics (where Rosenzweig made
particularly important discoveries), but according to a new methodological
principle expressed in the astronomical image of the book's title, and in the
three-part division it presents: the Elements, the Course, the Configuration
(Elemente, Bahn, Gestalt). The theory appears here at the heart of concepts familiar to all of us. "The theological problems," says Rosenzweig,

> seek to be translated into human terms and the human problems seek
> their way into theology's domain. The problem of the tetragrammaton,
> for example, is but a part of the logical problem of names in general, and
> an aesthetics that has no ideas on the question of whether artists may at-
> tain salvation may well be a decorous science but is certainly incomplete.[15]

We saw above how the All or Whole of idealism was shattered. Philosophy was left with three separate and distinct "wholenesses" given to it in the reality of experience since time immemorial: God, the world, and man, and to them the first part of *The Star of Redemption* is devoted. Three sciences—theology, cosmology, and anthropology—deal with these separate "elements" until philosophy and its criticism came along and proved to us that our knowledge of them is—nothing. The negative theology of Nicholas of Cusa, the negative cosmology of the sophists and of Spinoza, and the negative psychology of Kant with the misgivings about the I it uncovered—these are the product of reason's criticism of the living content of experience. Faith saw the world, man, and God, and what it took for granted was stamped by knowledge as absurd. This threefold nullification of the elements is the point of departure for Rosenzweig's analysis, which does not maintain the negation of knowledge as a conclusion, but turns it into a springboard from which to lead into existence, into affirmation. God, world, and man—the three cannot be proven, every proof leads knowledge toward negation. They form the triaxial system, the coordinates, from which knowledge cannot escape, within which all its lines are drawn. In the first part Rosenzweig tries to show that these three subjects, the first and last of all philosophizing, are not to be set alongside one another and cannot be reduced to one another, that the old game of philosophy, which teaches that everything is "really" "in its essence" something else, is baseless and futile, and that in fact it is the game of the wholeness we have left behind: that God is "really" the self or that the self is the world and the rest of these combinations and permutations called standpoints *(Standpunkte)*, which are no more than the deception of the one cognized wholeness. In the thought that thinks the world, nothing but world will be found. No matter how far one burrows, how deep one penetrates, and how many divisions one makes, the world will not stop being the world and turn into something other than itself. Thought seizes upon objects given to it in their experiential context, in living reality, and sets them up in their elementary isolation, turns them into essences, into substances. Into such an essence thought may descend and gaze upon the holiest of holies—for God as an essence, not the living present God, is no more hidden from thought than the "essence" of the world or of man. How profound was Rosenzweig's observation of these essences, which he found to be the elements of the world as conceptualized in the three chapters titled "God and His Being, or Metaphysics," "The World and Its Meaning, or Metalogic," and "Man and His Self, or Metaethics." But pure thought cannot escape its isolating wholeness and link essence with reality, that reality of our experience within which the el-

ements combine and where they appear only so combined. A phenomenon has no essence! Immersed within their infinity and mute, without
outward expression, the essences develop, each of these elements from its
negation and from the negation of its negation, which determines its "be-
ingness." The unprovable dialectic process that shows us the way from an
"absence of knowledge" to the factuality of the fact of the body of the
essence never leads us out. This world of the mute elements, which cannot
project its voice outside, is called by Rosenzweig "the ever-enduring proto-
cosmos" *(die immerwährende Vorwelt)*. The organon for attaining it, the
guide with whose aid we descend, like Faust, to these "Mothers" and lift
up the depths of their nothingness, is mathematics, the language of mute
symbols. With the help of this proto-language, which precedes all language, we bring to expression these mute symbolic essences. From the
three "primal words" that are not yet a language—from *yes, no,* and *and*—
Rosenzweig extracts with both mystical and mathematical precision the
secrets of the nothingness that stirs in these words and arrives at the existent in all three of the elements: the living God, who is nothing but living;
the specific plastic world in nature; and "defiant" man enclosed within a
substance, in his self *(Selbst)*. This proto-world, which contains all the objects we also find in our world, but contains them with a desiccative
strangeness, in a mute isolation, Rosenzweig recognized as the world of
the pagans. In their world, and especially in Greek antiquity, he found
these elements, fragments of the broken Whole, as forms of life and as a
living reality, and he presents them to us here as the elementary forces of
the Greek world: the living god of myth, the plastic world of art, and the
defiant hero immersed in the muteness of tragedy.

Using these deductions, the first book offers what Rosenzweig calls a
"philosophical defense of paganism" *(eine Philosophie des Heidentums)*. The
living god of myth is not the God of Creation, and however deeply we
delve into his essence, layer after layer, we will not find the Creator, for
that god is fully absorbed in his life, in his self-radiant timeless youth; the
mute man of tragedy, who is not permitted to express himself in speech
but is seen and heard from within his muteness, is not the speaking soul,
the living man created in the image of God; and the specific plastic world
enclosed in its display is not the work of creation. These are in fact elements, but our world, our reality contains something more. If thought will
not link them, take them out of their isolation, and create an idiom for
them, where shall we find them bound together?

The second part of *The Star of Redemption,* called "The Course or the Al-
ways-Renewed Cosmos" *("Die allzeiterneuerte Welt")*, proposes an answer.
The orbit within which the elements are joined in reality cannot be formu-

lated by pure thought, that pretentious thought whose concepts are not time-dependent. To know the orbit is to know their course in time and through time. Thought that wants to know the orbit must get up from its haughty chair and find for itself a new way; henceforth all of its concepts shall include concrete time, which cannot be turned into something else— and what appears absurd to autonomous thought is precisely what is taken for granted by theological thought, by the thought of belief whose classic terrain we enter here, by what is nothing other than natural thought uncorrupted by the conceit of the dream of its independence, thought that knows it is created thought and the thought of a creature—"creaturely thought," as Rosenzweig calls it *(kreaturliches Denken)*. In the broken Whole, in the world of the "shatterings of the Wholes," each fragment has its virtual time from which it cannot escape, and only in existing time, historical time, which is the Day of the Lord and is divided into its periods—the morning of creation, the noon of revelation, and the evening of redemption—do the elements leave their isolation. Upon departing from their muteness and submersion for the orbit, the forms of the ancient world of paganism of which I have spoken are transformed, and from this transformation and turning *(teshuvah,* a Hebrew theological term not chosen idly by Rosenzweig) a new Wholeness develops, the world that belief had always seen and that theology described as creation, revelation, and redemption—these regions into which Rosenzweig penetrates here constitute the Star's orbit.

If the language that preceded language, within which the elements of the Whole's silent departure from the depth of their isolation was expressed, was, as I said, the symbolic language of mathematics, the order of creation must be developed from ordinary language, that which is spoken and heard. If mathematics served as a guide to the "Mothers," the "higher mathematics" of theology, which is language, will act as the guide for discerning the Star's orbit by the movement of the elements' return; for while the idealistic world was born and created in thought by thought, the existing world was created by speech. On the gates of this theology I would inscribe the profound words of Johann Georg Hamann: "Language is the mother of reason and revelation." True, Hamann was a mystic and Rosenzweig did not have regard for such—the great introduction to the third part of his book bearing the motto *in tyrannos* (against the tyrants) is directed against them, and generally, there is a marked attempt by many associated with the philosophy of the "new thinking" to draw a sharp line between themselves and the world of mysticism. However, we can reply with another Latin phrase, *amica veritas* (truth is friend), and the truth is that in his comments both on language and on time-bound thought, Rosenzweig is in very close agreement with the disdained Kabbalah.

As for language, it is well-known that the theory of language is, in the words of one of the early luminaries of Kabbalah, "the wisdom of the inner logic";[16] as for time, it is worthwhile recalling the remarks of Rabbi Isaac Ibn Latif, one of the foremost Kabbalists, who, writing on the essence of mystic thought, said the following:

> Whatever be in the heart of a wise man and is without duration and without time, that is called wisdom, and every picture of a genuine thing that does not occur of itself without time—that is not wisdom and he who puts his trust in it is not a wise man, he is a Kabbalist.[17]

This Kabbalist had already attained the secret of the time-bound thought, and the minor difference between him and Rosenzweig is that what Rosenzweig and others call experience these earlier figures called— Kabbalah!

But let us return to the matter at hand. Through that transformation by which the elements enter reality, by which they arise in experience, every interior side becomes an exterior. When the mute elements are given language, everything is reversed, and Rosenzweig, who came out of Hegel's world, twisted the formation of the content of the existing world of religion by dialectic antitheses. By this dialectic, however, he gained something that would have been difficult to extract by any other means, namely, the deduction that Islam is that conception of reality in which the elements go into their orbit without any transformation of the constitutive structure they had in their isolation. Alas, according to Rosenzweig, Islam knows of no interrelationship among the elements; God, man, and the world remain locked in mutual isolation.

Acknowledging reality to be time-bound, genuine biblical faith (embodied in Judaism and Christianity) does, however, affirm a vital interrelationship among the elements. To be sure, "the times of reality," says Rosenzweig,

> cannot be exchanged. The elements we found in their isolation have no order, among them there is none that came earlier and none that came later. But just as an isolated event and occurrence has its own present, past and future, and without them cannot be known or understood, or if so only in a distorted way, so too the generality of reality, which is the course. It too has its past and its future, albeit an eternal past and an infinite future. To know God, the world and man—that is but to know what they do at these times of reality and what is done to them—what they do to each other and what is done to them by each other. It is quite clear that their pure "beingness" is distinct, for if not—how could they act on

each other? Who benefits when I am enjoined to love my neighbor, if I love not my neighbor but myself, and what that I do not already know can a god tell me who is nothing but my "higher self"? They are distinct, and in the world of the shattering, the world of the "elements," we know them in the distinctness of their essences. But in reality, and it alone and not essence is what arises in our experience, we bridge this distinctness. Every attempt of ours is an attempt at such bridging. We try to attain God and He is hidden, man and he is closed, the world and it is an open riddle. Only in their interrelationships, only in Creation, Revelation and Redemption, do they open up.[18]

"Philosophy as narrative" is Rosenzweig's name for what he is doing in this part, which begins with a new theory of miracle *("Über die Möglichleit das Wunder zu erleben")* and establishes a new philosophical and theological attitude. The highest point of the book is reached in this part, in the chapter "Revelation, or the Ever-Renewed Birth of the Soul" *("Offenbarung oder die allzeiterneuerte Geburt der Seele")*. I am not ashamed to say that I regard this chapter in particular as one of what may be called Judaism's "definitive statements" on religious questions. I cannot describe here the details of his "narrative," which explains to us how the living god of myth becomes the God of Creation who creates the world anew every day, and how the mute, stubbornly self-absorbed object that is tragic man becomes the speaking and hearing soul, loving and beloved, that has been opened by ever-renewed revelation ever since God called to Adam and said to him: "Where are you?" and ever since the words of the poet about man were fulfilled: "Going forth towards you, I found you / Coming towards me."[19] The story also explains how the plastic world of art, which became the work of creation by the speech of creation, will be restored to *malkhut,* that is, will become God's kingdom, in the redemption that is always to come—not idly did the Kabbalists interpret the "world to come" as the "world that is always coming." Here, from a comprehensive philosophy of language, a veritable fountain of concepts of belief is developed and the system of philosophy becomes a property of revelation. Had Rosenzweig appeared in our world to do no more than reinstate belief and restore miracle, the divine sign concealed in letters, to show us that and no more— that would have been enough. At the end of this part we understand how the restored world, which the Kabbalists call the world of *tikkun,* is made, in redemption, and we have departed from the world of the shattered Wholes we have left.

Only in redemption, God becomes the One and All which, from the first human reason in its rashness has everywhere sought and everywhere asserted and yet nowhere found because it simply was nowhere to be found yet, for it did not exist yet. We had intentionally broken up the All of the

philosophers. Here in the blinding midnight sun of the consummated redemption it has at last, yea at the very last, coalesced into the One.[20]

We have passed through two worlds: the world of concept and muteness and the world of reality and language. The historical forms of revelation have not yet been spoken of. There are no fixed configurations
(Gestalten) in the course. It goes on, continues, and changes. In the world
of living reality, according to Rosenzweig, there is only the present moment, every past merely has been, and every future will only come; there
is no time in the living sense other than the present. But just as forms of
the past, forms of the world of elements of paganism to some extent still
reach into the present, so too, by eternal forms, we anticipate the redemption that is to come.[21] This anticipation, this bringing of redemption
into the present via the fixed cycle of days of the religions, creates a new
dimension in the world, its last dimension: truth. Revelation takes on an
historical guise: time, the "river which flows and issues from its source,"
extracts from its three hidden fountains, which we called elements, lumi-
nous and enduring forms *(Gestalten)*. These forms, Judaism and Christianity, and their relationship to the truth, are taken up in the third part,
entitled "The Configuration or the Eternal Hyper-Cosmos" *("Die Gestalt
oder die Ewige Überwelt")*. This part, a logical further step up in the system's
development, searches once again for the eternal present, after the one
eternal Being of idealism had shattered in our hands, the remaining temporal reality being, after all, time and not eternity. Rosenzweig, the sworn
enemy of philosophical irrationalism in whatever guise, scoffs at the des-
perate suggestions that we hurl ourselves into the stream of life, indeed at
all suggestions and slogans of that sort. He is in search of the eternal that
does not need thought in order to be. The necessary anticipation of redemption in revelation, according to its two worldly forms in Judaism and
Christianity, provides Rosenzweig with what he wants: the form, or more
precisely the forms, for these two are but forms, configurations of the one
eternal truth, the truth that bears witness unto itself—the seal of God.

Judaism and Christianity are conceived here as two different rhythms
by which time in its worldly course—creation, revelation, and redemption—takes on a fixed form in accord with the respective type of anticipation of redemption each embodies. To present and portray them as
fulfilling this vital role, Rosenzweig does not consider differences in their
dogma but rather the materialization of each of these religions, the guise
they actually assume in the cycle of life. The order of prayer in the traditional Jewish prayer books and in the Catholic liturgy—that is the organon
acting as guide to Rosenzweig in the third part of *The Star*. Prayer, by

which man anticipates redemption in his life and for that moment sets up God's kingdom, is the language of the heavenly world, the hyper-cosmos. The depths of Judaism and of Christianity are bared to us by con-sidering the order of their prayers. Here what they share can be discerned, as can the profound differences between them, especially in the doctrine of redemption. Rosenzweig describes Judaism at length in terms of the cat-egory of eternal life or the fundamental fire burning within the Star—a world reality of the Jewish people founded on the natural reality of their life as the eternal people—and he describes Christianity in terms of the category of the eternal way or of the rays of light emitted by the Star. The Jew is always at home, in the sense of "among my people I dwell," because he and his faith are rooted in the fertile and constant soil of the people; the Christian is always on his way, for he has no refuge in this world save for the Church founded on the one event, which being an event is not enduring and which the Church is always having to renew and become what it once was. Jew and Christian stand before God; to both of them eternity within time has been revealed by means of the division of the cycle of their life in the liturgical year of Sabbaths and holy days; both partake of the one truth, each having the part that has become for it the principle of time's rhythmic division. To this, the one truth, and the pos-sibility of change and variance in it in revelation, the last chapter of *The Star* is devoted, which includes Rosenzweig's theory of knowledge. Noth-ing illuminates the unique structure of the system more than this situating of the theory of knowledge at the end and not at the beginning of the book, as is ordinarily done in philosophical systems.

A "messianic theory of knowledge" is what Rosenzweig calls this the-ory. The one truth—that is his final conclusion from long debates on the place of truth and on its bearer, after it turned out here that it too requires a bearer—is truth only for the One, for God. And if truth has only one bearer, one subject, our truth is not truth, is not *the* truth. Truth bears wit-ness to itself. But our truth requires existence. Our truth has more than one face, is variable, like the two elements other than the Creator: man and the world. This variability, necessary for flesh and blood, does not—not in Judaism and not in Christianity—place its bearers at a disadvantage, and it is in it that Rosenzweig finds the principle that explains the unfold-ing of the difference in the conception of redemption in Judaism and in its rival. Our partial truth is not had by logical acumen; the truth theology speaks of is not a conditional truth, like that of mathematics, dependent on its axioms. The existence of our truth depends on the price we pay for it and pay for it daily, and the existence of the Jew's truth depends on his acceptance of the yoke of the kingdom of heaven in his daily life.

Here the book ends, and I could do no more than try to compress within remarks a faint reflection of its brilliant light and abundant ideas, for the entire Jewish world is as if folded into this book. The system is not autonomous, does not stand on its own. It has been completed but has not come to an end, for at the end its gates open onto life, simple concrete life in which it must find its justification and existence, for it does not stand on its own.

The book was created and behold it is very good—and that *very* is death, thus constituting an affirmation of death and human finitude in general as an essential aspect of existence. Rosenzweig's book became a prophecy of his life, and he was compelled to pay for its truth in a most awful way. The life he went into from the gates of his book was soon to be death. After he had devoted only a small measure of time to Torah, he was stricken with a terrible disease and for more than seven years he lived among us in death's clutches. One after another, movement and speech were taken from him, the power of movement and the power of speech. Totally paralyzed except for two or three slight movements with his head and slight movement in one of his fingers, totally paralyzed in speech— that is how this man lived. Were it not for the absolute devotion of his wife, who, with an inestimable intuition born of love worthy of being called the holy spirit, understood his thoughts from hints and the faintest of cues, the divine voice echoing from the living soul in this dead body would never have reached us, that voice from the life of a soul that remained full and radiant as on the day the star of redemption was revealed to him. He became mute, and everything in the poem by Hölderlin with which I prefaced my remarks came to hold for him: the living sound was taken from his speech, but his seed was sown and from the fire of his muteness we heard the sounds of the words of the living God. Whoever once was in that room in Frankfurt and heard his questions answered and heard the eloquence of that mute saint surely knows what a miracle happened to us here. Rosenzweig hardly stopped working at all, and he bestowed upon us very important gifts, among them the precious delight of his lengthy and profound comments on the poems of Judah Halevi, which he translated into German—theological and aesthetic comments illuminating for us the world of Judah Halevi in light of the star that shone for him. For four years he worked with Martin Buber translating the Bible, applying a linguistic principle that can be formulated in the biblical phrase, "A [sky] light *(tzohar)* shalt thou make to the ark *(teivah),*"[22] which the Kabbalists interpreted as follows: Make *zohar* (brilliance, splendor) for every word *(teivah)* until it shines like the noonday light.[23]

In his death he fulfilled his truth, and not for naught did he request that words from Psalm 73 be engraved on his tombstone, the same psalm in which it is said:

> For all the days have I been plagued
> And my chastisements came every morning
> If I had said I will speak thus
> I had been faithless to the generation of thy children
> And when I pondered how I might know this
> It was wearisome in my eyes
> Until I entered into the sanctuary of God
> And considered their end.

Chapter Twenty-four

Does God Dwell in the Heart of an Atheist? (1975)*

I wish to express my admiration for Ernst Bloch, a restless, aged thinker who has become a sage. I do this, notwithstanding the fact that I may be reasonably certain that my own praises are of no interest to him, just as it is doubtful that my criticism will move him to critical introspection. The water that separates us is too shallow to provide the necessary depth for the development of a true encounter.

Yet, nevertheless: the first meeting between us—a nocturnal conversation which took place in Interlaken in 1919 and which continued for many hours, some of them quite tempestuous, at a time when I had already decided to dedicate my scholarly life to the study of Judaism—ranks among the most unforgettable hours of my youth. It is fitting that I should record here the opening tones of that encounter, as during the first moments of my meeting with Bloch I was afforded an unanticipated glimpse into my own spiritual world.

Walter Benjamin, whose acquaintance I had made a short time earlier, suggested that I visit Bloch. I entered his room, and to my amazement saw on his desk Johann Andreas Eisenmenger's *Judaism Uncovered (Entdecktes Judentum;* Frankfurt am Main: J. P. Andreae, 1701)—the most notorious, learned, and thickest volume in all of antisemitic literature.

* An essay written to honor the ninetieth birthday of Ernst Bloch in July 1975. Published in 'Od Davar, 453–60.

Upon seeing my astonishment, Bloch explained to me that this was in fact the most marvelous book concerning Judaism, from which one could learn any number of things. Its author, however, was a simpleton—a learned fool who understood nothing, damning with hideous blasphemy the magnificent images of an abundant imagination. These remarks appealed to me, kindling in me an idea which I have not forgotten to this very day: that one must also learn to read books against their declared intention.

I read most of Bloch's books with a feeling of great admiration and, if I may say so, with an equal measure of criticism and head-shaking. Forty-seven years have passed between our second and third meetings. It may be that, after so many years, the time has now come to push ourselves in from afar among the ranks of his well-wishers.

The young Bloch, a striking phenomenon both physically and spiritually, was a fearless pioneer who, without fear of the baroque, stormed into the realm of the apocalypse, where there perished the mystical scenes which he so cherished. At the age of ninety he has become a kind of blind visionary, a master who has survived after the struggle with the dragon, a struggle continued over forty years. He has become a sage, true to the spirit of the ancient Jewish definition of an "elder" as "one who has acquired wisdom"—something which Job already complained was almost impossible to attain.

The impetuous mystic was seemingly transformed into a preacher of Marxism. But has he really become such a figure? Bloch has in fact allowed various different spirits, some of them quite reprehensible, to whisper into his ears. But his decisive inspiration remained that of mysticism, which he interpreted as a turning towards an anarchistic messianism. Drawing upon ancient sources, he attempted to conquer virgin territory and thereby also fructify forgotten pastures (without covering them with super-structures).

It is clear to every reader of the "first version" of his book, *Utopian Spirit (Geist der Utopie),* written between 1915–1917 and already published at the time of the First World War, that this was the Archimedean point from which the young Bloch wished to shake the stultified bourgeois world off its axis. The field of music is not very well-known to me, for which reason I am unable to express my opinion concerning his *Philosophy of Music (Philosophie der Musik),* which constitutes nearly half of this thick volume. The manner of its presentation, which is frequently of an almost prophetic character, made Bloch's name in the vistas of the world of culture. At the time, the book was seen as an astonishing incursion of mysticism into the field of philosophy, in which Bloch attacked their academic guardians.

One finds there (a phenomenon which occurs repeatedly in his other writings) a daring expressionist struggle to develop new processes of thought, meant to concretize the mystical experience.

This was followed by the second great turning-point, in which the anarchist-mystic was transformed into the spokesman for a new melody within Marxism. This change in world-view left its impression upon his work from 1927 on; the tension between these poles was to determine Bloch's image for the next fifty years. We find here the only case in which a sworn convert to Marxism (a Bolshevik, to quote his own early phrase) attempted to preserve his own mystical inspiration within a fragile Noah's ark by means of an awesome flood of Marxist rhapsody—much of his later writing may be characterized thus. The daring revealed by Bloch in this paradoxical attempt demanded extraordinary spiritual powers, inspiring amazement even for one who held distinct reservations toward much of the substance of his discussions.

The complex Marxist structure of his second major work, *The Principle of Hope (Das Prinzip Hoffnung;* Berlin: Aufbau-Verlag, 1954–1959), stands in barely concealed opposition to his original (and ongoing) impulse to escape from all of the traditional categories of enlightened thought. It was this impulse which moved the disciple of Georg Simmels, the rebel and apocalyptic. Notwithstanding his willingness to march behind the flag of the party, his theosophy of Bolshevism inevitably turned him into one who was rejected from the camp. Indeed, one is astonished by the length of time required by the Stalinists of the party of socialist unity to "discover" his mystical face, which is his true face. The "inner light" of human dignity and of the divine image of man shone in him with great clarity, remaining with him throughout all of the distortions by which, unfortunately, he so frequently attempted to hide and to obscure it.

His opponents smelled the *homo religiosus* concealed within the atheist—and they were right. His own image of the revolution was far different from theirs. It was not for naught that this declared atheist was suspected of harboring God in his heart, to use the language of the Psalms. Bloch and Walter Benjamin shared a central common goal which, notwithstanding their fervent efforts, neither of them succeeded in realizing—for the very plausible reason that it was one inherently impossible. They attempted to superimpose the mystical experience upon the coordinates of the Marxist system, which was based entirely upon its obliteration. It is therefore not surprising that the numerous pages in Bloch devoted to this attempt draw their power precisely from their transcendence of this self-same system. In Bloch, this happened without his admitting it; in Benjamin, through a process of deliberate forgetfulness.

THE HEART OF AN ATHEIST

In 1968, Bloch published a book that sheds brilliant light upon the situation we are speaking of. It is a disappointing work if we attempt to evaluate it on the basis of the declared goal implied in its title, *Atheism in Christianity (Atheismus in Christendum)*. If, on the other hand, we ignore the title, it is a powerful and impressive work. Quite a few sections mark it as a great book—but one that has not the slightest connection with the assumption that it claims to represent.

IS IT POSSIBLE TO EXORCISE GOD THROUGH MARXISM?

One of the six sentences which Bloch uses as a motto declares: "The best thing about religion is that it gives birth to heretics." It is clear that even in their wildest dreams none of the Church fathers, the mystics, or the heretics upon whom he pours praises thought to deny the existence of God. God was for them a living being; even if they did formulate various paradoxical statements about Him, for them He was not a "projection of man," nor a "God who dwells in the depths of the Nothing," nor the bearer of the unusual title of the mystical Nothing, nor even the "God who is becoming" of Schelling—who was Bloch's spiritual forebear, and not only in the area of philosophy of religion.

Of course, the statement declared by Bloch's motto is not true: "Only an atheist can be a good Christian, and only a Christian is able to be a good atheist." A nice sentence, but one lacking in all meaning. No proof is given in support of this statement; Bloch seems excessively addicted to the game of his "atheism," and it is perhaps superfluous to add that he was enamored thereof.

Not since Gottfried Arnold's *History of the Church and of Heretics (Kirchen- und Ketzerhistorie;* Frankfurt am Main: T. Fritsch, 1696)—that old, unforgettable and truly revolutionary book, which advocated the thesis that the heretics, when examined against the background of the decadence of the Church, were always right—have many people written about God with a fervor similar to that of Bloch. This is so, even when he seeks to exorcise Him with Marxist oaths or to deny Him. May Bloch forgive me, but I do not believe in his atheism.

The sections of Bloch's book dealing with the Bible are deserving of attention. On the other hand, one needs to have an extremely narrow understanding of the concept of religion, one which has undergone Marxist treatment, in order to argue that recognition of the God who said to Moses "I am that I am" may no longer be defined as religion. This biblical sentence, one of the key expressions of Jewish faith, may not lead toward the Christianity of the "Son of Man," but it most certainly does not lead toward atheism—not even after 354 pages of heretical rhetoric infused with deep faith, which plumb its depths and lend it a pure utopian brilliance.

LUTHER WOULD HAVE CALLED HIM AN ENTHUSIAST

In speaking of Bloch, one must also say something of the master of style and the incomparable narrator. Bloch's early works and articles, up to his book, *The Heritage of This Time* (*Erbschaft dieser Zeit;* Frankfurt am Main: Suhrkamp, 1935)—with the exception of his dissertation on Rickert, whose style is deliberately dry and was omitted from the general collection of his writings—serve as a rare example in philosophical literature of linguistic intoxication, which was the prerogative of the expressionists, and of course resembles that found in certain levels of mystical writing. This linguistic lava cools down considerably later on, but even then it continues to gush from him now and again.

On the other hand, the later Bloch, of *The Principle of Hope,* of the explanations of Hegel (one of his particularly impressive philosophical discussions), and of *Natural Law and Human Dignity (Naturrecht und menschliche Würde;* Frankfurt am Main: Suhrkamp, 1961), becomes more didactic—although even in these writings he occasionally attempts to storm the heavens. In his expositions of the concepts of hope and of human dignity, which lend momentum to the style of the later Bloch, one can sense a substantial transition from enthusiasm to balanced judgment and calmness of mind. Thanks to these qualities, these distinctly encyclopedic works attracted many readers whose ears were jarred by the ecstatic drunkenness of their predecessors.

Of course, Bloch still remains what Luther would have called an "enthusiast," so that one should not be surprised that Bloch failed to particularly praise him. The mystical version of materialism to which he was devoted placed constraints upon his ability to speak and upon his creative impulse, to the advantage of both. In the characteristic expressionist orchestration of the opening sentences by which he leaps up toward the reader, there is still preserved something of the character of those artistic instruments whose purpose is "to upset the bourgeoisie." "Cooperation with something is definitely liable to be cowardice"; "The desire to suffice with seeing alone still places you upon the side"; "The water which flows in its due time, is not." The reader encounters such enigmatic rhetoric frequently, until his most recent book, *Introduction to Philosophy (Einleitung in die Philosophie),* where it is coherently explicated. How pleasing is Bloch's style of philosophic presentation, compared with the intolerable "didactic" note to which his lifelong friend Georg Lukacs became addicted in the 1930's! Even though they belonged to the same camp, debates continued between the two friends, whose literary opinions concerning realism and expressionism diverged so definitively. But their use of allusions and codes was modest compared with the debates between Brecht and Lukacs, so similar in spirit. Even today, one finds in them something of the nature of arguments between an unrestrained rebel and a dogmatic authority, between a child of nature who thinks profoundly and a chief research commissar of literary Marxism.

In his literary and philosophical writings, particularly in *The Heritage of This Time,* Bloch remains one of the outstanding spokesmen of the avantgarde in all spiritual areas. His distinct talent for barrages of curses and far-reaching dismissal is revealed to us in that book in a rather exciting way in his efforts to save for the future that which has passed away and is no more—and at times even that which has passed away and gone beyond the point of restoration. In a pleasant, and even touching, conversation in one of the last issues of *Kursbuch,* Bloch defended the basic approach of this work, which was the object of many severe attacks.

WHAT CAN THE NON-MARXIST LEARN FROM HIM?

Already in those days when I first heard about him, he had the public reputation of being an incomparable storyteller. In the two versions of *Traces (Spuren;* Berlin: P. Cassirer, 1969), we have his most brilliant, and at the same time rather entangled, accomplishment, as befits a philosophical storyteller.

In *Traces*—the title alludes to the traces of truth, to the utopian, to that which has passed away—these are explained with an intellectual freshness, almost without Marxist encumbrances. By this, he demonstrates to the astonished reader that hidden treasures may be found even among the most lowly stones. And if they are no longer to be found there, then they have at least left behind the traces of their brilliance. This is the most easily approached of all his creations, the most "popular" work. Jewish theology knows how to tell very strange things about the "traces of Messiah." In these stories he pursues such messianic traces, which he designates "utopian." They are frequently designated by other names as well, but in this work, the finest of his creations, he speaks of that brilliance which is anticipated from the beginning, of redemption, which is expressed by the narrator through the most innocent and peculiar stories.

What can a Marxist learn from Bloch? I am obviously not qualified to express a clear opinion on this subject. But against the artificially sustained, self-enclosed wisdom which renders so much of Marxist literature regarding spiritual matters absolutely unreadable, Bloch can contribute a certain convincing openness even regarding that which has not yet been included in those categories. To use his language: a progressive openness towards the past.

What can the non-Marxist learn from Bloch? That the various explanations current in the public, which present themselves as Marxist explanations, are not Marxist in his eyes? That he thinks, moreover, that they are not proven and are not capable of being proven in any serious sense of the word? That he finds it difficult to understand or does not at all understand their application to the phenomena of spiritual life, even when the proposals come from such impressive thinkers as Lukacs, Bloch, or Benjamin?

The unbiased reader approaching Bloch's work will find it difficult. He will attempt in vain to discover any meaning whatsoever in many sentences stated with authority and enthusiasm. They will leave him at a loss, as if listening to the speech of disembodied spirits. Does the "mastery of the melody-leading soprano and the agility of the others" indeed correspond to "initial receptivity"? From whence does he know this? Or may this be perhaps a parody of Marxist aesthetics? Mozart as an ideological super-structure of initiative? At the same time, one finds certain basic assumptions in his thought which have fructified the philosophy and theory of art: the doctrine of the darkness of the lived instant, and the ontology of that-which-does-not-yet-exist and is not-yet-known—projected in his first period, and preserved throughout all of the storms which he underwent—which he stressed as central goals in the philosophy of history and aesthetics.

TEACHINGS FROM THE TREE OF KNOWLEDGE

Thus, for one who is not a Marxist, Bloch's oeuvre becomes an incomparable acid test for everything relating to Marxist approaches and perspectives. He learns to recognize the boundaries of these systems even with regard to serious attempts to apply them, boundaries which it is possible to cross (to use an infelicitous formulation) only with the help of acrobatics or declarative dictates. Can we really believe that that which was beyond the ability of men of spirit of his stature can be successfully performed by people of lower caliber?

But more than all this, I value the positive side reflected in studies such as those of Bloch (and also of Benjamin, notwithstanding the differences between them in details, in spirit, and in the conclusions of their thoughts): here there dwelt, in a truly Procrustean bed, a series of remarkable studies and metaphysical approaches to reality, which at times broke through their fetters.

We must express our admiration and respect for the strength to stand firm and to defend views such as these, which Marxist orthodoxy persecutes with a degree of intolerance toward heresy similar to that revealed by other orthodoxies. Read in this spirit, Bloch's works yield a double fruit. His books, especially his *Philosophical Essays* and the *Tübingen Introduction to Philosophy* (1970), contain chapters of teaching in which he succeeds in cultivating fruits and assuring that they will be pleasing to the taste, fruits whose source is doubtless in the tree of knowledge, even if they are wrapped in the garments of Marxism.

Notes

Introduction

1. Cynthia Ozick, "The Mystic Explorer," *New York Times Book Review*, September 21, 1980.

2. R. J. Z. Werblowsky, *Beyond Tradition and Modernity—Changing Religions in a Changing World* (London: University of London, 1976).

3. See M. A. Meyer, *The Origins of the Modern Jew: Jewish Identity and European Culture in Germany 1749–1824* (Detroit: Wayne State University Press, 1967); J. Weiss, "Some Notes on the Social Background of Early Ḥasidism," *Studies in Eastern European Jewish Mysticism*, D. Goldstein, ed. (Oxford: Oxford University Press, 1985), 3–26.

4. G. Scholem, *From Berlin to Jerusalem* (New York: Schocken, 1980).

5. See G. Scholem, "Mein Weg zur Kabbala," ein Credo—vorgetragen vor der Bayerischen Akademie der Schönen Kunste, *Feuilleton* 20 (July 21, 1974) (included in the present volume).

6. See, for example, Scholem's article "Be-mai ka Mipalqei" (1931) in *'Od Davar*, (Tel Aviv, 1989), 80.

7. This is what he said in a series of lectures on the Sabbatean Episode at the Hebrew University, 1955, as noted by R. Schatz, Jerusalem, 1975, 1.

8. On the meaning of paradoxes and dialectical processes in his world, see R. Alter, "The Achievement of Gershom Scholem," *Commentary*, April 1973, esp. 74–76.

9. See "With G. Scholem: An Interview by M. Tzur and A. Shapira," in G. Scholem, *On Jews and Judaism in Crisis* (New York: Schocken, 1976), 36. Dialectics have a prominent place in contemporary Jewish theological

thought. See, for example, A. J. Heschel, *The Theology of Ancient Judaism,* Vol. III (Hebrew, Jerusalem: H. H. Cohen 1990), 88–89. We shall merely present one demonstration of this approach of his. In a letter to Hannah Arendt, in response to her *Eichmann in Jerusalem,* he wrote: "I am aware that there are aspects of Jewish history (and for more than forty years I have concerned myself with little else) which are beyond our comprehension; on the one hand, a devotion to the things of this world that is near-demonic; on the other, a fundamental uncertainty of orientation in this world." *Encounter* 22 (January 1964), 51, collected in Hebrew in *Devarim be-go,* (1976).

10. See Y. Baer, "The Doctrine of Original Natural Equality Among the Ḥasidim of Ashkenaz" (Hebrew), *Zion,* 1967.

11. See "Memory and Utopia in Jewish History" (Hebrew), in *'Od Davar,* 189. Included in the present volume, Ch. 18.

12. "Judaism itself is an unbroken relationship to sacred text ever fertilized by fresh commentary, . . . a canon without closure." I. Schorsch, "The Legacy of Martin Buber," Keynote address delivered at Heppenheim, Germany, on the occasion of the twenty-fifth anniversary of Buber's death (July 18, 1990), *The Jewish Week* (New York), September 21, 1990.

13. See "S. Y. Agnon: Last of the Hebrew Classics?" in *'Od Davar,* 341–62.

14. See the poem and fragment about Kafka in this volume, Chs. 21–22.

15. See *'Od Davar,* 51–54.

16. See the essays in *'Od Davar,* 363–415, and, in English, "Martin Buber's Interpretation of Ḥasidism," in his *The Messianic Idea in Judaism* (New York, 1971), 227–50.

17. G. Scholem, *From Berlin to Jerusalem* (New York: Schocken, 1980), 104.

18. "What Others Discarded." Included in this volume.

19. See D. Flusser, "Gershom Scholem and His Work" (upon his reaching the age of eighty), *Davar,* February 20, 1978.

20. E. Neumann, *Krise und Erneuerung* (Zürich: Rhein-Verlag, 1959).

21. *Mekhilta de-Rabbi Yishma'el, Parashat Va-yehi be-shalaḥ.*

22. G. Scholem, *Sabbatai Ṣevi: The Mystical Messiah, 1626–76.* Trans. R. J. Z. Werblowsky (Bollingen Series 93; Princeton: Princeton University Press, 1973).

23. On the Eranos conferences and Gershom Scholem's participation in them, see W. McGuire, *Bollingen—An Adventure in Collecting the Past* (Princeton: Princeton University Press, 1982), 119–81 and esp. 152–54.

24. G. Scholem, *Walter Benjamin: The Story of a Friendship* (Philadelphia: JPS, 1981), 136.

25. D. Sadan, "Revealer of the Lights Which Have Disappeared," *'Al Ha-Mishmar,* November 22, 1974.

26. See "The Meaning of Torah for Us Today" (1939), in *'Od Davar,* 95–97.

27. G. Scholem, "Kabbalah and Myth," *On the Kabbalah and Its Symbolism* (New York: Schocken, 1967), 117.

Chapter One

1. Franz Joseph Molitor, *Philosophie der Geschichte, oder, über die Tradition* (Münster: Verlag der Theissing'schen Buchhandlung, 1857).

Chapter Two

1. A movement based on the belief in divine power and higher centers of consciousness, attained through spontaneous and ecstatic exercises. Founded in 1933 in Indonesia by Muhammed Subud, known as Bupak, who was influenced by Sufism, it was spread to the West by followers of Gurdjieff (*Encyclopaedia Britannica*, Vol. 11, 345).

2. Cf. *Zohar* III: 79b and Rashi to B. Sanh. 90a.

3. For a discussion of the interplay of "earthly" and "spiritual" elements in the thought of such secular Zionist thinkers as Berdyczewski, A. D. Gordon, Berl Katznelson, and others, see Ehud Luz, "Spiritual and Anti-Spiritual Trends in Zionism," in *Jewish Spirituality II*, A. Green, ed. (New York: Crossroad, 1987), 371–401.

4. The reference is to his *Leaves of Grass.*

5. Richard M. Bucke, *Cosmic Consciousness: A Study in the Evolution of the Human Mind* (New York: E. P. Dutton, 1956).

Chapter Three

1. The individual referred to here was Phillip Bloch (1841–1923), whose writings include *Die Kabbalah auf ihrem Höhepunkt und ihre Meister* (Pressburg: A. Alkalay, 1905); *Geschichte der Entwicklung der Kabbala und der jüdischen Religions philosophie* (Trier: S. Mayer, 1894).

2. Franz Kafka, "Josefine, die Sängerin, oder das Volk der Mäuse," *Gesammelten Schriften,* Bd. 1 (Berlin: Schocken Verlag, 1935), 240–60. English translation in N. N. Glatzer, ed. *Franz Kafka: The Complete Stories,* (New York: Schocken, 1971), 360–76.

Chapter Four

1. An artificial language invented by the German cleric Johann Martin Schleyer, which enjoyed a certain vogue in the 1880s until it was displaced by Esperanto.

Chapter Five

1. Aḥad Ha-Am, "'Avdut be-tokh Ḥerut" (1891). In *Kol Kitvei Aḥad Ha-Am* (Jerusalem-Tel Aviv: Devir, 1947), 64–69.

Chapter Seven

1. Nitchevo—evidently an allusion to the Russian type of anarchist; or, those who are habitually indifferent or apathetic, as if to say, "Nothing matters."

Chapter Eight

1. *Iggerot Ḥayyim Naḥman Bialik,* F. Lachover, ed. (Tel Aviv: Devir, 1938), Vol. III, 48–49. Item No. 459, July 20, 1925.
2. The reference is to his "Questions Concerning *Zohar* Criticism on the Basis of His Knowledge of the Land of Israel" [Heb.], *Me'asef Tzion* 1 (1926), 40–55.
3. "Shekhinah," *'Al Gevul Shenei 'Olamot* (Tel Aviv: Yavneh, 1965), 113–26; "Yofi shel Maa'alah," ibid., 127–68.
4. Fischel Lachover, *Toldot ha-Sifrut ha-'Ivrit ha-Ḥadashah* (Tel Aviv: Devir, 1928), I: 14–44.

Chapter Nine

1. The term "Science of Judaism" is used specifically in reference to the school of nineteenth century German Jewish scholarship, known as *Wissenschaft des Jüdentums*. In the twentieth century, in the new centers in the United States and Israel, the preferred term is "Jewish studies" or "Judaic studies."
2. While this is not the place for references and notes, one cannot refrain from noting in brief the important sources developed by Zalman Rubaschoff [later Shazar—J. C.]: "The First Fruit of the Destruction," and by Sinai Ucko, "The Foundations of Jewish Studies in Terms of the History of the Spirit." Both of these appeared in German in journals which it is difficult to find today, and which have unfortunately disappeared almost entirely.[—G. S.]
3. *Kitvei Rabbi Naḥman Krochmal,* S. Rawidowitz, ed. (London-Waltham, Mass: Ararat, 1961 [reprint Berlin: Eynot, 1924]), Ch. 17, "Ḥokhmat ha-Misken," 284–334; "Kitzurim mi-Sifrei Rabbi Avraham ibn 'Ezra," 335–94.
4. *Moreh Nevukhei ha-Zeman,* ibid.
5. Joshua Heschel Schorr (1818–95), prominent scholar and thinker of the Haskalah in Galicia; editor of the influential journal *He-Ḥalutz* between 1851 and 1887.

6. Max Wiener, *Juedische Religion im Zeitalter der Emanzipation* (Berlin: Philo Verlag, 1933).

Chapter Ten

1. Oxford MS. 1664 and Budapest-Kaufmann MS. 290.
2. D. Kaufmann, in *MGWJ* 42(1898), 38–46; J. N. Epstein, *Mavo le-Nusaḥ ha-Mishnah,* II (Jerusalem, 1948), 1248ff.

Chapter Eleven

1. The reference is to Giulio Racah (1909–65), head of the Department of Theoretical Physics at the Hebrew University from 1939 on; and Hans Jacob Polotsky (1905–91), a highly versatile linguist and Orientalist on the Hebrew University faculty from 1934 on, who made significant contributions in the fields of Semitics, Egyptology, etc.
2. "Alchemie und Kabbala: ein Kapitel aus der Geschichte der Mystik," *MGWJ* 69 (1925), 13–30, 95–110; "Nachbemerkung," ibid., 371–74. Reprinted in expanded form in *Eranos Jahrbuch* 46 (1977).
3. The person referred to here is Phillip Bloch. See above, Ch. 3.

Chapter Fifteen

1. Y. Zakovitch, "Poor and Riding on a Donkey (Zech. 9: 9–10)" [Heb.], *The Messianic Idea,* 7–17.
2. I. Gruenwald, "From Sunrise to Sunset; The Image of Eschatology and Messianism in Judaism" [Heb.], *The Messianic Idea,* 18–36.
3. S. Rosenberg, "The Return to the Garden of Eden; Notes on the History of the Idea of Restorative Redemption in Medieval Jewish Philosophy" [Heb.], *The Messianic Idea,* 37–86.
4. Y. Leibis, "The Messiah of the Zohar: On R. Simeon bar Yoḥai as a Messianic Figure" [Heb.], *The Messianic Idea,* 87–236. An abbreviated English version of this lengthy paper, translated by the late A. Schwarz, appears in Leibis' *Studies in the Zohar* (Albany: SUNY Press, 1993), 1–84.
5. Ch. 7: "Isaac Luria and His School," (New York: Schocken, 1961), 244–86.
6 I. Tishby, "The Messianic Idea and Messianic Tendencies in the Growth of Hasidism" [Heb.], *Ḥikrei Kabbalah u-Sheluḥoteha,* II (Jerusalem: Magnes, 1993), 475–519 [also found in *Zion* 32 (1967), 1–45]; Scholem's view is articulated in "The Neutralization of the Messianic Idea in Ḥasidism," *The Messianic Idea in Judaism and Other Essays on Jewish Spirituality* (New York: Schocken, 1971), 176–202 [also found in *JJS* 29 (1970), 25–55].

7. M. Piekarcz, "The Messianic Idea During the Flowering of Ḥasidism as Viewed Through *Derush* and *Musar* Literature" [Heb.], *The Messianic Idea,* 237–53.

8. "Toward an Understanding of the Messianic Idea in Judaism," *The Messianic Idea in Judaism and Other Essays on Jewish Spirituality* (New York: Schocken, 1971), 35–36.

Chapter Seventeen

1. It would be foolhardy to attempt to list the scholarly literature written over the past half century dealing with the numerous topics touched upon in this essay. The interested reader is referred, first of all, to Scholem's book-length introduction to the subject, *Major Trends in Jewish Mysticism* (New York: Schocken, 1971). For as good an overview as any of the state of research in the various fields of Kabbalah since the publication of this paper and of *Major Trends,* see *Gershom Scholem's Major Trends in Jewish Mysticism: 50 Years After.* Proceedings of the Sixth International Conference on the History of Jewish Mysticism [Berlin, 1992], P. Schäfer and J. Dan, eds., (Tübingen: J. C. B. Mohr [Paul Siebeck], 1993).

2. In his *Meḥkarim u-Masot be-Toldot am Yisra'el* II (Jerusalem: Israel Historical Society, 1986), 175–224; originally published in *Zion* 3(1938), 1–50; English translation: Yitzhak Baer, *The Socio-Religious Orientation of Sefer Ḥasidim* (Binah: Jewish Civilization University Series, Joseph Dan, ed.; Jerusalem: International Center for University Teaching of Jewish Civilization, Everyman's University, Israel, 1985).

3. Scholem elaborates upon this theme in greater detail in his essay, "The Meaning of the Torah in Jewish Mysticism," *On the Kabbalah and Its Symbolism* (New York: Schocken, 1965), 32–86.

4. According to the theory of Y. Baer, the appearance of this doctrine also reflects the influence of the great religious movement initiated by the Franciscans during the thirteenth century in southern Europe. [G.S.] See his paper, "The Historical Background of *Ra'aya Mehemna*" [Heb.], in his *Meḥkarim u-Masot* II, 306–49; originally published in *Zion* 5(1940), 1–44.

5. On this entire subject, see Scholem's essay, "Gilgul: The Reincarnation of Souls," in *On the Mystical Shape of the Godhead* (New York: Schocken, 1991), 197–50.

Chapter Nineteen

1. H. Heine, "Zur Geschichte der Religion und Philosophie in Deutschland," in his *Sämmtliche Werke,* Bd. 8/1 (Hamburg: Hoffmann und Campe, 1979), 443–61, on 454.

2. Eccles. Rab. 4:1; Lev. Rab. 32:8: "'Again I saw all the oppressions . . .' [Eccles. 4:1]. Daniel Hayata explained this passage as referring to the bas-

tards [*mamzerim;* i.e., those born to incestuous and adulterous unions, who were barred from marriage with non-'tainted' Jews]. 'And behold, the tears of the oppressed' [ibid.]. The mothers of these committed a sin, and these luckless ones suffer. The father of this one had incestuous relations, this one, what did he do, and what concern is it of his? 'And they have no one to comfort them' [ibid.], but rather, 'On the side of their oppressors is power' [ibid.]. This is the Great Sanhedrin of Israel, which comes to them by power of the Torah and separates them out, in the name of 'Let no bastard enter the assembly of the Lord' [Deut. 23:3]. 'And they have no one to comfort them' [ibid.]. The Holy One blessed be He said, 'It is incumbent upon Me to comfort them. Because in this world they are unfit, but in the world to come, Zechariah said, 'I have seen a [thing] of pure gold. And he said to me, What do you see? I said, I see, and behold, a lampstand all of gold, with a bowl on the top of it'" (Zech. 4:2). [—note by G.S.]

3. Scholem seems to be referring here to the contempt which Maimonides felt toward those who "consider withal that you may understand a book that is the guide of the first and the last men while glancing through it as you would glance through a historical work or a piece of poetry—when, in some of your hours of leisure, you leave off drinking and copulating" *(Guide for the Perplexed,* I. 2; Pines, 24). [—note by Shlomo Zucker]

4. This "quotation" is evidently a paraphrase of things Scholem had read in Baeck, quoted from memory. I wish to thank Prof. Rivka Horvitz, Dr. Ephraim Meier, and Mr. Shlomo Zucker for their assistance in the futile search for this source. [—J.C.]

5. *Degel Maḥaneh Efraim* (Jerusalem: Defus Hadar, 1963), 165–66.

Chapter Twenty

1. B. Baba Batra 8a.

2. B. Menaḥot 29b.

3. *Kad ha-Kemaḥ,* Ch. Breit, ed. (Lvov, 1892), Vol. II, fol. 10a.

4. J. Gikatilla, *Sha'arei Tzedek,* 1785, fol. 16a.

5. M. Avot 5.14.

6. In his *Commentary on the Mishnah,* on Avot 5:7.

7. Cf. my *Major Trends in Jewish Mysticism* (New York: Schocken, 1945), Ch. 3, 91–99.

8. This holds true even for later periods. Isaac Markon remarked (in his article in the final volume of the *Monatsschrift für Geschichte und Wissenschaft des Jüdentums,* 1939, published without pagination), how restrained the use of the term *Ḥasid* still was between 1650 and 1750.

9. Vital, *Sha'arei Kedushah,* I. 3. His source was Maimonides, *Shemonah Perakim,* Ch. 6.

10. *Mesillat Yesharim*, Ch. 18.

11. Genesis Rabbah 35:2; 49:3; and parallels. [—J.C.]

12. B. Sukkah 45b. [—J.C.]

13. Cf. my essay on the concept of the hidden *tzaddikim*, "Die 36 verborgenen Gerechten in der jüdischen Tradition," in *Judaica* I (Frankfurt am Main: Suhrkamp Verlag, 1963), 216–25.

14. This is stated by Benjamin of Zalozits, *Torrei Zahav*, 1816, fol. 34b, and idem., *Amtaḥat Binyamin*, fol. 78c.

Chapter Twenty-three

1. "Patmos" ("Zweite Fassung"), in *Hölderlin: His Poems*, Michael Hamburger, ed. and trans. (London: Harvell Press, 1952), 222–25.

2. For a critical evaluation of Rosenzweig's thesis, see C. Jamme and H. Schneider, eds., *Mythologie der Vernunft: Hegels "älteste Systemprogramm des deutschen Idealismus"* (Frankfurt: Suhrkamp, 1984).

3. Franz Rosenzweig, *Kleinere Schriften* (Berlin: Schocken Verlag, 1937), 56–78. English translation in Franz Rosenzweig, *On Jewish Learning*, Nahum N. Glatzer, ed. (New York: Schocken, 1965), 27–54.

4. Franz Rosenzweig, "Einleitung," in *Hermann Cohens Jüdische Schriften*, (Berlin: C. A. Schwetschke,1924). Also in Rosenzweig, *Kleinere Schriften*, 244–350.

5. Neḥemiah Anton Nobel (1871–1922), a much respected Orthodox rabbi and scholar in Frankfurt.

6. B. Megillah 31a.

7. Rosenzweig, *Kleinere Schriften*, 373–99. Excerpts are included in Nahum N. Glatzer, ed., *Franz Rosenzweig: His Life and Thought*, (New York: Schocken, 1961), 190–208.

8. In Leo Shestov, *Le pouvoir des clefs*, trans. from the Russian by Boris de Schloezer (Paris: J. Schiffrin, 1928), 307–96.

9. An image from the Kabbalistic doctrine of Isaac Luria (1534–1572). The repair *(tikkun)* of this supernal event, he taught, is effected through the pious and mystical deeds of man and leads to redemption.

10. In German philosophical parlance *Erfahrung* refers to knowledge mediated through the five senses.

11. Scholem here refers to the physicist Werner Karl Heisenberg (1901–1976), who published in 1927 his thesis on "the uncertainty principle."

12. Salomo Ludwig Steinheim (1780–1866) published this four-volume work between 1835 and 1865. Moritz Lazarus (1824–1903) published the first volume in 1898, the second posthumously in 1911. An English translation of the first volume was published by the Jewish Publication Society in 1900.

13. The reference is to Pirkei Avot 2:2, which Samson Raphael Hirsch (1808–1888) read thus: "The study of Torah is excellent with *derekh eretz,* that is, worldly occupation, or secular education" *(derekh eretz* is usually understood as "good manners" or "decorum"). "Torah with *derekh eretz"* became the general slogan of the neo-Orthodox movement founded by Hirsch in Germany.

14. Published posthumously in 1919.

15. Franz Rosenzweig, "Das neue Denken," in *Kleinere Schriften,* 389.

16. Cf. Abraham Abulafia, *Iggeret sheva' Netivot ha-Torah,* in A. Jellinek, *Philosophie und Kabbala,* Erstes Heft (Leipzig: H. Hunger, 1854), 14–15. [Note supplied by Moshe Idel]

17. Cf. Ibn Latif, *Rav Pe'alim,* in A. Jellinek, *Kokhavei Yitzḥak,* Vol. 25(1860), 10, par. 39. [Note supplied by Moshe Idel]

18. Rosenzweig, "Das neue Denken," 385ff.

19. The reference is to a hymnic poem by Judah Halevi, "Lord Where Shall I Find Thee."

20. Franz Rosenzweig, *The Star of Redemption,* trans. W. Hallo (New York: Holt, Rinehart and Winston, 1970), 238.

21. See introduction to ibid., Part 3, 265–97.

22. Gen. 6:16.

23. The Hebrew word *teivah* means both ark and word; for the Kabbalists, each word of Scripture, understood in all its hidden meaning, is the Ark of the Torah.

Glossary

Aggadah—lit., "telling" or "relating." The non-legal portion of talmudic literature, encompassing tales of the Sages, ethical maxims, folklore, etc.

Ashkenazic Ḥasidism—A pietistic-ethical movement in twelfth century Franco-Germany, discussed in Chapter Seventeen of this volume, and in greater detail in Scholem's *Major Trends*. Not to be confused with the popular mystical movement of eighteenth century Eastern Europe of the same name founded by the Ba'al Shem Tov.

Devekut—clinging or attachment to God, at times described as the ultimate goal of the mystic's journey.

Halakhah—lit., "walking" or "the path." Refers both to the literature of Jewish law and to the process of legal elucidation and interpretation itself.

Ḥasid—Pietist; an individual of super-exemplary devoutness and piety. In Eastern European Ḥasidism, the meaning was inverted to refer to any follower of the Ḥasidic sect. See Chapter Twenty.

Haskalah—Enlightenment. Used to refer to the modernization movement in modern European Jewry: in Western Europe, one of acculturation and Emancipation; in Eastern Europe, the "Hebrew" Haskalah, associated with the national and cultural renewal revival that preceded and in a sense heralded political Zionism.

Kabbalah—The movements of Jewish mysticism. Specifically, used of the mystical movement that emerged in southern France and Spain during the late twelfth century, whose best known literary expression was *Sefer ha-Zohar*.

Midrash—lit., "exposition." Generic term used to refer to the homiletical literature of classic rabbinic Judaism, whether focused upon the "literal," normative implications of Scripture ("halakhic Midrash") or involving far-reaching flights of imaginative fancy ("*aggadic* Midrash").

Mishnah—the compendium of Jewish law edited by Rabbi Judah the Prince in the early third century; forms the core text around which developed the Talmud.

Pilpul—talmudic dialectics or casuistry (literally, "pepper"). Especially, the highly sophisticated, abstract dialectic method that reached its culmination in the talmudic novellae of seventeenth and eighteenth century Poland and Russia.

Piyyut—religious poetry; refers specifically to the genre developed in Byzantine Palestine and medieval Spain, used as addenda to the regular liturgy on fast days, special Sabbaths, festivals, and, especially, the High Holy Days.

Sefirot—the ten emanations of the Godhead that, in Kabbalistic theosophy, represent the essential building blocks and moving powers in the cosmos. The sefirot are variously understood as part of the Godhead or as separate entities emanating from it.

Shulḥan 'Arukh—Handbook of Jewish law abstracted by Rabbi Joseph Caro of Safed in 1560 from his larger opus, *Beit Yosef*. Over time, it came to be regarded as the authoritative guide to Jewish law.

Talmid Ḥakham—sage; learned person or scholar. See Chapter Twenty.

Talmud—the voluminous collection of legal material and other rubrics recording the discussions in the Jewish academies (yeshivot) of Babylonia and Palestine during the third to sixth centuries; it forms the core curriculum and pinnacle of traditional Jewish religious studies.

Tanakh—Term used to refer to the Hebrew Bible, taken from the acronym referring to its three sections: *Torah, Nevi'im, Ketuvim* (i.e., the Five Books of Moses; the Prophets; the Holy Writings).

Tzaddik—appellation for "the righteous man." In Ḥasidism, used to refer to the "rebbe," the charismatic leader of the congregation. See Chapter Twenty.

Index

Note: Page numbers in boldface refer to glossary entries.